# Hobo Roads

# Hobo Roads
Two Accounts of Living Rough in Early 20th
Century America

## The Adventures of a Woman Hobo
Ethel Lynn

## From North Carolina to Southern California
Without a Ticket and How I Did It Giving
My Exciting Experiences as a "Hobo"
John Peele

LEONAUR

*Hobo Roads*
*Two Accounts of Living Rough in Early 20th Century America*
*The Adventures of a Woman Hobo*
by Ethel Lynn
*From North Carolina to Southern California Without a Ticket and How I Did It*
*Giving My Exciting Experiences as a "Hobo"*
By John Peele

FIRST EDITION

Leonaur is an imprint of Oakpast Ltd

Copyright in this form © 2022 Oakpast Ltd

ISBN: 978-1-915234-26-1 (hardcover)
ISBN: 978-1-915234-27-8 (softcover)

**http://www.leonaur.com**

Publisher's Notes

# Contents

# The Adventures of a Woman Hobo

# Contents

## CHAPTER ONE

# April 18th, 1908, Chicago, Illinois

"Doctor Lynn, you are in the incipient stage of tuberculosis. You should return to California immediately."

That is what Dr. Graves said to me today and he is in a position to know what he is talking about. But I can't believe it! Why, I can do the work of two women. Haven't I supported myself since I was fifteen years old, worked my way through Medical College and built up a city practice by my own, unaided efforts? Besides, everyone says I am the picture of health. My five feet eight of energised muscle, my high colour, my breadth of shoulder, all seem to give such a diagnosis the lie.

Yet a still voice whispers in my heart, "It is true." Since that last severe attack of grippe, the buoyancy has vanished from my step. Life has become a drag.

But then, why not? The last two years have been strenuous. Just two years ago today San Francisco went down in earthquake and flames, scattering my growing practice to the winds. And of course, Dan's position went too. But we celebrated with an earthquake wedding, and it was not long until my husband had worked out his great invention, and we came here; he to gain financial backing for his project, and I to profit by the abundance of clinical material in a great city.

And then the panic of 1907 struck us. Why, the earthquake was nothing to that. Poor Dan was crushed. How can I tell him of this new calamity? And what will it profit to add to his burden, helpless as he is? For months now, he has walked the streets looking for any kind of employment at any wage, but none is to be had. This hopeless seeking, added to the stunning blow of the collapse of his company and the deadening pressure of debt incurred last fall when we borrowed to the utmost limit of all our friends' capacity in a frantic endeavour to save the invention, only to lose money, company, invention—all in one universal crash—has completely unnerved him.

To see his wife forced into the depths through his failure, even though that failure was no fault of his, has been gall and wormwood to him. Those days when we pledged every pawnable article in a dogged desire to hang on for just one week longer in the hope that the tide would turn; when we moved from lodgings to lodgings, each meaner and more squalid than the last, until the fathomless pit of hell itself seemed reached in this slum; when I gave up my work in the college where the wonderful experience gained was ample compensation except to those driven by grim necessity to seek for any work that would keep this vile tenement over our heads and put food in our mouths;—all these things have left him a broken-hearted man.

And there are many such. Months of idleness, a diet of bread and coffee, all the horrors of shivering nights in the open or in vermin-infested flop houses, the morning rush for the "help wanted" pages of the daily papers, the standing in line for hours waiting to apply for a job—a hundred men for a single position—would these things not take the heart, nay, the very soul itself, out of a man?

When I was discharged last month, losing my position because of a general retrenchment, never shall I forget the scenes at the Public Library when with scores of others I sought the protection of its sheltering walls at early morning to thaw the night's coldness out of my half-frozen body, and search the papers for a possible chance of employment.

One young man in the huddled group interested me immensely. When the doors swung open, he bounded up the stairs like an athlete, well in the lead of the rushing horde who refused to wait for the elevator in their frenzied scramble for the first chance at a paper and possible employment. Well-dressed, palpably clean living and efficient, he was an excellent type of the successful young business man. I could picture him as a broker, in an insurance office or bank, or filling some responsible position in a business house. But in the fall of many such houses, his had evidently gone down to ruin and now the lad was beginning to feel the pinch that comes from weeks of idleness.

Morning after morning he appeared. His well-tailored suit gave way to a misfit piece of shoddy; his hat was replaced by a cap which failed to conceal his need of a hair-cut; his face became lean and haggard; no longer was his expression one of energy and confidence. A three days' growth of beard on his jowls will take some of the confidence out of any man when looking for employment.

12

Then for days he disappeared.

Came a day when I saw him. It was blizzard weather; a sleety rain was carried on a high wind which swept through the city streets and wailed and whistled round the entrance to the Library building. A gaunt figure dragged its feeble way up the front steps to the semi-shelter of the pillars; from a face, piteously thin, hollow eyes looked out, their glance filled with a deep, an utter despair; a short coat pinned together at the throat revealed the absence of a shirt or underwear; through the cracks in the run-over shoes the bare flesh peered; wet to the skin as he was, he shook in the icy blast like a dog in a wet sack. As the doors swung wide at nine o'clock, he did not lead the upward dash, but half-way up the stairs sank down, overcome by a choking fit of coughing.

I never saw him again.

To live in a hovel; to drag my weary body for miles in search of work; to cough my lungs out like the man next door; to be submerged like a drowning rat in a sewer; this will be my life in Chicago. My eyes ache from gazing at confined spaces; across the way the bare walls rise; down the canyon streets I see the black ants of humanity crawl; overhead the sky is leaden.

Oh, my beautiful, my California! The whistle of the quail on the open benches is calling me; the mating songs of the mocking birds vibrate in my heart. Up the wide valley the warm wind sweeps, heavy with the fragrance of blossoming trees; on the uplands' brilliant masses of filming poppies and the silvery blue of slender lupines spread a feast of colour for my weary eyes; oranges blaze out in golden glory against the dark green foliage of the thrifty groves; the deep blue of the cloudless sky seems infinite in depth; and in the purple distance the white-capped peaks of San Bernardino and Gray-Back rear their lofty heads.

## Chapter Two

# April 27th, 1908

Eureka, I've found it—the Great Idea—the craziest scheme that ever popped into a woman's head!

We're going home—back to California on a tandem bicycle. We'll carry a cooking and sleeping outfit with us, stop wherever the night finds us, work when we can get it, and somehow, with God's help, we'll win through.

And it has come about in the strangest way. Dan got a chance to help a man he knows clean out an old barn which is to be converted into a garage, and in the loft along with the accumulation of years, they ran across a tandem bicycle which is in excellent condition. The owner gave it to Dan's friend who thought he could sell it for something, even though cycling is out of date.

When Dan told me of the occurrence an intense longing for the open road leading into the west surged over me, but I could see no way of securing the wheel since our funds totalled less than five dollars.

Then I said to myself, "There is a way. You must find it," and resolutely set my subconscious mind to the task.

A day passed and another. Then over the threshold of consciousness came the recollection of my one cherished possession—a beautiful opera cloak.

On that fateful morning in April, 1906, after the rush to escape from the tottering building, I found myself on the streets of San Francisco in somewhat scanty attire, but folded warmly in my new biscuit-Negro evening wrap. Many thanks I offered up for its protection in the chilly days and nights that followed. Then, when conditions had returned somewhat to normal, a good cleaning and remodelling restored almost its pristine glory, and again it gave good service on the honeymoon. While the panic was sweeping away all our possessions,

I laid it aside, resolved that it at least should be retained throughout the storm.

But a sterner necessity compelled, so taking it from the drawer, I wended my way to Oak Street and there held a colloquy with our friend's wife. The cloak caught her fancy at once, the bargain was struck, and I trundled home my prize in triumph, to lean it carefully near the door of our crowded quarters.

Here at dusk, Dan, entering hurriedly, collided violently with an outstanding pedal. He hopped agilely about on one foot, clasping his left shin in an affectionate embrace.

"What in hades is that thing I just fell over?" he demanded hotly.

"That? Why, that's our through ticket to California."

As I turned up the ineffective gas jet, he recognised the graceful lines of the machine.

"Well, I'll be darned!" he ejaculated. "So you got the blooming thing from Dave, did you? How'd you manage it? And what do you mean, anyway, by a ticket to California? You can't be aiming to ride that contraption."

"Don't you dare to call my beautiful green tandem a contraption. You'll be glad enough to take your seat on a bicycle built for two as soon as I've explained my perfectly scrumptious scheme to you. We'll fix up a light cooking outfit, tie our blankets on behind, and away we'll glide out into the west. We'll work along the way and have lots of interesting experiences; I'll get rid of this tiresome cough, and after a while we'll get home—home, do you hear? Back to California."

"Ride that thing to California! Why think of the country between here and the coast; look at the desert, look at the Rocky Mountains, to say nothing of the little old Coast Range. What do you think I am, anyhow, a cross between a camel and a mountain goat?"

"I'll be sure you're all goat if you butt into my cherished plan in that rude fashion," I responded gaily. "Never mind. Wait till your shin feels better and you've had something to eat and we'll talk it over."

I drew the table closer to our tiny stove and set out the meal while Dan prepared for supper.

"You remember my telling you about that poor little couple that I used to see at the Public Library," I began when we were comfortably settled, "the ones that used to come in about two or three o'clock and go off in a corner somewhere to eat a bit of lunch when the librarian wasn't looking? She's been going down very fast for the last few weeks, hasn't been able to look for work at all, but waited in the library till he came in, half-crazy from the continued failure to find anything, and then she'd try to comfort him while they shared the part of a loaf of bread that she'd have hidden beneath her old cape.

"When I was warming up in the library this morning she was coughing terribly and I talked her into trying the charity hospitals again. It seemed as if they must take her. You know she went a while back, but couldn't get in; she was an ambulatory case. He came in about noon, all used up and they didn't have even a crust of bread.

"We started out and just on the edge of the sidewalk she had a haemorrhage and before we could get the ambulance, she was dead. I had taken her in my arms, her little body was light as a feather." My voice failed.

"I'll never forget the look in his eyes when he realised that she was dead. . . . Dan, I can't die as she did. Before I go, I want to see the open fields, feel the soft earth beneath my feet, draw a few breaths of real air. Since I've lived in this slum, I'm getting so I can't even believe in God."

"Ethel, you're getting morbid. What's all this talk about dying? You're simply upset over these people's trouble."

"No, I'm not morbid, Danny boy. I hate to tell you, but Doctor Graves says I have consumption and must go back to California at once if I'm to get well."

"What utter nonsense. You're the strongest woman I've ever seen. It's ridiculous to talk of a strapping girl like you having consumption."

"I know it sounds ridiculous, but I'm afraid it's true just the same. I've had a good many symptoms . . . but I won't die like an animal in a trap. I won't die in this pest hole. I've a fighting chance and I'm going to take it. We'll ride that tandem west! or die in the attempt. When I think of the terrors of the journey, the miles and miles of desert that I know so well, when I picture those tremendous mountains, my heart almost fails me, but nothing, nothing can be so terrible, so horrible to our souls as well as destructive to our bodies as these loathsome slums.

"We've got to get away from here, Dan. That's all. And I believe we can go to California on that wheel. I've heard of people making the journey on foot, and in the early days whole families went with all sorts of conveyances. What we need is a little nerve and grit like the pioneers."

Well into the night we argued, until Dan was finally silenced, if not fully convinced.

Then the question of equipment confronted us. A matter of a few

16

tools for repairs on the journey, extra tyre and other insurance against accidents reduced our finances almost to zero. Also, the problem of bulk and weight is a serious matter when clothing, bedding, cooking utensils and other necessaries must be carried on one small frame.

As usual, the front seat of the bicycle is arranged for the woman, and on the handle bars we have rigged a holder for the cooking outfit. This consists of a heavy frying pan with the handle removed, a fair-sized potato kettle with bail, useful for carrying water, nested inside, and within that again a strong tin pan with close-fitting cover which may be used as coffee pot, cocoa kettle or dish pan as occasion warrants. Dan has a pair of long-handled pliers to remove these from the fire.

Inside the pan lie two tin plates and two tin cups for coffee; also, a couple of forks, a sharp steel knife, one large and two small spoons and a small tin of salt. A cocoa can of sugar, one of coffee and one of cocoa fit together very nicely and complete the collection. Directly on the rack rest two heavy pieces of wire sharpened at the ends which are bent at right angles to the body, forming prongs about nine inches long. When the points of these prongs are driven into the ground so that the lengths are parallel and about eight inches apart, a convenient little support for frying pan and kettle is formed, under which a small fire can be kindled to great advantage.

Then Dan contrived a case to fit within the body of the frame, which, with careful packings holds a small emergency case, fitted with simple instruments, bandages, etc., a few toilet necessities and a change of hose and underwear for each.

Behind the rear seat there is a large rack with leather straps for bedding, which is our worst problem. Dan made a trip to a big machine shop and returned triumphant with two large sheets of black oilcloth which had covered electrical equipment. To each sheet I sewed a woollen blanket, thus giving our future bed protection from damp above and below. When an extra shirt for Dan and a waist for myself was added to this bed roll, we found that we could just crowd in one soft old blanket for extra covering. When I consider sleeping on the ground with a combination oilcloth and woollen blanket below, and the two blankets above, my teeth fairly chatter with anticipation. But even a frozen death would be preferable to our present hopeless existence.

Inasmuch as our rent is due next Sunday, May 3rd, we have decided to start on that date. What the future holds, God alone knows, but at least we will live in the open, which will compensate for much.

CHAPTER THREE

# May 4th, In a Big Barn

We are off!

Sunday dawned bright and clear and Dan and I were up with the first light. The neighbourhood assembled to receive our few poor sticks of furniture and household goods, for we deemed it best to give the things to our poverty-stricken neighbours rather than sell them for a few pennies to some second-hand dealer.

Our friends think us insane, as well they may, but crazy or no, we will see this thing through.

We surely made a picture at the start. Dan's blue eyes were alight with eagerness, his fair hair tousled, while his sturdy body showed to good advantage in sweater, corduroys and cap. I wore a dark shirtwaist, short plaid skirt, blue sweater and straw sailor hat. At the last moment we fastened a small parcel of groceries atop the bedding roll—a bit of bacon, a loaf of bread, a pat of butter and one or two other odds and ends. Altogether, the machine was well loaded.

Then, followed by the cheers of the crowd who were busy carrying away, the contents of our room, and accompanied by a horde of shoving, shouting urchins, we made our way up the street. At the corner of Division Street we paused to weigh ourselves and wheel, and found the combination tipped the scales at just five hundred pounds.

Pushing on to a clear bit of pavement, we mounted and were off toward the west side. Both Dan and I had ridden bicycles at earlier periods in our career, and had spent a little time in Lincoln Park practising on the tandem, but we were far from being expert riders. The double steering gear which should enable the man to help the woman steady the front wheel was broken, so, loaded as we were, I found the task of steering a difficult one.

As we wobbled our serpentine way through the streets, fortunately nearly empty at that early hour, it seemed to me that this was the strangest nightmare that ever vexed the soul of woman. There was a weird beauty in the morning light, the breath of freedom in the gentle breeze. The spirit of adventure rode with us. I had a feeling of detachment from earthly things while realising to the full the perils and difficulties of the venture.

An ash can in the street caught my eye. With incredible accuracy I headed for it.

"Hi!" cried Dan, "look where you're going."

"Good gracious," I answered desperately, "that's just what I'm trying not to do."

*Bang!* Quite a spill, but no harm done luckily.

When we reached Humboldt Park, we decided to take a short rest. Propping our machine against the curb, we sat on a bench beneath a tree. While aimlessly poking the litter at its base with my toe, I saw something glitter.

"Look, Dan!" I exulted. "See what I've found. Talk of manna in the wilderness." I held up a silver dollar, a half and two dimes. "I feel sure it is an omen."

"Yes, an omen of fresh eggs for breakfast tomorrow morning," replied Dan prosaically.

Once again, we were off. The day wore on. Streets gave way to dusty roads full of ruts, into which the wheel appeared possessed to stagger. Dust rose; sweat poured; our throats ached with unquenchable thirst. My arms seemed wrenched from their sockets. Human endurance reached its limit as the sun set.

Wearily we searched for a camping place. Finally, in a grassy hollow, screened from the road by trees, we unpacked our equipment. While Dan took the potato kettle to a nearby house for water, I set up our wire rack and kindled a tiny fire beneath.

After a meal which we were almost too tired to eat, we spread our scanty bedding on the ground and composed ourselves for slumber. An owl settled on a branch near our heads and surveyed us with amazement. Back and forth he flew, studying the strange intruders from every angle. Then with a "hoot" of protest and derision, he winged away to attend to the business of the evening.

"Ugh, this ground is hard," grunted Dan.

"And none too warm," thought I, but neither cold nor discomfort could prevail for long against our utter exhaustion.

I sat up with a start. A grey day was breaking; the trees rustled in a wind that moaned and muttered with chilly breath. Big drops of rain beat on my face.

"Quick, Dan, get up!" I cried to the snoring partner of my dreams. "It's going to pour down rain in a few minutes."

We scurried around, collecting and packing our scattered belongings, then decided to make a dash for a big barn which stood not far down the road at the foot of a hill, for the rain was beginning to fall heavily. Reaching the highway, we sprang to saddle and sped down the hill. With a sickening lurch the front wheel struck a slippery patch of mud at the bottom, the hind wheel skidding sideways. The heel of my right shoe caught in the pedal shaft and in a trice was torn from my foot and sent spinning ten feet away, Dan went sprawling on the wet earth, while I hopped awkwardly along, bruising my shins, but clinging desperately to the handle bars with both hands.

Dan picked himself up and came to my assistance.

"Pick up my heel, please," said I, standing like a stork on one foot. Dan stared at me dazedly. "Pick up my heel," I cried impatiently. He reached for my foot. "Do you think I'm a horse waiting to be shod? Don't you see the heel of my shoe lying over there in the mud?"

With that he retrieved the loosened heel and we hurried through the steady downpour to the barn. The owner came out and, having listened to our tale of woe, gave us some shingle nails to repair the torn shoe and bade us build a fire beneath a shed to prepare breakfast. Dan fulfilled the augury of the previous day by the purchase of some fresh eggs, and soon we were feasting on bacon and eggs and pints of steaming coffee.

Good? Why nectar and ambrosia were stale beside it.

After the meal, we repaired to the barn loft and, easing our weary bones into the prickly depths of hay, awaited the end of the storm.

## CHAPTER FOUR

# May 6th, 1908

Dan found work! Only a day and a half, but a few hours were better than nothing, and gave us hope.

The sun was setting as a wagon rattled up the road with Dan dangling his feet over the end-gate,

"Come on, Ethel," he cried, "our friend here has offered us a place in his barn and plenty of dry corn cobs for the fire."

I sprang up and we loaded the wheel into the wagon. Soon the driver entered a lane which ended in a large barnyard, and as Dan began to help with the team, I unloaded the cooking outfit.

The farmer was pulling some grain sacks from a large tub in the wagon bed.

"Here's plenty of fish," he said. "Just pitch in and help yourselves."

Our eyes bulged in astonishment at sight of the silvery heaps that filled the tub.

"Where on earth did you get so many?" gasped Dan.

"South o' the road where the river has overflowed its banks. The boys are heaving them out with pitchforks and spears and even bare handed. Take all you want. I've three times as many as Sarah Jane and I can eat."

Nothing loath, I lifted out sufficient for our needs, and as Dan set to cleaning the fish, I collected corn cobs and kindled a tiny fire beneath the rack.

A short, roly-poly woman bustled out of the back door of the small but comfortable farmhouse and approached us.

"Dear me, dear me, a lady tramp!" she exclaimed. "Bless us, if they haven't gone to running in pairs like animals entering the ark."

Catching sight of the tandem still loaded with part of our equipment, she paused in amazement, pushing back her red calico sunbonnet and revealing wonderful masses of snow-white curls.

"But you're not a tramp after all, are you? Tramps don't ride bicycles. What a disappointment! I've always wanted to meet a lady tramp. But what are you up to anyway? Must be something interesting. You look interesting."

I assured her that we were, indeed, up to something interesting, just how interesting we would probably fully realise later on.

"So, you're really going back to that strange California where it is always summer? What awful monotony. Come fall, I'm always glad, for I feel that summer has been here plenty long enough."

She seated herself on the wagon tongue.

The barnyard world was settling for the night with much cackling, grunting, lowing and stamping. Under a nearby shed a flock of fowls was clucking and fussing as they sought the highest perches.

"Look at those chickens, now. Aren't they just like humans?" demanded our visitor. "I sit out here and watch them by the hour."

"*Caw, caw-rr*," croaked a haughty grenadier of a hen, taking a sharp peck at a handsome young pullet who had endeavoured to perch on the topmost roost.

"Hear what she says? I'll tell you," the little woman interpreted eagerly.

"Get right away from here, you impudent, upstart Dominick. Go back with the lower clawsses where you belong and don't try to crowd in here with your betters.'

"Do you know, we got a woman living on the other side of town who's the perfect spit and image of that old hen. There, hear her talking?

"'These nobodies try to push in everywhere.'

"Now the old rooster is a cuttering. . . . 'She seems rather a nice little thing, but of course, as you say, she'll never be able to attain to any position in life, but really for one of her social standing, she's quite chick.'

"Now the old hen's talking again. 'Fowls of quality can't be too careful nowadays. These plebeian climbers are everywhere.'"

The haughty Plymouth Rock settled herself and preened her feathers with the conscious air of duty well performed, while the little woman lauded gaily.

"Now she feels that she has maintained all the traditions of her class. Oh, yes, they have classes in the chicken yard just as in the American nation. I was thinking of getting a good likeness of that hen and

22

sending it to the *Chicago American* so's they could print her picture on the society page.

"You know, I find lots of interesting characters out here. There's a hog over yonder. He's stuffed so full he can't swallow another mouthful, yet he keeps wallowing over the food so the shoats can't get any, and they stand back and first one tries to get a bite and then another, when if they'd all rush him at once they'd get aplenty. When he grunts like that, he's telling them to be contented and industrious little pigs and that if they just start rooting early every morning, after a while they'll be eminent and respected like he is and able to wallow in the feed trough.

"And Father's got the big kettle all ready, and Saturday he's going to butcher him."

"Hi, Serjane, I've got the fish ready for the pan and there you set on the wagon tongue aletting the fire go out." It was the querulous voice of the old man.

Sarah Jane hurried into the kitchen as Dan placed a fine mess of fish over the coals. We had just gotten well started to eating when the back door flew open with a bang and the little woman scudded toward us.

"Oh, I'm too late," she cried breathlessly. "You're already eating. Now why didn't I ask you to eat with us before? Why? Why? Why?"

Each word was a tiny explosion.

"Just because I didn't think! Didn't think! That's what ails the world. We don't think, won't think and can't think. Now, which do you consider is the worst?"

"The *won't thinks* are the worst to my mind," I assured her gravely, "because the *don't thinks* get waked up now and then, and after a while the *can't thinks* will grow some more brains, so that there is a chance of them getting started right, but as for the fellow who just naturally refuses to think at all, there is not much hope for him."

"Dear me, dear me. I would just love to talk to you. You must come into the sitting room as soon as you are done eating and spend the evening with me. I'll hurry and wash the dishes."

She spun around and scurried into the house. We hastily finished our meal and prepared sleeping quarters in the hay mow.

Then, as darkness fell, the old man ushered us into the neat living-room. The soft rays from a large lamp glimmered on the walnut furniture and illumined the family groups upon the walls. Braided rugs, round and oval, were scattered about the floor and a cheerful blaze in an open-front stove radiated a pleasant welcome in the chill of evening. In a few moments our hostess was extracting all the details of our journey with the neatness and skill of long experience.

After a while Dan rose with a sigh of weariness. "Come, Ethel, we'd better hit the hay. I've got to work tomorrow, you know."

"Hay—hit the hay! No such a thing. Go right into the spare room and make yourselves uncomfortable." Sarah Jane rushed to open the bedroom door.

I explained our plans for roughing it and said we should rest very comfortably in the hay mow.

"Dear me, dear me, you should always put off till tomorrow what you can get out of doing today. You can do aplenty of roughing it when you get to Wyoming. Go on to bed now and enjoy a good spring mattress while you have the chance."

Daylight came all too soon, with Sarah Jane summoning us to a breakfast of cornmeal mush and cream, fried perch, buckwheat cakes with maple syrup and cups of amber coffee.

"Let me know if you find anything that I can do to help along. I'd like to be of more use in the world than I can be hibernating here," she called after us as we pedalled down the lane.

I can still see her merry smile as she leaned over the gate, vigorously waving her sunbonnet in farewell.

CHAPTER FIVE

# May 7th, At Crab-Apple Hedge

We are in a new world. All day long we press forward, sometimes riding and again on foot, for the roads are rough and often muddy; and on every hand the beauties of an Illinois spring unfold before our enraptured gaze.

With the western spring I am familiar. In March and April acres on acres of greasewood blossoms and wild lilacs were all swaying in the ocean breeze that sweeps the wide reaches of our Southern California valleys each afternoon. A wild spirit of freedom, an almost Pagan joyousness and gaiety is manifest, which speaks of primitive things and appeals to the elemental essence of the soul. But here Nature approaches in more tender intimacy. Little love flowers snuggle on her breast. The whole earth palpitates with a sweet warmth and promise of beauties to follow.

On our right stretches a crab-apple hedge in full bloom, a veritable glory of beauty and fragrance, which crowns a ridge whence rolling acres fall gradually away, revealing, here and there, farmhouses surrounded by kitchen gardens and groups of fruit trees, billowy plumes of soft colour, some outlined by the tender green of spring. The smoke of noontime fires lazily ascends from the chimneys, the cackle of hens and other barnyard sounds come faintly on the breeze. My heart aches with the homing impulse. My mind turns to the experiences of the past few days.

Wednesday the air was clear and balmy, and as night approached, we stopped beneath a bridge where thick trees screened our camp from view. The wires were driven in the ground, the modest campfire lighted, and soon the delicious aroma of boiling cocoa and grilled steak whetted appetites already ravenous. Our hunger appeased, we were settling for the night, when I was seized with foreboding of a

25

coming storm. Dan laughed and called it a crazy notion and beyond all reason. But the feeling increased in intensity until I insisted on seeking the shelter of some building. Dan acquiesced reluctantly, but by the time we had repacked and loaded the wheel, night had fallen.

At the nearest farm we asked permission to sleep in the barn, but were abruptly denied. At the next house the inmates refused to answer our knock.

"Well, what are you going to do now? Walk all night?" expostulated Dan.

On our left a dark mass appeared in the darkness and proved to be the ruins of a race track grandstand. As I stumbled beneath the tiers of seats, hoping for some promise of protection, a man leaped up almost at my feet.

I sprang back, startled.

"Come," said the stranger, "I know the way."

As though in a trance I followed him, my hand guiding the wheel, while Dan pushed behind. We immediately came on a narrow board walk at right angles to the road. The man led on into the thick darkness, the two of us following blindly after. On and on we travelled as though impelled by some force outside our own volition. A huge building loomed on our right. Silently we skirted it, the clop, clop of our feet on the boards giving way to noiseless progress over grassy turf.

Suddenly the front wheel of the tandem struck some obstacle, and in the deepened gloom I could faintly discern the outlines of another building, the steps of which were before me. These I mounted, preceded by our strange guide, who said not a word, but rapped loudly on the door.

From some remote region came a scuffling, then the bang of an inner door, and down a long hall shuffled a tall, lean figure wrapped in a trailing dressing gown. An oil lamp in its hand gave forth a yellow gleam, which lifted up the old-fashioned interior and shone through the glass panelled door. The old man, for such it was, peered through the glass at our mysterious attendant, and then, after prolonged fumbling with lock and bolts and chain, slowly swung open the door.

"And who might yez be?" he inquired in a rich brogue, directing a keen Irish eye on Dan and me.

We explained our situation as briefly as possible and asked for the shelter of some outbuilding for the night.

"Faith, and ye're wilcome to the house. Sure, and it's large enough for ten and but three av us to fill it."

As he spoke there came a tapping and a little old woman with snapping black eyes skipped like a bird to his side.

"An' indade they shall not come inside this house the night. Murdthered in me bed I will not be."

"Hush, Katie," querulously chided the ancient. "This is no time for to be exercisin' yer conthrary timper."

But the little old woman braced herself in the doorway as though to defy the world, and I hastened to state that we only wanted to sleep in the barn.

'Well, if so ye will. Arrah, the house is open save for this old spalpeen." With that he shuffled off to fetch a lantern.

I turned to thank our guide, but he had disappeared.

Soon we were inside the big barn that we had passed coming in. The wavering rays of the lantern disclosed huge, cob-webbed recesses, rows of empty stalls, a tumble-down carriage, and near the sliding door, a small hillock of well packed hay. Otherwise the place was empty. On this hay we made our bed and were soon asleep.

I was awakened by the drumming of rain on the roof. Another wet morning was upon us. I leaned over to ask Dan what he thought of my "crazy notion" now. But he was sound asleep, so I conquered my feminine impulse and decided to get up and scout a dry place to cook breakfast.

"Ow-wow!" My bare foot splashed into a lake of cold water which, concealed by a layer of floating straw and chaff, covered the floor of the old barn to a depth of eighteen inches.

My startled howl brought Dan up with a jerk.

Hastily we dressed and moved our footgear and bedding to the top of a grain bin. As we perched forlornly on this refuge in a watery waste, the door opened and the little old lady of the night before came in.

Perhaps we appeared less murderous by the light of day, or what is more likely, her "conthrary timper" was less in evidence when acting on her own initiative; at any rate, after a short chat, she cordially invited us in to breakfast.

Then followed a most interesting day. Jim, her husband, who was unusually well read, struck up an immediate friendship with Dan, and while waiting for the rain to cease, Katie and I visited in the kitchen.

There were but three in the family: the old man, his wife and the feeble-minded chore man who had brought us to their dwelling the previous night. Outside of an acre of orchard, a chicken run and a small garden, their great holdings of hundreds of acres were rented to tenants, one of whom supplied them with milk and butter.

The couple had emigrated from the old country when very young; had met and loved on the long voyage, and were married soon after their arrival.

James Grogan was a remarkable man. Keen, shrewd, ambitious, he worked and saved and invested with all the energy and acumen that has enabled so many of his race to rise in the world. He homesteaded the original Illinois farm and to these hundred and sixty acres he constantly added. His passion was to leave his children educated and rich. He himself had learned to read and write when past the age of thirty; the struggle upward had been a hard one; his children should be spared all this.

And eleven babies were born to them. With bitter words old Katie painted pictures of the heart-breaking toil; the lack of ordinary conveniences; the goading tongue of her lord and master driving her on through the years while acre was added to acre, and the herds increased, and no barn was large enough to hold the abundant crops. Modern farm implements were purchased in plenty, but there was no money for the simplest household conveniences; outbuildings were snug and well built; but the home itself was ramshackle and poor.

It has been said that in earlier days the size of a man's farm could often be estimated by the number of wives' tombstones in his lot in the cemetery. But it was not true in this case. Katie had lived, but her babies died. Her love for her husband turned to a cold hate, but still the babies came. Ten had been born and ten had died before Jim realised that Katie needed as good care as his animals—that she was more than any animal—that she was, in truth, the mother of those children—his children—whom he worshipped—and lost.

So, the youngest boy was born and grew—a slender, delicate, brilliant lad—and all the facilities for education, and all the riches of cattle and horses and broad acres were his to command.

He was educated for the Bar. And while he was in college and while he studied law, his father and he built up a wonderful library and still more wonderful plans for the future, when James Grogan, Junior, should be a great jurist and statesman with a reputation nationwide.

Abruptly his health failed. Lack of vitality, his inheritance from his mother, made itself felt. He went to California and there died.

James Grogan, Senior, brought home that library and installed it in the old ramshackle house with its addition here and lean-to there. And here, alone, he read each volume.

28

## CHAPTER SIX

# Monday, May 11th, In the Mud

To you, and you alone, little diary, will I confess a sense of deep discouragement. Mud! Mud! Seas of mud and oceans of rain!

We have been out eight full days and have covered but sixty-five miles. The appetite that I have developed is truly amazing. As I sit by a fence, waiting for Dan to investigate those streaks of ooze and slush called roads, I'm hungry enough to eat Limburger cheese, which is saying a good deal for me. Yet I finished a hearty breakfast but an hour or so ago. I am ravenous, morning, noon and night, and Dan is nearly as bad. When I compare the size of our appetites with the cost of bread and eggs at farmhouses, the dollar and a half that Dan sweat like a stevedore to earn, looks woefully inadequate.

Saturday afternoon we cycled through the town of Morris, stopping long enough to purchase a few supplies. Two miles from town we passed a neat farmhouse, and just beyond found a most beautiful meadow surrounded by trees. The long shadows of late afternoon lay across the thick green sward which rose in a gentle slope.

Delighted with the spot, we cooked our evening meal and lay down to enjoy the glory of the moon, which, floating above the trees, bathed the earth with its soft radiance. The peaceful chorus of night insects and the gentle whisper of the wind in the tree tops soon lulled us to sleep.

I dreamed that we were riding over a long bridge that suddenly gave way with a deafening crash, precipitating us into the rushing stream below. I wakened with a start. Alas, it was more than a dream. The night was like ink. Lightning crackled, thunder crashed and rolled, rain descended in torrents and a fine young rivulet was bounding down the hillside and pouring directly over our bed.

Bewildered, we stumbled around in the darkness, collecting such clothing as came to hand.

"Come on," cried Dan, "let's make for the big barn up the road."

Guided by the flashes of lightning, we hastened across the field and approached the barn from above. A momentary gleam disclosed a black opening before me. I made a dive for the shelter within. Followed a sickening sense of falling, and I spread-eagled onto some yielding, hairy object which heaved and scrambled madly with much blowing and bellowing. Thus, I was made aware that my unseemly arrival had disturbed the gentle slumbers of a cow. At least I sincerely hoped that the creature belonged to the gentler sex as I backed out of the stall with more haste than elegance.

Dan, meanwhile, had located the hayloft and, guided by his voice, I groped my way to him, and notwithstanding the stimulating companionship of barley-beards and thistles, contrived to snatch a few hours' sleep.

The rain ceased about daybreak, and we returned to the scene of the evening before to collect our scattered utensils and spread the soaked bedding in the brilliant sunshine. Most of our recent purchases were ruined, the bread especially being reduced to a soggy mass, so Dan sought the farmhouse to renew our supply. He returned rather indignant with less than a half loaf of bread, for which he had paid ten cents. It then developed that the bacon had disappeared and our dozen eggs were badly scrambled, so Dan reluctantly went back to buy eggs and bacon if possible.

In a few minutes he was back empty-handed, angry right through. The farmer had demanded twenty-five cents for a half dozen eggs, which had cost us twenty cents a dozen in Morris the day before, and when Dan declined to buy had grown insulting.

We made coffee and were drinking it when a roughly dressed man approached.

"Say, folks," he began, "you better clear out of here. The boss up there is hitchin' up a team to go to Morris after the constable. I heard him vow to have you run in for trespassin' on his land."

We looked at one another in alarm. Hastily swallowing the last crumbs of bread, we rolled up our wet blankets and made ready for the road, the stranger doing all he could to help. Once on the highway we found riding out of the question because of the mud, and what to do we didn't know, especially as our friend said that the constable would be glad enough to arrest us for the fee.

"But if your wife don't mind," he concluded, "you might come down to the river with me. We're choppin' wood down there and the bunch'll hide you till the constable gets tired nosin' around and goes back to town."

No sooner said than done. The men took the wheel, and away we went through the underbrush to the woodchopper's shack. There were four men there, washing clothes, shaving and attending to the usual Sunday chores. Our adherent explained the situation and they all hustled around to make us comfortable. One built up the fire to dry our things, another hid the wheel, one went out to the road to keep watch, while the fourth arranged a place of concealment for us in the rear of the room. Hardly were the preparations complete, when the watcher reported the coming of the farmer and the constable.

We ducked to cover, the door was shut, and after a bit we heard our hosts parleying with the newcomers and demonstrating their skill in the art of graceful lying. Soon they announced that the coast was clear, but advised us to remain in retirement for an hour or two at least, and, to pass the time, suggested a trip on the river. One got out some fishing tackle, another dug bait, while a third cut rods from the willows. We all followed a winding path to the river where row boats were tied, and stepping in, were off for a little fishing excursion.

The hours flew by on the wings of delight, while the men fished in cool, shady coves or rowed upstream with the oars glinting in the sun. We had a good catch, when dark shadows athwart our course and a gusty breeze that set the water rippling proclaimed the coming of another shower.

Returning to the shanty, the men prepared the glistening spoils, and before the savoury dish was ready for the table, the rain was pounding on the roof.

As the day waned, I became the prey of serious misgivings, but about an hour before sundown the rain slackened and four of the men declared their intention of going to town to see a show, adding that they did not expect to return till morning. Our first acquaintance cooked a hearty meal, then rigged a blanket curtain across one end of the room, and warmed and dried and fed, we retired to rest, giving thanks for the spirit of true brotherhood which often manifests itself in unlikely places.

Next morning our benefactor packed a substantial lunch and started us on our journey. But so far, we have made poor progress.

Dan has just come up with the news that our one chance to proceed lies in following the railroad track, so I must up and away.

31

Well, we are making a little better time along the track than in the slush of the road, though this method of travel is far from ideal. We push the wheel between the rails, and the poor thing goes bump, bump, bump over the ties, while the cooking outfit jingles and clinks and the whole load threatens to fall off. When nerves can stand the strain no longer, we try the path at the side of the track. This we essayed to ride, but a shelving ledge where the path almost disappeared nearly sent us down the embankment, so we trundle the wheel and walk. The pedal barks my shins and I feel like saying something wicked. I hear Dan muttering under his breath and fully second what he is thinking. Just when I can no longer endure the pangs of starvation, he declares that it is time to stop for lunch. Sweet sound!

Luncheon over, I throw myself face down on the gravelled siding. When I consider the lack of money, the scarcity of work, the wretched roads and never-ending storms, my beloved California seems very far away.

CHAPTER SEVEN

# Thursday, May 14th

Before the open door of a "side-door Pullman" I sit at ease on our bedding roll with my diary on my knees, watching the Iowa prairie billow past. What a relief to view the stretches of gluey, sloppy road, serene in the knowledge that for the present at least we are free from its sticky toils.

We lunched last Monday beside the Stockdale siding and while packing our belongings preparatory to another tussle with the bike, a freight train pulled in. The train crew surveyed us with vast interest, and as the engine backed slowly past, the engineer leaned far out of the cab window.

"Whither away?" he queried.

"California or bust," yelled Dan.

The long train jarred to a stop on the siding. A brakeman appeared and entered into conversation.

"It must be pretty fierce to ride a wheel through that mud," he volunteered.

"You bet it is," agreed Dan, "and the track isn't much better. If I bark any more hide off my shins, I'll have to buy a pair of crutches."

With a shriek and a roar, a passenger train thundered through. The freight pulled slowly off the siding. The engineer leaned out as before, his big, good-natured mouth stretched in a broad grin, his right arm swinging with a scooping motion.

"Get aboard! Get aboard!" he shouted.

Dan and I exchanged glances. With one accord we jumped for the wheel which stood loaded for the start, and ran it along beside the track. Car after car groaned past. The caboose appeared. A brakeman leaned from the step and grasped the handle bars, the conductor lent a hand, and in a moment our old machine was being hoisted upon the platform while Dan and I scrambled up the steps.

Followed a detailed account of our aims and adventures, which was listened to with keen attention. The train crew held a council of war to determine the best means of procedure. About half way up the train was situated an empty box car, and to this we were transferred as soon as darkness had fallen. We spread our blankets on the floor and composed ourselves for sleep.

But alas and alack! A new crew had come aboard, who had chosen our resting place for a bumper and appeared to be switching all the cars on the middle division with it. We would enter a siding with much grinding and jarring, coming to a stop with a jolt. The train would be uncoupled in the middle, our car would advance with increasing speed, then—*whang*—we would bump the standing *gondolas*, the train would buckle at each coupling with a resounding thumping, the engine would jerk us backward, and we were off to repeat the performance.

Towards morning the door of the box car slid softly open and several men piled in. Dan asked them what they wanted and one replied, "It's all right. Bo. We're westbound bundle stiffs same as yourself."

Great was their amazement when the morning light revealed the presence of a woman. About sunrise, two jumped out to "rustle some grub" while the engine stopped for water.

The train was moving out and we had given them up, when here they came, helter-skelter, and leaped aboard the speeding car. One had some slices of meat and bread in a newspaper, while the other carried part of a loaf of bread. The food was unhesitatingly divided among the five of us and was greatly appreciated.

The scant meal finished, we settled down to talk. I was amazed at the mentality displayed by the smallest fellow, a member of the I. W. W. He seemed conversant with all the questions of the day, and expressed in, excellent language clear cut opinions on industrial subjects that were both novel and startling. They were all workers, but jobs were scarce where they came from, so they were going west in the hope of bettering their condition. The fact that thousands were at that moment travelling in the opposite direction, impelled by self-same conditions, failed to deter them.

One was a big, husky chap with rugged, honest features and the true brown eyes of a Collie. His story interested me greatly.

Born among collieries, he was driven to work as a breaker boy at a very early age by the wretched poverty of his parents. After several years of deadening toil at a time when he should have been in school, he drifted away to join the great army of migratory workers. He worked on a threshing machine while the harvest was in progress, and at its close what little money he had been able to save was consumed while searching for another job. Perhaps he got work with pick and shovel in some construction gang, but the contractor's system of low wages, high board bills, charges for physician's care—which most do not receive—and the like, kept him destitute.

He called at an employment office, where he paid two dollars for a job, was worked just long enough to pay for transportation, board and monthly fees, then discharged without wages, his employer and the agent dividing up the original fee. From coast to coast he wandered, sweating in the dust and heat of summer through long hours of racking labour, in order to escape starvation in the idle months of winter.

His eyes grew dark and wistful as he shyly confessed his one love affair. He had secured employment in a little lumber mill and made such a good impression on the boss, who was also the owner, that he was taken to board in his own home. Here the poor fellow got his first idea of what home life might mean. He fell in love with the daughter of the house, who seemed to reciprocate, but before they could enter into any formal engagement the lumber trust put the mill out of business, ruining the owner, who was forced to leave that part of the country.

Try as he would, the young man could secure no steady employment and marriage without such foundation was out of the question.

"I saw enough of getting married on nothing when I was a boy," he concluded. "Wages are set for single men, I reckon. And after a bit a fellow can't earn a living for his family, so the wife and kiddies have to rustle out and work. Easy enough for them to get a job," he added bitterly. "Many a time I've seen kids doing work that I'd been glad to get. But they can beat a man all out at working cheap. They got to work cheap or starve. I may be a good-for-nothing bundle stiff, but I've never got so low as to live off the work of little children."

"Our good business men are not so finicky," broke in the I. W. W. "A big profit looks good to them. If it comes from the coined sweat and blood of women and children, so much the better. Yes, women are cheaper than men, and kids are cheaper than women. After a bit they'll get machines that are cheaper than kids, and then the brats can rot in the slums for all they care."

"Why not let the people in general own the machines and run

35

them for use instead of for profit? Then the men could do the work, the women could stay at home and the children go to school." Thus, spoke the quiet member of the trio.

"Shut up, you crazy socialist!" exclaimed the I. W. W. "You fellows won't do anything but vote. You leave it to us. We're the boys who'll fix the machines, all right, all right. Yes, and the plutes, too."

I remembered the many I. W. W. signs and notices that were posted along the way; the groups of men beneath the water tanks who listened eagerly to the harangues of such as he. Some even had told me that they had given up liquor because it blunted their faculties at a time when brains were needed in the workers' fight against the capitalists. I seemed to hear a muttering as of a gathering storm; perhaps in the days preceding the French Revolution a similar murmuring rose.

There are so many like my dark-eyed acquaintance. He lost touch with his sweetheart, lost hope, lost ambition and now drifts aimlessly about the country in search of a bare subsistence.

It is he and the millions of his class who quarry the stone and hew the timber for our cities; they build the roadbed and lay the tracks for swiftly turning Pullman wheels; they mine the coal that warms our dwellings; they harvest the wheat that nourishes our bodies; without their labour industry would cease.

Yet life to them holds out no hope, no promise; their meagre earnings forbid the thought of marriage; their only home is some saloon; their final rest the potter's field.

About ten o'clock a trainman poked his head inside the door.

"Hey, clear out, you fellows. This is no place for you when we enter the yard. Better beat it."

The hoboes bade us *adieu* and sprang from the car. The brakeman leaped in beside us.

"We finish our run at the next stop," he said. "The engineer will slow down at the outskirts of town and you jump off and hike out. You'll find the main road over to the north."

We thanked him warmly for his kindness and made ready to follow his advice. Soon the train slowed to a mere crawl. Dan leaped down and ran alongside, I swung out the wheel, which he seized, and in an instant, I was standing beside him.

Waving farewell to the train crew, who had all turned out to see us off, we struck out for the main road. The straggling outskirts of a good-sized town lay before us.

"Tell you what," I remarked after we had traversed some distance.

"Suppose we stop in the residence section and look for work. I'll offer to do washing or cleaning by the day, and you can cut the lawn, wash the automobile or something."

Dan replied with a snort of righteous indignation. "Ever since you were bit by the crazy bug and started out to be a lady hobo you have lost all your natural pride, Ethel. It was bad enough for me, a high-class electrical engineer with a paid-up union card in my pocket, to stoop to the job of a common labourer as I did last week for your sake. Now I'll be damned if I become a dirty roustabout and have some old hen ordering me around while I sweep off the front porch."

"Oh, all right," I answered cheerily. "But the interesting hour of high noon approacheth. Will you please be so kind as to furnish me with exact information regarding your financial standing? I am pained to confess myself the victim of a too familiar craving which calls aloud for attention."

Dan thrust his hand into his pocket and withdrew a solitary ten cent piece, nor did a prolonged search of numerous pockets yield further riches.

"'Tis sad," I sighed, "but a still voice tells me that that bit of silver will prove strangely inadequate to the demands of nature. However, no doubt you can dine off your natural pride, served up on your paid-up union card, while I eat a dime's worth of doughnuts or something."

We approached a rather pretentious place as I spoke. A large brass sign announced "J. Stanchley Loane, M.D., Physician and Surgeon." I paused to study the white house with the red-roofed garage in the rear.

"This looks like a good place to make a start. Think I'll just go in and call on my fellow practitioner and see what happens."

Dan stepped in front of me. "Now see here, Ethel!" he began angrily. "Don't go to pulling off foolish stunts. You are my wife and I absolutely forbid you to go about like an Irish washerwoman and—"

"Now see here, Dan!" I mimicked, breaking in upon his authoritative harangue, "I am your wife, 'tis true, but sad to say, the fact does not prevent me from growing hungry. 'Tis also true that I am only a graduate physician with a high-class appetite. I have no paid-up union card to stand between me and possible employment with its promise of a square meal. Moreover, I have never felt myself to be so wonderfully superior to the Irish washerwomen who earn an honest living by honest labour. At any rate, I shall not attempt to hold myself above them unless I can prove by my conduct that I have that right. Just now

I fail to see how either you or I can do better than by marching up to that back door and asking for work like the genuine bundle stiffs that we are. Of course, if you desire to remain here on the curb, upholding your dignity while I ask for employment, you are entirely at liberty to do so. As for me, I'm going in right now."

As I turned up the concrete driveway Dan leaned the wheel against the fence and followed. I rapped at the door of the screen porch. The inner door was opened and a heavy-set man with bristling, reddish hair stepped out.

"Good morning, Doctor Loane," I began. "My husband and I are cycling to California, and being short of funds are looking for employment. My husband is an excellent mechanic and will be glad to go over your car for you. I can cook, wash, scrub or do any kind of housework."

The doctor looked us up and down with an insolent stare.

"So, you can cook, can you? Suppose you come in and show what you can do. I'm alone in the house today. We have a devilish time with servants. Our last maid—a pretty little fool—got on her high horse and quit us yesterday, and the old harridan of a cook followed suit. My wife's gone to town to get another bunch."

"Sit down on the porch, you," he ordered Dan, "and you step in here. There is the pantry and the ice chest. Throw together some sort of lunch and call me when it's ready." He waved his hand with a lordly air and disappeared into the front of the house.

A short inspection enabled me to determine on a suitable menu, and soon a very fair lunch was spread on the dining table.

"Humph! You are quite a clever piece of goods," the doctor volunteered, as I summoned him to the meal. "Go and feed your man now, and later we'll find something more for you to do."

The meal concluded. Dr. Loane took Dan to the garage, while I whisked the dishes away and tidied the kitchen. The doctor entered as I finished my task.

"There is some work to be attended to in my private office, and you are just the one to do it for me," he grinned ingratiatingly.

I felt my face growing hot as I realised what he meant.

"What work do you want me to do?" I asked, rising to my feet.

He advanced with outstretched arms, a bestial demon looking out of his red-brown eyes. I backed behind the table, fury and dread causing my heart to beat tumultuously.

Just then a short ring came at the side entrance. Dr. Loane drew back with a muttered curse. We stood motionless for a moment. The bell rang again, insistently.

"You, you keep quiet now. Remember what you are," he hissed, and strode to the door.

I lost no time in dashing to the garage, where I found Dan tinkering with the car.

"Come, Dan, quick! Let's get out of here," I cried.

"What's up, Ethel?" He came out wiping his hands on a piece of waste.

"Never mind an explanation. I'll tell you later." I spoke imperiously. "Get the wheel now and don't stop to talk."

We started in the direction of the business section of the city.

"I think we had better take the wheel over by the railroad yard, Dan, and see if you can't arrange for us to take a freight out of here. I'm a trifle nervous about that old beast of a doctor. He impressed me as the kind of man to make us trouble if possible, have us arrested or something."

At the station I waited for Dan to see what arrangements he could make. In a few moments he returned to the waiting-room door with a troubled countenance.

"A freight is going to pull out in about an hour, but I haven't been able to make any impression on the crew. You know, the rules are pretty strict against carrying passengers on freight trains and the boys are afraid of their jobs. I think we'd better give up the idea and ride out on the bike. I cached it down at the end of the yard."

"I think I'd better talk to the trainmen, Dan," I replied seriously. "I'd like to get away as soon as possible. I am afraid the doctor may make trouble for us."

We walked up the track to where a freight engine was puffing back and forth placing cars in a long train, like a fussy old woman stringing beads. A lean-jawed man in blue denim with a conductor's cap pulled over his eyes turned at our approach.

"Good evening, Conductor," I began, looking him full in the face. "We have no money and we must get out of this town immediately. I should like to put our bicycle, which is down at the end of the yard, in some empty car that you are going to take out tonight, and get a lift for fifteen or twenty miles."

His keen grey eyes bored into mine. "What's the trouble that you got to get out of town? Been holding up somebody?" he queried gruffly.

"My husband and I rode into town this morning and started to hunt work as usual. We stopped at a doctor's house over on the north side, Doctor Stanchley Loane's and he gave us work for the day. His wife was out, my husband was cleaning the auto in the garage, and while I was at work in his private office, he attacked me. I gave him the slip and got away. Now, if we ride the wheel out of town, I'm afraid he'll make trouble for us. He expects us to go that way."

"The old son-of-a—" the conductor stopped abruptly. "He's a bad egg all right. We all know that, but I scarcely thought he'd dare go so far. Of course, your being a sort of hobo—" He stopped again. "Reckon he didn't take a very close look at those shoulders of yours, or he wouldn't have tried to get fresh. Well, we'll see what can be done. Where did you say your wheel is?"

Dan described its location.

"All right. You go there and be ready. We'll shunt an empty down that way and when the coast seems clear, you pile aboard and lie low. It's a risky business, but it's all in a lifetime." He turned away and began signalling the engineer.

Dan and I scuttled down the track. When we had the wheel in hand, ready for loading, he turned to me.

"Did that old devil actually try to lay hands on you? Why didn't you tell me when you came out to the garage? I'd like to go back and crack his nut for him."

"I'm glad enough to get out of the nasty scrape without any skull-cracking. You must remember that we are looked upon as hoboes, and hoboes have no rights. I do wish the men would hurry with that car."

As though in answer to my thought, a box car rolled gently down the track and came to a stop not ten feet from where we waited.

"Good shot," said Dan as we slid back the side door, which was ajar.

A long look around and I scrambled in, while Dan, hoisted up the wheel and quickly followed. The bottom of the car was packed solid with radiators, which were piled almost to the top in the rear end, each tier held in place by heavy braces. We stacked the tandem in a convenient corner and crouched in silence on the crates.

Soon there came a clinking rumble, there was a slight jar, and our car moved up the line to take its place in the outgoing train.

An hour or more passed while the train roared on. Dan sat by the door, while I, lulled by the clank of wheels and the panting breath of the engine that was whirling us homeward, leaned against the radiator braces in the centre of the car and lost myself in dreams.

Came a shriek of the whistle, a grinding crash, and the floor of the car seemed to buckle under me while something dealt me a terrific blow between the shoulders, lifting me clear into the air and flinging me headlong against the front timbers.

Consciousness struggled back from the void of nothingness and I heard Dan's agonised voice in my ear.

"My God, Ethel, speak to me. Are you hurt? Oh, she doesn't answer! She can't be dead! Ethel! Ethel!"

As he dragged my limp body toward the door a flaming torture seared my lungs, my mouth filled with a hot, brackish fluid. "Wait," I gasped, half strangled. "Let me rest a moment. I'll be all right in a minute." He must not know my plight; I turned my head away as his groping fingers caressed my hair, thankful for the thick darkness as I freed my mouth of blood.

"Oh, thank God! Thank God!" he was whispering softly as he tried to lift me in his arms.

'Let me lie flat for a little while, dear. Then I'll get up. Are you all right?"

"Yes, I'm O. K. It wasn't a regular wreck. We must have run into something. The shock threw the radiators about. The air seemed full of them, but I got off scot free. You and the tandem and the radiators were all in a scramble. I thought I should never get you out. You're sure you are not hurt?"

"I feel rather shaken, but I believe there is nothing serious the matter. I had a rap that put me out for a few minutes, that's all."

"What happened?" called Dan to the conductor who approached with a lantern, as I finished scrubbing the blood from my face.

"A drunken bum stalled his team on the crossing. The engine rounded the curve and was within a hundred feet before Sam saw the wagon. The good-for-nothing sot was off in front of the horses, else he would be in kingdom come. How did you come out? Did it shake you up much when Sam set the emergencies?"

"My wife had a pretty thorough pounding. The blamed radiators broke loose and piled up in the front of the car. Guess we'd better try another Pullman or clear out altogether. What do you want to do, Ethel?"

"Oh, let's ride as far as we can. Even a freight train covers ground so quickly compared to our slow old wheel."

"All right, but we'd better hunt another carriage."

The conductor stood hesitating. "This radiator car is billed straight through to Frisco," he informed us. "I picked her out for that reason. There ain't many cars left open like she is. Don't know how it comes she ain't sealed shut. But if you have real good luck, you might be able to skate right through to Frisco in a week or ten days. It'll be a pretty rough trip, but if you want to get to Cal in a hurry, it'll beat pumping a bike."

"Oh, Dan, we must try it. I'd ride the bumpers or the cowcatcher to get home in a week," I cried, forgetting my pain in such a joyful prospect.

"It seems a trifle risky to trust those radiators again, but you're the doctor, so here goes."

As Dan settled down beside me the conductor slipped a bill into his hand and ducked away. The engineer signalled that he was ready to be off. When the train took the next siding to permit repairs on the engine, Dan secured a lantern and we straightened our tangled possessions and made ourselves as comfortable as possible for the night.

I was glad when Dan slept, for I feared he would notice my restless seeking for some posture in which I could forget my aches and pains in sleep. But my hopes were in vain, for mind and body conspired to hold my nerves at a tension. The events of the day, which seemed of a month's duration, formed a kaleidoscopic jumble in my brain.

Morning dawned at last and I lay prone on the radiator crates, while Dan busied himself with the tandem, which had also suffered in the *mêlée* of the evening before.

It was nearly dark when we pulled into the railroad yard at Des Moines. Our car was switched off the main track, and Dan immediately got out to purchase provisions for the western trip. Trembling at every noise, I awaited his return, and it was not long till he was back with an armful of bundles and a kettle of water. Another train was being made up and soon our car was shunted into place. The engineer had given the signal for the crew to assemble and my breath had begun to come easier, when the door was jerked open and a man thrust in his head.

"Hey, yous! Come out of that," he snarled. "Here, Tim, I've found a couple of boes. Come on out now," as we made no move. "If you don't, you'll wish you had in about two seconds."

Slowly Dan clambered out. I followed.

"What to hell have we here? Blamed if it ain't a woman!" the detective cried.

Tim, meanwhile, advanced with a lantern, and having given us a close inspection, leaped into the car.

"What in blazes is this?" he exclaimed, catching sight of the wheel. Dan explained shortly.

"Well, yank her out of here. This car moves in about two minutes."

Dan sprang inside and lowered the wheel to me. Tim threw our bundles to the ground. "*Toot, toot*," whistled the engine. The train pulled out.

As the familiar car moved away, my heart seemed breaking. All my hopes of reaching California in a few days crashed to the ground; thoughts of the fierce railroad detectives, the waiting jail, the courtroom in the morning, surged over me. I burst into tears.

"What ya goin' t' do wid 'em, Joe? Run 'em in?" queried Tim.

"Naw, don't believe I will. Come, now," turning to us. "Beat it out o' here and don't let me catch yous fooling around this yard any more. Go on. Beat it quick."

Glad enough to escape, we stumbled up the track through the darkness.

"Aw now, aw now," said a hoarse voice at my elbow. "It's pretty fierce luck, all right. But never you mind, lady, we'll get you out of here all right. Just come right along to our shack and we'll fix you up fine."

In a few minutes we came to a tiny one-room shanty, formed from an old car, which was fitted up with a stove, bunks, a table and chairs. My kindly guide set out soap, clean towels and a fine, big basin of hot water. What luxury! I plunged my grimy hands into the grateful depths and laved my blackened, tear-stained face.

When Dan had made a refreshing toilet, we sat down to the first real meal in two days. Our friends, the car inspectors, watched us eat with much satisfaction while discussing the best method of getting us safely out of Des Moines. Picking up his switchman's lantern, one stepped out and soon returned with the report that an empty car would go out in a freight that left about two o'clock.

The men conducted us by a circuitous way to a cattle car, the bottom of which was covered with a thick layer of clean straw. The detectives had already examined and passed this car, so under the protection of the car inspectors, it was quite safe to climb aboard. Our wheel was hoisted in and laid flat in a corner, and after an attempt to express our gratitude—really too deep for words—we ourselves lay down and were well covered with straw. I fell asleep immediately.

The rays of a lantern, which was thrust within a few inches of my face, aroused me. The train was grinding to a stop, and as I blinked stupidly in the sudden light, I heard voices deep in argument.

"I tell you, they're no spotters. She has an honest face."

And another voice answered, "Well, let 'em ride to the next station and ask 'em a few questions."

The lantern flashed the signal, and once more we were under way.

The "brakie" settled himself in the straw. Dan produced his union card, our marriage license and other papers to prove our identity; the wheel was uncovered for inspection, and a few questions confirmed the brakeman in his opinion of our honesty. At the next stop the conductor joined us and agreed to move us into a closed car before daylight.

So today we rest in comfort and despite the ache of bruised and stiffened shoulders I am happy in the thought that tomorrow's dawn will see us close to Council Bluffs.

## Chapter Eight

# June 3rd, Somewhere in Nebraska

At last I know the joys of domestic service. The pleasures of the "hired girl" and all the privileges and emoluments pertaining to her high estate have been mine.

Our good friends, the train crew, who carried us out of Des Moines, dropped us off at the first little station east of Council Bluffs early in the morning of May 15th. We determined to cycle into town, get breakfast and look for work. We were making good time and had entered the suburbs when, as we spun around a corner and approached a large red house, surrounded by a tall hedge, a series of brain-piercing shrieks rent the air. My control of the wheel was none too steady that morning and the shock was too much for frayed nerves and stiffened muscles. The tandem took the bit in its teeth and in a jiffy had buried its nose in the thick branches at the base of the hedge. I landed on my feet, and through a break in the shrubbery saw the cause of the commotion.

In an angle of the enclosure a red hen was flapping and squawking, her brood of downy chickens dashing hither and thither, pursued by a large mongrel dog. Within a high wire fence, evidently the chicken yard, a moon-faced woman stood like a marionette, her fat hands shooting into the air with a rhythmic precision which synchronised perfectly with the dropping of her lower jaw which opened widely with each vocal effort.

As I stared, the dog captured a tiny chick and tossed it high in the air. I dashed forward and seized the brute by the scruff of the neck and dragged it, growling and struggling, to the break in the hedge where Dan came to my assistance and sent the animal howling down the road.

I turned back to the frightened brood and was joined by the female calliope. Together we gathered the cowering mites from their places of concealment among the grass and weeds and at last saw the mother safe in the coop, her decimated family huddled about her.

"You know chickens, oh, you know," the lady puffed. "These are prize birds—all, all prize stock—I paid an outrageous price for them—Tamas said it was very short-sighted to do so—but you know chickens."

"I couldn't stand idly by while that hateful dog mangled the little things," I interrupted.

"Of course not, with prize stock like these. You know, oh, you know."

Dan approached with the tandem, the front tyre of which was sadly flattened.

"Got a puncture when you rammed the hedge. Guess we'll have to camp here till I can patch the inner tube. Maybe you can buy a few eggs and cook breakfast. I'm nearly starved."

"Not these eggs. Not these eggs. These are all prize stock, every one a prize winner." The arms of the moon-faced madam made an upward sweep. I clapped my hands over my ears instinctively. But a compassionate Fate in the shape of a young girl intervened.

"Breakfast's ready, Ma'am," she sang out "Mr. MacBride says he will be right in."

A tremendous struggle was mirrored in my lady's open countenance. She looked at the "prize chickens," turned toward the house, shot a covert glance at Dan, gazed anxiously at the chickens again. It was a solemn moment. But fear and hospitality triumphed.

"Maybe you better come in. I don't know what Tamas will say. But the dog would have killed more—all prize stock—so short-sighted of me . . ."

Thus, rambling on, she led the way into the house, while the maid stared unbelievingly. It came my turn for wonderment when I caught sight of the breakfast table. It was loaded with great bowls of oatmeal, cream, sausage, eggs, potatoes, and a heaping plate of graham or oatmeal gems. An odour of hot cakes spoke of more food to follow.

"You must wait till Tamas has finished. Just sit down here. I hear him coming now."

Our hostess turned in much agitation as a long, cadaverous individual entered the door. He halted and fixed us with a hostile glare.

"Now, Tamas, now—this lady saved my prize doggins from a chick—oh, dickens from a chog—oh, oh, what am I saying!"

Dan uttered a strangled snort. The mingled horror and wrath on Tamas' face was indescribable. His unfortunate wife once more essayed an explanation.

"He—he was going to suck the eggs. But I told him they were all—all prize eggs. Then I thought it best to bring them in here."

"Probably under the circumstances it was the safest thing to do, ah. So, you go about the country begging, do you?" He turned to Dan. "I am surprised, surprised and pained. Your wife—I presume she is your wife?—appears quite intelligent, ah." He dragged out each word as from the depths of ultimate wisdom.

"Well, I'll admit that my wife does show gleams of intelligence at times," Dan responded gravely.

"Those thoroughbred fowls are provoking, most provoking, ah." Mr. MacBride turned to his palpitating wife. "You see, my dear, how very short-sighted it was of you to bargain for them while I was in Omaha. Such a waste and loss—no profit. I shall be compelled to foreclose on old lady Martin's poultry farm next week, which will give us some of the finest fowls in this county—and at absolutely no expense for feed and care, no bother, no annoyance. All profit, clear profit, mark you that."

He licked his lips physically and metaphorically as he seated himself at the table and attacked a bowl of oatmeal and cream. His performance reminded me of a dredger I once saw at work in the Sacramento Valley. The spoon work was wonderful—his only rival in endless chain effect being a Chinaman with chopsticks.

The girl removed the empty bowl and replaced it with a plate heaped with sausage, eggs and fried potatoes, which Mr. MacBride fell upon with undiminished zeal, his wife meanwhile plying us with questions.

"You, I take it, are presumably working people—that is, you will no doubt accept employment if such is presented to you," he began after a prolonged period of uninterrupted labour. "Now, there is one grave failing to which the working classes of America abandon themselves, ah. They eat too much."

With consummate skill he flipped into his thin-lipped, rapacious mouth an enormous forkful of sausages and potatoes, which he swallowed at a single gulp.

"I have read scientific articles, articles written by experts, which prove with mathematical accuracy that a workingman can live comfortably on nine cents a day, ah."

"Tamas knows, oh, he knows," chirped his wife delightedly.

"But the average workingman's outlay is far, far beyond reason. This whole nation is suffering from extravagance and overfeeding, ah."

"But thousands of people, in the cities especially, eat scarcely enough to sustain life," I ventured.

"Slums, bah, slums, human dregs unworthy of an intelligent man's consideration. Of course, they live in poverty. Why not? It is all their own fault—lack of thrift, extravagance and laziness." He paused to drain a cup of tea.

"But there is never any real poverty in the country districts. Now this community, for instance, is prosperous, most prosperous. I never get less than 8 *per cent*, on my loans."

"That certainly does speak well for the community and yourself," I conceded.

"I flatter myself that I am a good business man, an excellent example of the pure American type, conservative, patriotic, a solid all-round citizen. But our low, ignorant foreigners must be educated. I have endeavoured to collect a fund among our leading merchants to secure a teacher to inculcate an idea of thrift. Such work should really be done by the government. Thrift, ah—the lack of thrift is the curse of this nation. Just imagine the business gain if our extravagant working class could be brought to live on nine cents a day."

"But I don't understand," I murmured, eyeing him with interest. "If your patrons ate less, they might save money, and then they would not borrow money of you at 8 *per cent*, interest, and the prosperity of this community would suffer."

"Not at all, not at all." He leaned forward with a first suggestion of animation. "With the price of land as it is, the cost of farm implements, the high taxes on improvements and the irregularity of crops, it is simply impossible for a man of small capital to escape a mortgage. Now the point is this. With the present high cost of living, the farmer pays even a moderate interest of 8 *per cent*, say, with extreme difficulty. But with proper instruction in thrift, I have no doubt rates could be raised to 12 *per cent*, and still not prove prohibitive." He paused to butter a muffin.

"I hold land that I purchased for a song years ago. I hold it unimproved as the advance in land values, as the small farmers come in, amply repays me. But some of it I subdivided and sold at fat prices. Why, one of those farms has been foreclosed on five times in the last fifteen years. Each owner has added improvements, of course, but not what they should have done. If I could have had a series of really ambitious men on it, I now would own one of the finest farms in this section. But my farmers don't seem to understand thrift."

He sighed heavily as the maid set out the remains of the meal for our consumption. Dan, no doubt deeming imitation the sincerest flattery, seemed bent on equalling his host's remarkable performance as trencherman. Mr. MacBride eyed each mouthful with scowling anguish, while with each succeeding minute his wife's agitation increased.

"Really, my good man, your appetite is excessive, positively abnormal. I had thought of permitting you to work a few days for your board and lodging, but that is manifestly impossible. It would never do. Moderation, my good man, moderation should be the keynote in all things."

We passed from the MacBride domicile in comparative quiet.

Dan soon had the puncture repaired and the wheel ready for the road. We mounted and presently were gliding through the streets of Council Bluffs.

A few hours' inquiry convinced Dan of his inability to get work at his trade, but he heard that there was a chance of employment on a truck farm east of town, so we rode out to locate the place.

After some argument, we were engaged, I to do the housework, Dan to work in the fields. The farmer first offered a dollar a day between us, but we finally secured a dollar and a half a day and board. We were immediately put to work tying bunches of radishes, onions and other vegetables for market.

About ten in the evening, as we went to the bare room assigned us, the woman handed me an alarm clock set for four a. m. with orders to serve breakfast promptly at five so the men could be at work by five-thirty.

Nightmare days followed. Always up at four in the morning, I was kept constantly at work until after I had cooked the nine o'clock supper for two men who made the late trip to town each evening.

The house was a large one. There were four children, the man and his wife, an old aunt and five hired men besides Dan and myself to cook for. The laundry had remained undone since the last girl left, and present opportunities were not to be overlooked. Such heaps of soiled clothing I never saw before. Then, when cooking, cleaning, washing and ironing were done, if perchance there was half an hour to spare, I was set at the never-ending task of tying vegetables. On Sunday the mistress of the house wanted to know whether I could darn stockings, as I ought to be able to do a good deal of mending on that day.

To cap it all, the couple quarrelled constantly, nagged the children and one another and railed at the poor old aunt by the hour. When not so engaged, the woman would snoop through our scanty belongings, ask me all manner of personal questions and follow me about with talk of the good home she was giving me and how few people there were who would take tramps and hoboes right into their own comfortable houses and care for them. Poor Dan was driven like a slave from dawn till dark and after, so at the end of a week, we concluded to take to the road once more.

When Dan informed the man of our intentions and asked for our money, such a storm of invective was loosed as is seldom heard. We were lazy, good-for-nothing bums who were too shiftless to do honest work, but wanted to live off thrifty, economical people who had some ambition in life. The woman declared that I was an ungrateful dog—only she did not say dog, but referred to the female of the species—that I had imposed on her hospitality for a whole week, but she supposed that was all one could expect for trying to do a good turn to dirty sewer rats. The man then burst into shocking profanity, which Dan cut short by suggesting the imminence of a stiff punch on the jaw.

As we were riding away from the "good home," I recalled experiences related by servant girls with whom I had come in contact in the practice of my profession. I remembered the little maid who was on duty habitually sixteen hours a day in the mansion of a San Francisco millionaire. She became violently insane and was sent to the Napa State Hospital. I thought of the great number of household workers to be found in such institutions, and of the terrifying increase in insanity. Then my thoughts turned to those who go astray and others who lead lives of shame, and the large percentage that are recruited from the ranks of servant girls. My mind dwelt on the attitude of friends who counted the "good home" given a girl a large part of her reward for service rendered.

A good home. What is it? Food and shelter? Yes, but it is something more. Personal comfort, the exercise of individual taste in the choice of one's intimate surroundings, the joy of ownership, the privilege of entertaining one's friends, a sense of privacy, a certain liberty of habits—all these, added to that greatest of all great gifts, love, and the presence of the loved ones, make a true home.

We were approaching the Missouri River when black clouds heaped themselves across the horizon, and soon blasts of wind and rain forced us to seek the shelter of a rude shack on the river bank. A bent, white-bearded man opened the door and invited us in with all the warmth and grace of real southern hospitality. There was scant room the wheel beneath the tiny porch, and the two rooms were already overcrowded.

A feeble old lady, swathed in shawls, sat in a rough box chair at the window. A young girl with a baby but a few days old on her arm lay on the bed, while a woman, evidently the daughter of the old couple, fussed about her. A tall, incredibly lanky girl was kept busy placing pots and pans to catch the drippings from the roof, which leaked in a dozen places.

In ten minutes, we were chatting as freely as lifelong friends. The old man was a Confederate veteran, who had been wrecked financially and physically by the Civil War. He and his invalid wife had moved by degrees from Kentucky across Illinois and Iowa to their present location. One child only had survived the many privations. She had married young and been left a widow with two little girls. The eldest of these, the pale girl in the bed, had married a youth of eighteen when little more than a child. The baby which formed the fourth generation in this home of poverty awakened with a feeble wail. The mother showed me the wriggling red mite with an air of pride, but suddenly she turned her head away and burst into tears.

"Oh, Tony, Tony," she moaned, "how can they keep you away from your own beautiful baby boy?"

"Her Tony's in the jail," the old man volunteered with slow bitterness. "In the jail because he couldn't see his wife and unborn baby starve. We had bad luck last winter. I'm an old man. My right hand never has been worth anything since the war." He extended his withered arm, drawn and distorted by an old wound. "I've done all I could, but work is scarce for such as me."

"Folks won't give Grandpap a job. They call him an old Copperhead." The younger girl spoke for the first time.

"I fought for the South. I love her. Should my great-grandchild be starved for that?"

"The children had typhoid fever, Tony and Sadie and Stella." The quiet, brown-eyed widow took up the story. "Tony took sick at the camp—he'd only been there a few weeks—and came home the last of October ready to die. Sadie took it next. She was carrying little

Tony and it went hard with her, Then Stella came down. I thought we would lose them all. We had no money for anything. It was weeks and weeks before Tony got better and then he wasn't strong. I took in washing when the worst was over, and Pap did all he could. Tony, he's an orphan and Italian besides,—a *Dago* they call him." Her voice trailed off despondently.

"Tony is as good an American as ever lived," Sadie spoke up fiercely, "a sight better than the scrubs around here. Supposing his folks was Italian. What difference does that make?"

"Tony got work teaming," the old man spoke again. "We had no food in the house, the weather was cold, Sadie was weak from the fever and crying with hunger all the time. He got to taking things from the cars and bringing them home. One time he brought a case of canned soup. How the girls did go for it. It was their salvation.

"Then one night it was snowing hard. Tony came in all tuckered out—he never was one of these husky boys—and he was sitting over the stove, with Sadie trying to cheer him up. All of a sudden, the door flew open with a bang and in walks a couple of men—didn't knock or nothing, just walked in—and put the handcuffs on him and dragged him away. I'll never forget his black eyes, looking so big in his white face as he stared back at Sadie who had fallen in a faint."

"And now he's in jail, my Tony. He never knew what it was to have a single soul to love him till he met me. Just an orphan and a bound boy. He was always so good to me, working hard for a home and children. And now he can't see his own son. Oh, Tony, Tony!" She flung herself about in agony.

"Hush, honey, hush. Think of little Tony. You'll poison the milk if you take on that away."

The frail mother quieted her grief and clasped her baby in an ecstasy of mother-love. "I must take good care of you, mother's little angel. Daddy will come back to his own little baby boy someday."

The rain had stopped, so we said goodbye to the unfortunate family and resumed our journey.

"There is no real poverty in the country districts, is there now?" I remarked as we pushed the wheel along the sloppy road.

"Oh, Tamas knows—he knows," returned Dan grimly.

The old Confederate had told us of another truck farm not far distant where we could probably find employment, so we located a convenient clump of willows and made camp for the night.

Early next morning we applied for work at the farm and were set to the task of weeding onions, ten hours' work for a dollar a day and board. Slowly the hours dragged past. The noon hour found me far too weary to eat, so I flung myself face down under a tree, while Dan sought the cook house with the other hands.

Once more I began work on the interminable rows. The sun beat down with intense heat, my back seemed literally broken. As I weeded in a daze, a peculiar illusion took possession of my mind. I saw a cosy room in San Francisco, caught a whiff of cooling, bracing fog, fresh from the Pacific, heard the unctuous tones of a well-groomed, fat-jowled, long-haired gentleman who was declaiming to a group of adoring females, lengthy verses of his own composition on the "Joy of Labour." Oh, grave and paunchy poet, would that thou wert here to busy thy soft white hands with gummy weeds and thistles and reap a harvest of joy and onions in my stead!

About three o'clock something happened. I found myself lying under the tree at the side of the field, with Dan pouring water over my face.

"What's the matter, Dan?" I demanded, bewildered by my new and strange sensations.

"Oh, nothing much. You pitched forward on your head about half an hour ago and I thought you would never come to. You mark my words now. This ends it. You don't do any more weed pulling or washing or scrubbing on this trip. If I can't earn the living I'll beg or steal."

"It was my back, dear. I haven't recovered from the thump I got that night in the radiator car. As soon as that spot gets well, I'll be able to do any kind of work."

"You may be able, but you won't do it. I'll see to that after this. You lie here and meditate on what I've been telling you while I finish this infernal day's work. We'll beat it into Omaha in the morning and I'll look for a white man's job." With a farewell pat he returned to the weeding, leaving me to fall asleep in utter exhaustion.

We trundled over the long bridge across the Missouri River and passed through Omaha early the following morning. In a grove of trees on the western outskirts of the city, Dan pitched camp and made me as comfortable as possible, then mounted the wheel and rode into Omaha to search for work.

I was stretched full length on the ground, enjoying the rustle of the wind in the tree tops and the murmur of a tiny brook, when my attention was attracted by the sound of footsteps and a moment later a dainty child in a blue pinafore appeared at the edge of the little hollow. I smiled a welcome and she came closer and leaned against a nearby tree,

"Are you having a picnic all by yourself?" she asked, fingering her apron.

"Yes, a kind of picnic. I'm all by myself because my husband has gone to Omaha. You come over here and sit down by me and then I won't be lonesome anymore."

She approached and snuggled by my side. We introduced ourselves and soon were deep in an interchange of confidences. She located various birds' nests for me, described the latest family of kittens, discussed the number of eggs laid by her white pullet and many other matters of interest. Then I noticed that she seemed uneasy, examining our luggage with searching glances. Finally, eight-year-old flesh and blood could endure no more.

"Is the picnic in that bundle?" she asked wistfully. "When are you going to eat it?"

"There isn't very much in that bundle. All I have is bread and butter, but I'll get you some of that," I replied, sitting up.

Her face fell, then brightened. "I know what I'll do," she cried, springing to her feet and clapping her hands joyously. "I'll run home and ask mother to put me up some cookies—and some jam—and some hard-boiled eggs—and maybe some animal crackers, horses, you know, and cows and things—oh, I'll get lots and lots of good things to eat, and then I'll come back and we'll have the very nicest picnic ever you saw in all your life." She danced away with fairy-like grace, leaving me to picture her mother's expression when informed of the woman who was holding a picnic all by herself on nothing but bread and butter.

Some fifteen minutes passed. Then I heard a gay "hoo-hoo," and down the hillside came my girlie, skipping up and down and hastening the footsteps of a woman whom I knew at first glance to be her mother.

"This is Ethel, mother," she cried as I rose to my feet. Then turning to me, "Now you can't be lonesome any more, 'cause mother's come her own self."

There are persons to whom no introduction is necessary; we recognise them at once as old friends. Thus, it was with Mrs. Patton and myself. She was soon in possession of my story and invited me to her home to rest and spend as many days as circumstances would permit. I pinned a note for Dan on the tree trunk, gathered our belongings, and set off for the house. Hazel piloted us over the ridge, through orchards and across fields until we came to a long, low farmhouse, cuddling between two hills and almost hidden by masses of vines and trees.

Mrs. Patton was a trained nurse and at once set to work to demonstrate her capabilities. She heated water, gave me a prolonged hot bath, followed by a thorough spine-stretching and massage, tucked me into bed, fed me a bountiful lunch, and then left me to dream away the afternoon in blissful comfort.

I awakened about six o'clock, wonderfully relieved and refreshed and found that my hostess had sent her son to watch for Dan at the crossroads and guide him to the house.

At dinner we were introduced to Mr. Patton and John, who were greatly interested in the story of our adventures. I told them of the old Confederate soldier, of Sadie grieving for her Tony in the jail, and they were horrified to learn that such misery existed so close at hand.

"Of course, I've been aware that there were all kinds of suffering and wretchedness in the slums of large cities," Mr. Patton sighed, "but I thought there was no real poverty in the country districts."

Dan shot me a covert glance.

"You'll get the poor man out of jail, so he can see his little baby, won't you, father dear?" Hazel inquired eagerly.

"Well, well. I'll see what can be done. It's a shame that such conditions should exist in a country as rich as this."

When we had repaired to the living room, Mrs, Patton suggested music, and upon my delighted acquiescence, John set the Victrola to playing. Then for the first time I recognised one cause of my persistent heart-hunger. My soul was starving for music. Thrills of ecstasy agitated me almost to tears as the passionate strains of Tchaikovsky's "Melodic" flooded the room with pulsating harmonies. Raff's "Cavatina" seemed the divine expression of universal longing for home and love—*heimweh* incarnate.

Once, when we had first moved into Chicago's slums, I took my guitar and sang. Simple songs came to my lips, lullabies, songs of the South, the old, old songs that caress the heart strings. A noise at the door startled me. I swung it open and started back in surprise. Porch, stairway and area below were packed with children all absorbed in my poor performance. Many times, thereafter I sat at the narrow entrance and sang while children and adults crowded about, always asking for more. But at last the increasing pinch of hunger goaded me into carrying the precious guitar, relic of girlhood days, to the pawnbroker, there to bid it goodbye forever.

Millions of acres of land lying barren in the hands of speculators, hordes of idle men roaming the country in search of employment, tons of delicious fruit rotting on the ground in California, hungry women, billionaires, destitute children, great masses of wealth producers starving mentally and physically while the fruits of their labour are denied them.

Would to God that the people of this nation could learn to think!

Dan's efforts to find work in Omaha were unavailing, so after another day's rest we struck out on the military road leading away from the city. Two days' travel convinced us that we were hopelessly wrong.

I now look upon myself as something of an expert in mud, and I can truthfully recommend the Nebraska article to be superior in cohesion, adhesion, weight and quantity to any known combination of earth and water. After a few hundred yards of travel, the wheels and skirt guard would completely disappear in great masses of reddish *adobe*, while our feet assumed elephantine proportions. Standing first on one foot, then on the other, we would rid ourselves of a few pounds of mother earth and scrape the wheel as free as possible from its accumulations. A struggle onward of a quarter of a mile forced us to repeat the process.

A day passed—and another. Food ran out and farmers refused to sell; there were no stores, and the situation grew desperate.

We approached a schoolhouse one evening and stopped under a horse shed for the night. The teacher was passing and stopped to chat. Later she returned with a bottle of malted milk tablets, which constituted our evening meal.

Next morning, we turned south to reach the railroad. About one o'clock we came to a little blacksmith shop, and after some haggling, bought a half loaf of mouldy bread for a dime. Pushing on for perhaps a mile, we stopped in a lonely spot to make tea. Everything was dripping with moisture from recent rains, so, despite Dan's vigorous efforts, the fire refused to burn.

We were both on our knees blowing lustily when a shadow falling athwart the rack attracted our attention and, glancing up, we saw a bareheaded man standing with folded arms, fixedly regarding us. We sat back and stared, for we had seen no house in that vicinity.

"When you get tired exercising your lungs," began the stranger, "just follow me and get a surprise."

Thinking that any change must be an improvement on our situation, we gathered up the cooking utensils and obediently dragged the wheel after our guide, who plunged into a thick growth of trees on our right.

A few minutes' walk brought us to an immense tent, from which issued a great noise of crunching, stamping and snorting. Passing around to the far end, we beheld, stretching down one side of the interior, a long row of horses and mules—perhaps twenty in number—busily munching their noonday feed, while the other side of the tent was fitted with a kitchen range, a gasoline stove, cooking utensils, table and chairs, and in the rear some bunks and a great pile of hay. Leading the way through the kitchen, the stranger pulled out a curtain strung on a wire, closing off the rear compartment, and brought a huge kettle of hot water, buckets of cold, a large tub, towels and soap, with directions to enjoy ourselves while he prepared a meal. And what a delight it was to have the use of such conveniences, crude as they were. My opinion of "dirty hoboes" has undergone a radical change since I have seen for myself the difficulties that beset the man who has nothing, in his efforts toward cleanliness.

Our ablutions performed, we entered the kitchen and found our host deep in the labour of cooking. And what a meal he set out. Hot biscuits, mashed potatoes, broiled ham and cream gravy, fried eggs and a pot of delicious coffee.

The meal was nearly over before his strange manner impressed me. Opening a large bread box, he took the entire contents and going down the row of animals fed the loaves to them, talking meanwhile in a most astounding fashion. Returning, he escorted us to the rear room and insisted on our lying down, saying that we must be tired, as indeed we were. The words were scarcely spoken when a heavy rain beat a tattoo on the tent walls.

"Confound this weather," began our host, settling himself in a chair; "I'm two-thirds crazy now, and another three days of this beastly rain will drive me completely nutty."

He held a large contract for road construction, the grading outfit was his, and "the damned cattle were eating him out of house and home while he was sewed up by the weather." It seemed the grading crew had gone to Omaha to celebrate their enforced holiday, but should be back that day.

Reaching under the bed, the boss produced an empty demijohn and informed us that he had drunk the contents to cure the blues. He congratulated himself on our opportune arrival, declaring that he intended to keep us so long as the rain continued as an antidote to loneliness and its alcoholic consequences.

Just then the smith who had sold us the bread, appeared on the scene in search of the usual hospitable stimulant. Our host at once produced another demijohn and stood treat, imbibing freely himself. While the two men were thus engaged, a foaming horse, hitched to a covered buggy, dashed up to the tent door, and two women followed by a couple of half-drunken men clambered out. Fishing under the seat, one fellow drew out four good-sized jugs of whiskey.

Night had fallen and the rain was beating heavily, but Dan and I exchanged one glance, seized our hats and made for the wheel, which stood, still packed, just within the entrance. Hastily we backed it out and plunged into the stygian darkness. We had covered a bare hundred feet when wild yells and shouts for our return showed that our flight was discovered. The drunken crew came boiling out of the tent with lanterns in their hands and rushed hither and thither. We drew up behind a clump of bushes and cowered down with our hearts in our mouths. With an oath, the smith discovered the track of the wheel in the soft earth and with a howl of delight started to follow it. Attracted by the outcry, our erstwhile host lunged madly round the tent and collided violently with one of the newcomers. Over and over they rolled in the mud, cursing and slugging one another in drunken frenzy. The smith paused within a yard of our hiding place to watch the battle. The yellow rays of a lantern cast a circle of light at the tent door and illumined the struggling forms.

Cautiously we lifted the wheel, and guarding each step as best we might, made off in the direction of the main road. Doggedly we stumbled on, making as rapid progress as the rain and darkness would permit, falling at times in the slippery ruts, but always driving desperately ahead.

After what seemed an eternity, a light shone off to the left. Following a private road, we came to a gate. The shrill bark of a dog sounded from an outbuilding. I opened the gate and entered. A cold nose touched my hand and I felt the pressure of another against my skirt. I have no fear of dogs and have never been bitten, but Dan is not so fortunate, so he remained in the background while I explored the premises. Accompanied by the dogs, I marched boldly to the front door of a large house and rang the bell. It was opened by a man who stared at my dripping figure in amazement. His eyes travelled from me to the dogs, a Great Dane and an Airedale, and I realised the full significance of his glance. I explained the situation and asked leave to sleep in his barn.

"Well," he answered uncertainly, "as a rule, I never let anybody sleep in my outbuildings, but a person who can get past those dogs must be all right, so wait till I get a lantern and I'll take you and your husband over to the hay mow and make you as comfortable as I can."

He turned into the house and soon came out with a lantern and an armful of bedding beneath an oilskin. Calling Dan and quieting the dogs, he conducted us to a large barn where we were soon settled for the night and glad enough to be under the shelter of a safe roof.

I was awakened this morning by the romping of two kittens and the fox terrier I heard barking last night. The sun is shining brightly and everything looks fresh and clean after the storm. The farmer showed us where to build a fire with dry corn cobs and supplied us with a brimming pan of new milk, a basket of eggs and a crusty loaf of fresh, homemade bread, for all of which he refused compensation.

## CHAPTER NINE

# June 6th, With a Good Samaritan

While waiting for our things to dry, the day after the experience in the grader's camp, we visited our host and his family, who were shocked at the dangers we had encountered unarmed. The eldest son brought out a sharp lath hatchet, through the handle of which a hole had been bored and a stout leather loop attached to slip over the hand. This he handed to Dan with the remark that while it could hardly be called a deadly weapon, it would do good execution in case of trouble and at the same time be useful in making camp. Little did I think, as Dan thanked him heartily and strapped it on the wheel, how soon that hatchet would prove the means of saving my life.

Later in the day we reached the railroad and that night camped in a ravine. The next day dawned hot and clear. Mile after mile we trudged down the track, for the roads were still too wet for riding. Houses were scarce and stood far away from our course; there were no streams near or other places to obtain drinking water. Our thirst increased as the day wore on, and when at last we saw a farmhouse in a group of trees some half mile from the track, Dan suggested that I remain with the bicycle while he crossed the several pastures that lay between and brought back a kettle of water. So, I sat beside the wheel on the edge of the embankment while Dan climbed the fence and disappeared in the trees.

In a few minutes a dreadful commotion arose from the direction of the farmhouse. A great, roaring voice was booming like a cannon.

"Get out! . . . ornery hide. You . . ." Inarticulate outcries and oaths mingled with scattered words and phrases.

I listened appalled. I knew the attitude that some farmers maintained towards tramps, and I trembled for Dan's safety. The racket increased in violence. I became frantic and determined to go to the rescue. Unstrapping the hatchet from the handle bars, I slipped the thong about my wrist and plunged under the railroad fence and across the field, determined to take a short cut to the scene of combat. Worming a difficult passage through a barbed wire fence, I came to a black, sluggish creek or strip of mud perhaps eight feet wide, bordered by a thick row of trees, whose branches hung low over the surface. An extremely stout barbed wire fence stretched at right angles across this stream and joined a similar fence on the farther bank. I paused on the brink, for the black, slimy surface was repellent. The outcries redoubled and from where I stood whole sentences became intelligible.

"Come on now, you . . . son of a gun! Get out of that gate, you. Oh, if I could only reach you with a club. I'll shoot your hide full of holes in about a minute."

I gazed anxiously up and down. My only course was to wade across. Grasping the hatchet firmly, I swung my arms, made a little run, a jump and plunged in. Down, down I sank, deeper and deeper. I laboured furiously to reach the further bank, but my struggles only increased the rapidity with which I sank. The thick, black slime rose higher and higher about me. I tried to scream, but my parched lips could utter no sound. We have no quicksands or sloughs in my home country, but I have read of such places and heard of horses and cattle and sometimes human beings going down, never to be seen again. I thought of Dan escaping from the fanner and returning to find the abandoned wheel. Of his wife, there would be no trace. My end would always remain a mystery. As the black mud sucked me down, I could imagine it rising to my chin, my lips, my nostrils. I could picture the inky surface closing over my head, shutting out the sunlight forever.

In a frenzy, I threw my arms above my head. The blade of the hatchet caught over a bough. Cautiously I pulled. It held firm. A gleam of hope illumined my dark despair. Grasping the handle with my left hand, I tried to lift myself out, but the slough refused to give up its victim so easily. The blade slipped a little. My heart seemed to leap from my body. My senses reeled. Fiercely I called on all my forces of reason, will and self-control.

Placing just enough weight on the hatchet handle to prevent my sinking deeper, I studied the situation calmly. My one hope lay in securing a firm hold on the large branch above.

Little by little I began to spring the smaller shoot up and down. Harder and harder I pulled on the hatchet, at the same time forcing the blade firmly over the limb. The leaves swung closer and closer.

Emboldened, I worked harder than ever. At last I was able to abandon my hold on the hatchet and secure a firm grip with both hands on the tough wood.

But the slough dragged me down with a grip like an octopus. A ton weight pulled at each foot, my skirt seemed grasped by a thousand clutching hands. And then I gave thanks for my broad shoulders, and for the violent exercise of steering the tandem, which had developed the sturdy muscles of my hands and arms. Slowly, slowly I made headway against the treacherous depths; slowly, slowly, the vicious grip was broken, till with a gasp of relief I draped myself out upon the bank.

I sank down exhausted.

Then from the farmhouse the undiminished sounds of conflict forced themselves into my consciousness and suddenly I burned with a reckless berserk rage against the whole world.

Springing to my feet, I hurled myself upon the barbed wire fence that crossed the slough, and clinging with hands and feet to the thorny strands, edged my way across. Skirt and stockings were torn in a dozen places. My heavy coils of hair slipped down. My hands bled profusely. Forcing my way through the second fence, I started across the meadow. As I rounded a clump of bushes a large red bull, with head to ground and pawing hoof, barred my way. But I was far past caring for such as he.

Snatching up a stick, I began clapping wood and hatchet together and charged directly at his lordship. He stood his ground till the hatchet was almost touching his nose, then, with a bellow of fear, turned tail and raced across the field with me in close pursuit. Gaining the fence, I tumbled over and arrived panting at the back of the farmhouse.

In a beautiful kitchen garden, a farmer stood as though rooted to the ground with amazement at my grotesque appearance, as with hands and face streaked with blood, clothing in shreds and bedraggled with mud, I stood before him with a club in one hand and a hatchet in the other.

Eyes bulging, nostrils flaming, tail in air, a fine bull calf was careering madly among the vegetables.

"Wh—wh—why, my good lord, woman," began the man as he recovered his breath. "What's happened to you? Where in the world did you drop from?"

"Where is my husband? What have you done to him?" I demanded hotly.

"Well, now. Let me see." He scratched his head perplexedly. "Seems like I recall a man askin' for a bucket o' water something like a half hour back. Might he be your man now? I was so plum frantic with this here pesky calf, that I didn't pay no attention to the man."

"But who were you going to shoot?" I persisted. "I could hear you swearing clear over to the railroad."

"Sho, now. Is that so? 'Scuse me. I'm plum bad about swearin'. Wife, she's after me all the time, too," he apologised. "Now, the wife's right set on her posies, and this here ―― 'scuse me, seems like I just can't stop cussin'―got in and tromploed 'em all down, and while I was a trying my damdest to get him out, I'll be damned if he didn't bust through into the vegetables and cavort all over them."

Meanwhile, the innocent cause of the commotion had taken advantage of the lull in the storm to make his escape from the garden.

"You didn't get in the slough, did ye?" continued the farmer, eyeing my skirt. "Didn't ye see all them fences? We had so much trouble with the stock gettin' in the ―― hole―'scuse me, beats the devil how those words will come apopping out―that we fenced her all in. But what gets me is how ye come to get past that bull 'thout being gored to death. He's turrible dangerous. That's why we got all them high fences about. Kill't two men, he did, 'fore I got him. Bought him cheap, but the wife just raises a hell of a row―'scuse me―at keepin' him."

I asked for water, for my thirst was intensely and after drinking deep from the dripping dipper and washing off the worst of the blood and dirt, I followed the farmer to the main road, where he pointed out a short cut to the railroad.

There I found Dan rushing frantically about, for having found the wheel with the hatchet gone, he felt sure I had been kidnapped.

It seems that he had gone to the house, found the farmer chasing the calf, secured the water, then thinking it would be difficult to carry the kettle through the fences, tried another route and got on the wrong road. Before he could find the right path and return, I was in the slough.

We slept that night in a tumbledown shed—or rather, Dan did. Each time I dropped to sleep, I could feel myself sinking in the slough, and would wake up with a start.

Next day we rode a good deal and covered a long stretch of territory. The country was flat and uninteresting and my strained muscles occupied most of my attention as I tried to confine the rebellious wheel to the smoother stretches.

At noon we pitched camp near the railroad track and had the meal well under way when a passenger train pulled out of a station a mile or two ahead and thundered toward us.

"Look," exclaimed Dan. "What's the matter there? The train is going to stop."

Sure enough, it was losing speed. People were thrusting their heads from windows while the fireman was looking back at a group of men on the blind end of the baggage car. Just as it ranged alongside us, a small figure catapulted from the platform and rolled almost to our feet. The train gathered way and sped on.

I rushed forward and fell on my knees beside a grimy, tattered boy of some twelve years, who was clutching his fiery red head in both hands and cursing like a pirate. Blood was spurting from a deep jagged gash in his left wrist, which he had struck against the projecting fragment of a broken bottle in his descent. I seized his arm and applied pressure to control the haemorrhage. He fixed me with an uncomprehending glare. Then his eyes fell on his dripping arm.

"Oh, Lord," he gasped, "oh. Lord, I'm bleedin' to death—I'm goin' to die. Oh, Ma, Ma."

"Nonsense, kid, you won't die. That blood looks a lot worse than it is. Just be a good boy and hold still for a few minutes and I'll fix you all safe. Quick, Dan. Hand me that kettle of boiling water. Now, unpack my emergency case."

By the time Dan had the kit unpacked and contents laid out the water had cooled enough for use. I cleansed and sterilised the wound, tied the artery, and soon had the arm bandaged in scientific fashion. The boy had made no sound, but gazed in fascination at the shining little instruments, the vials of antiseptics and rolls of gauze.

"You see, this case proved useful after all," I remarked to Dan as I gathered up the implements. "If such things are needed at all, they usually are needed badly. This boy would have bled to death without proper attention."

At my words the lad burst into tears. "The —— sons of——" he sobbed. "They all jumped me at once. They wouldn't let me alone. I wasn't doin' no harm. It—it don't cost the old railroad nothin' if I do ride the blind. I want to go home. I want to go ho—ome." Tears washed pallid channels down his sooty cheeks.

"Do you think you can take a little nourishment, young man?" queried Dan as he busied himself with the meal.

64

The boy checked his sobs. "I dunno what that is, but I kin eat any old kind of chuck. You just try me once and I'll show you. I ain't had nothin' but one little old hunk of bread in two days."

"Well, take this pan of water and see if you can remove some of that make-up from your manly countenance and then pitch into the grub. I'll die of starvation myself if I don't eat soon."

I set another kettle of water to boil for tea, and we all fell to with avidity.

"Say, I made good time last night," the boy volunteered, as he finished his third helping of canned beans and bread. "Rode the Overland Limited. Gee whiz, but she does burn up the rails. If I only could a stuck, I'd been home tomorrow. But those boneheads chucked me off this morning. Then I landed that old hearse they thrown me off of just now. Suppose I'll have to hoof it till night."

"Why don't you catch a freight? You wouldn't be nearly so likely to get into trouble."

"Huh, a freight! Me? Not on your life! What do you think I am, a dead one? I'm a live guy, I am. No bindle stiff about me. Say, do you know, I've beat it clear from northern Wyoming. I've been workin' a long time there as a cowboy on a great big cattle ranch. Say, that's the life."

"Seems to me you're travelling in the wrong direction for a cowboy," I observed. "The cattle ranges all lie west of here, and you're heading east. How does that happen?"

"Well, you see. Ma, she wants to see me, so I thought I'd make a short trip home. Me and the old man had a falling out, and I beat it west. Say, do you know, he expected me to milk two cows, milk 'em and feed 'em and wait on 'em hand and foot. No fun nor nothin'. And weed the garden! Say, I bet you never saw as big a garden as we got— great long rows—and say, I bet you never saw weeds grow as fast as ours do—big, tall weeds. But Ma wants to see me, so I gotta go home."

"Did your mother write to you to come?" I enquired gravely.

"No, she didn't write. I've never stayed very long in one place so I never wrote to tell her where I was."

"Oh, my! She must be terribly worried about you. How long have you been away?"

"Why, let's see—it must be nearly six weeks now since I beat it. I met a gang of hoboes the first day I was out and they took me right along with 'em to northern Wyoming. Say, that's a great country, all right, all right. But, of course, when Ma wanted to see me, I had to leave.

"I tell you where's a bad town you gotta fight shy of. That's little old Cheyenne. There's a gunman there, Jeff Fair's his name. Say, he shoots a Bo for breakfast; every mornin'. You folks want to watch out when you go through. They run you in for nothin' at all. I met a n———r just the other side o' there. Say, he was runnin' in circles like a fitty cat. They had chucked his pal in the can just for nothin' at all—vag charge maybe—and no tellin' when he'd get out, and here's this poor Negro, can't go off and leave his pard, can't find work, can't get nothin' to eat, can't do a thing in the world but chase around and bawl. Say, I felt awful sorry for that poor Negro."

We raided our scanty stores to pack a lunch for the boy. I instructed him in the care of his wound, described the location of various houses along the road where I knew by experience he would be sure to find help, gave him a little note of recommendation and explanation to use when applying for assistance, then started him on the way to his waiting mother.

Just at sundown we came to the town of Wood River, a place I am destined to remember. Storm clouds were piling on the horizon as Dan hurried to the shop to buy some meat for supper. While he was gone, some Greeks approached and with much gesticulation endeavoured to explain something to me. I gathered an idea of trouble of some kind, but exactly what they were driving at I was unable to determine.

We camped on the outskirts of the village, and had hardly finished our simple meal when gusts of wind and great drops of rain proclaimed the coming of the storm. We looked anxiously about for shelter. There were no barns near, but not far from the railroad track stood a house in process of construction, and while doors and windows were lacking, the roof and outside walls gave promise of sufficient protection. To this we hurried and lifted the wheel onto the veranda just as a flood of rain burst upon us. After a little search we found some nail kegs and sat down in the front room. We were dozing when footsteps sounded on the porch. I strained my eyes, but could see nothing in the pitchy blackness.

Suddenly a light flashed in my face, the cold muzzle of a pistol pressed my temple, and a hand gripped my arm.

"Get up there. None of your tricks now," snarled a harsh voice.

The flash was turned on Dan, who was ordered to throw up his hands by a second man, who flourished a revolver in his left hand. We stumbled to our feet, dazed by the unexpectedness of it all.

"You're under arrest. Better come quietly," growled the first man gruffly.

Dan tried to explain that we had only taken shelter from the storm and had no intention of doing any damage, but was savagely ordered to shut up. Grasping me tightly by the arm, the first fellow led the way out of the building and down the road to the village.

Arrived at a tiny, wooden shanty, the man unlocked the door and crowded us in. They slammed and bolted the door behind us and we heard their footsteps retreating up the walk. As we stood, too bewildered to move, a match flared in the darkness and in a moment the feeble rays of a candle revealed the interior of the lockup. It consisted of a single room, partially divided by a partition, and containing two bunks. On one of these sprawled a man, while a big Negro held aloft the guttering candle end. At sight of a woman the recumbent man sprang to his feet and courteously bade us good evening. Without further ado or questioning, he removed his hat and coat from the bunk where he had been lying and suggested that we make ourselves as comfortable as circumstances would permit.

At once the Negro blew out the candle with the remark that we might need it before morning.

As we settled ourselves as best we might in the darkness, flashes of lightning revealed the dimensions of the one small, barred window, which furnished all ventilation to the unfortunates within. Furniture, drinking water or conveniences were utterly lacking and my flesh crawled at the thought of the straw-covered bunk on which we must rest in the confined space.

Hardly had we lain down, when the door was opened and a fifth person was hustled in. Again, the Negro lit his candle stub, and we saw that the newcomer was a boy of not more than sixteen years.

The officers had paused just outside the window and one remarked that it was time to go home. There were no occupied buildings near the jail and I could not help but consider what our fate would be should lightning strike the flimsy wooden shack or a fire start from match or candle. When I realised that I was locked within those constricting walls, it seemed that they were crowding in and smothering me. I wanted to scream, to beat my hands against the bars, but reason forbade. I settled down and strove to cultivate the non-resisting attitude of our cell mates, but my mind kept busy with the wonders of our boasted American civilisation that permits such occurrences as this. I thought of the churches throughout the land—no doubt there was one in this very community—and of the teachings of One who had no place to lay His head.

"*I was a stranger and ye took me not in . . . .sick, and in prison and ye visited me not.*"

How many of the good people of the nation have ever even so much as thought of visiting those cast into their barbaric prisons?

At sunrise our jailers returned, unlocked the door and set us free. There was no charge against us and no legal formalities to go through apparently. Retrieving the wheel, we hastened out of town.

Beside a small house some miles away we stopped to get water for breakfast. A motherly woman came to talk to us. Hearing of our recent experiences, she took us into her home, provided us with hot baths, and sent us to bed while she cleaned and sterilised our contaminated apparel. Completely exhausted, I slept the clock around and woke next morning to find my clothing, clean and neatly mended, piled on a chair at the bedside. So, thanks to our good Samaritan, we are able to go forward with renewed strength and courage.

CHAPTER TEN

# A Day in June, On the Open Road

The days go by as in a dream. We seldom see a newspaper and seem out of touch with the world. At night I am too thoroughly occupied with my blistered feet or else too busy "spouting for the eats," as Dan expresses it, to keep track of diary or calendar.

"Spouting for the eats" has come to be quite a joke with us. We stop near some farmhouse and Dan goes in for water. Presently along come the kids and watch our camp preparations with much interest. Usually they are followed by father or mother, or, perchance, a grown son, who at once becomes absorbed in the tale of our adventures. Soon the whole family may be seen crouched around our little fire, which illuminates the eager faces as they drink in every word with ears and mouth and eyes. Dan fumbles about with the camp kettle and I break off in the middle of some exciting incident to attend to the preparations for supper. Somebody wakes up to the need for milk and eggs, which, of course, are difficult to carry with us. It is usually about milking time, and at a word from some grownup child scurries off and proudly returns with a pail of new milk and a hatful of eggs, which he shyly presents to me. The eggs are boiled and eaten from the shell, and the cocoa made from undiluted new milk is a beverage fit for the gods.

In other instances, we are invited into the house and sit down to a real country supper. After the meal I resume the interrupted narrative and entertain our hosts with descriptions of life in Chicago, the San Francisco earthquake, and incidents of interest along the way. Quite frequently I advise a change of diet and care for some puny infant, or diagnose the case of an ailing mother and risk the leaving of a prescription to be filled when we are well on our journey.

Next morning the family assembles to see us start. We exchange

69

names and addresses, and as we ride away, we feel that a new bond of friendship has been established.

Near a little place called Gibbon our rear tire gave out, and while making the change, a farmer invited us to his home to eat supper and spend the night. After considerable trouble with the wheel, we started on shortly after noon next day, but had not gone far when we saw dense, black clouds piling up ahead. We rode hard for some time, then rain began to fall and we stopped beneath a cattle shed. The rain slackened and we rode on, but had not proceeded any great distance when we noticed a very severe storm raging in the northwest.

Soon great gusts of wind came whirling across the prairie, while rain and sleet whipped our faces. There was no shelter near, so we determined to struggle on and reach Kearney if possible. A train steamed past, with passengers leaning from the windows and waving their arms in great excitement. Glancing about to learn the cause of the commotion, I looked toward the south and nearly fell from the wheel. A cyclone was bounding across the country and as I gazed it whirled a building into the air, then dashed it to earth, where it flew into a thousand fragments.

Suddenly we were picked up, wheel and all, and the next thing I knew, were rolling over and over in the ditch at the roadside, while the tandem lay twenty feet away. As I struggled to my feet, I saw another cyclone, which had just given us a playful flip, scudding away in the north. Hailstones as large as pigeon's eggs now began to pelt us, and to add to our discomfort, we found that both chains and the steering gear had been broken in the crash and Kearney was still at least two miles distant.

We had pushed the damaged bicycle a scant hundred yards when a two-seated automobile, guided by a man with a white-faced woman at his side, drew up beside us. The man invited me to ride into Kearney with him while Dan brought in the wheel. Dan urged me into the back seat and the machine plunged ahead. With a wild yell, the driver whipped off his soft felt hat and began to beat the steering wheel with it.

"Whoop-la!" he howled. "Go it, Nellie! Go it, old girl! Show the natives what you can do."

The car careened from side to side across the wet and slippery road. At tremendous speed we struck the railroad crossing at a tangent. Tossing us high in the air, the machine leaped for the ditch. With a powerful wrench the driver whirled the car, which poised on two wheels at the verge, then headed straight for a telegraph pole on the other side of the road. Once more he veered, and the brass hub of the hind wheel bit into the wood as we shot past.

But Providence was with us, and in a few moments the car drew up in front of a hotel in Kearney, while the half-drunken owner staggered out and, conducting me within, engaged and paid for the best room in the house for Dan and me. The other poor woman, who had been picked up from the roadside like myself, made her escape.

Dan came in, drenched and weary from the buffeting of the storm, and threw himself on the bed. I heard a terrific, roaring, crashing, rending sound, and rushing to the window saw another cyclone sweeping through the outskirts of the town. Large trees swayed and whipped madly, then were whirled into the air.

"Cyclone! Cyclone! Quick, Dan, here comes another cyclone," I screamed above the roar of the tempest.

"Dam the cyclone," Dan replied; "I've seen enough for one day."

Nevertheless, he came to the window just as the great, black, swirling funnel passed from view, and, gazing at the sky, enquired where all the books had come from. Sure enough, something floated in the heavens that resembled the scattered leaves of volumes. An instant later these pages came down and disclosed themselves as the sides and roofs of houses.

Next morning Dan took the wheel to the repair shop while I studied the ravages of the storm. No lives were lost in that immediate neighbourhood, but much property had been destroyed. The brick foundation of one home had been scattered in every direction, while the wooden frame, apparently unharmed, had been set down on its original site. In another instance a parlour wall had been neatly removed and a marriage license torn from the frame which still hung in its place, while furniture and pictures remained untouched. This peculiar phenomenon gave rise to considerable comment and jokes concerning the domestic felicity of the married pair.

We were eating our lunch in a vacant lot when our friend from Gibbon drove up. He called Dan over for a short talk, then drove rapidly away. When Dan returned and held out his palm, I cried out in surprise, for in his hand lay four shining five-dollar gold pieces. When we had gone and the storm came up, this man had worried over our probable fate, and early next morning had driven the twelve miles into Kearney to overtake and give us this money to ease the journey across the Rockies. Thus, we were able to renew our shoes and stockings, which were in shreds, pay for new parts for the wheel, lay in a stock of groceries and still have a little money in our pockets.

If grateful, loving thoughts have power to benefit the recipient, then surely our benefactor will receive some reward, for my whole soul pours itself out in deepest gratitude for his gracious, generous act.

Leaving Kearney, we were able to do a good deal of riding, but suffered severely from heat in the middle of the day. For miles we rode beside stock fences where groups of horses with heads tossing, nostrils flaming, manes and tails floating like pennons in a breeze, raced beside us to the confines of their pastures, there to stand with stamping hoofs and outstretched noses, eyeing us with the greatest curiosity. Once a steer, grazing by the roadside, started to run ahead of us, and lumbered along a full mile, then, in a panic of fear, he reared and upended over the fence in a comical fashion and stood blowing wildly, watching his strange pursuer glide past.

The road became wretchedly poor. Again, and again the wheel would slip into the deep ruts filled with choking dust in spite of every effort. In places where the surface was hard, innumerable small gullies from the winter rains crossed at right angles, so that riding became unsafe from the strain on the heavily-laden tandem.

Mosquitoes bred in the sluggish streams, full-fed by recent storms, and when evening fell surrounded us in dense clouds. Their bites are almost as painful to me as bee stings, raising great, red wheals, which itch and burn for days, so that I was nearly wild from the irritation. To add to the general discomfort, my new shoes, which were very heavy for the coming trip across the desert, blistered my feet atrociously, so that when the rear chain broke in crossing a bad gully, I was scarcely able to hobble.

And each succeeding day made greater demands on one's endurance. The country became hilly with stretches of treacherous sand. High bench lands, seamed with narrow ravines, skirted rugged buttes, while to the south and west one caught vistas of barren plains. Small farmhouses perched on the hillsides, and here and there great fields of grain or sprouting corn appeared, with groups of animals grazing in the distance.

Dan had managed to mend the damaged chain, but his natural recklessness chafed constantly against my caution, so that each steep descent provoked an argument. At last I flung discretion to the winds and down the hills we flew, bounding from hummock to hummock, swaying, lurching, recovering ourselves by seeming miracles.

We had been riding across a jutting arm of bench land, and as we approached a sharp turn in the road, the ground began to fall away abruptly. I endeavoured to slow down, but Dan was of a different mind. Spurred on by his words of ridicule, I permitted the wheel to gain momentum and we spun around the curve at racing speed.

A tremendously long and steep declivity lay before us, the strip of road disappearing from our sight in another turn at the bottom of a ravine. My heart leaped convulsively as the wind whistled past my ears, but I had scant time to coddle fear. The strain of handling the heavy tandem at such a speed took all my attention. The pitch increased; we seemed to fly through space. Then the front wheel struck a bed of heavy sand at the curve, and I knew no more.

My next sensation was of a shaking, joggling motion and by degrees I discovered that I was lying on my back on the bottom of a farm wagon that was jolting slowly up a rutty hillside. Dan, very pale, was bending over me, and the wheel with twisted handle bars and dangling chain was propped alongside. In answer to his anxious inquiries, I undertook a few investigative movements and soon was able to assure him that I suffered from nothing worse than some severe bruises and slight concussion from alighting on my head. He had received a rather deep scratch in the *mêlée*, but otherwise was uninjured.

The wagon turned abruptly and I struggled to a sitting posture, as our driver, a lad of some sixteen summers, halted his team of mules in front of a low, unpainted farmhouse. A motherly woman hurried out in answer to his call, and in a moment was all solicitude. With tender care she guided my reeling footsteps into the house and I was soon ensconced on the living room lounge while Dan occupied a rocker at my side. After seeing that we were both as comfortable as circumstances would permit, our hostess left the room to prepare supper.

The outer door swung open and a handsome, blue-eyed boy about twelve years old, dressed from head to foot in blue denim, passed slowly through the room and, with a shy nod to us, entered the kitchen. Scarcely ten seconds later the same door opened and the boy again appeared and with another little duck of the head disappeared in the rear. I was marvelling at the speed he had shown in encircling the house in such a short time, when the sound of the latch caught my ear and I turned to confront the same blue-clad figure. But was it the same? No, this lad was larger. It must be a brother. He also passed through and vanished with the peculiar sideways nod. Almost before I could wink an eye, his double followed, using the identical gesture of his predecessors. I turned to Dan, who was staring round-eyed after the vanishing figure. Just as I opened my mouth to address him, the door opened and a fifth youth appeared. He too was blue-eyed, blue-clad and strikingly good to look upon. Dan rubbed his eyes; then ran his hand through his thick curls.

"That jolt must have done something to my brain," he declared with a worried look at me. "Do you see whole droves of kids, all looking the same, all dressed the same, all acting the same, all going from the front to the back of the house? First, I thought a kid was running round the house to fool us. Then I thought I was seeing double, but they keep getting bigger all the time, till darned if I know what to think. What in blazes do you suppose is the matter with me?"

"It's as much a mystery to me as it is to you," I replied. "Whatever it is, it affects us both the same way, for I saw them just as you did. There were five, all dressed in blue, all with blue eyes and light hair, and about the same size, though the first seemed the smallest and the last the largest. At first I thought they were twins, but there could scarcely be five twins."

At that instant the boy who had rescued us from the roadside appeared, and as he advanced to speak to us, another lad, a size larger, entered from the kitchen and was joined in a moment by boys number one, two, three and four. The room was of fair size, but it seemed to overflow with blue-clad youths.

"Well, what do you think of my little brood?" cried the laughing voice of our hostess, who had entered unobserved.

"Are these all your boys?" I gasped, gazing at her still youthful face and figure. "It doesn't seem possible. I had about concluded that the fall from the bicycle had affected my brain or my vision; I wasn't sure which."

"Indeed, they are all mine, and not all my family either. My two oldest sons are still in the fields. I have nine in all. The eldest has just turned twenty-three, while the youngest two are twelve. The next two are twins also, and only fifteen months older."

As the lads were introduced, it seemed that a more remarkable, handsomer group of youngsters would be difficult to find. In spite of the utmost care, I was unable to identify the younger ones, so that they must linger in my memory as a group.

All were eager to be of service and assisted Dan in putting the tandem in shape for further adventures. It was with regret that we bade them farewell next morning, and I often think with envy of the happy mother of such a delightful family.

One evening we stood beside the railroad track while the Overland Limited shot by. As we crossed behind the vanishing train, I saw a strange object moving between the rails. Closer inspection disclosed a large terrapin crawling over the ties as fast as he could scramble. I gathered him up and took him back to Dan.

"Now for some real turtle soup," cried he, making a grab for the creature. But the terrapin resented such tactics with so fierce a snap that Dan, perforce, released him.

Sitting beside the campfire that evening, I bored a hole in Mister Turtle's shell and attached a stout string. Next morning, we rigged a large square can atop the bedding roll and daily the turtle rode in state on a bed of fresh leaves, while at night he was staked out in whatever water was available. He attracted much attention along the way, for his shell was very handsome, but his jaws proved to be so savage that nobody dared to touch him but me. I named him Bird and, while resting, would frequently take him from his bed and gently stroke and tickle his neck or leg, which he would stretch out to be petted.

Sometime later we camped on the bank of the North Platte River and as usual I staked Bird out at the edge of the stream. Next morning, I was busy with the laundry, so did not call for Mister Turtle until nearly noon. What was my amazement to find him flat on his back at the extreme limit of his string, while a large bird stalked round and round him and aimed vicious pecks at the soft folds of skin between the edges of his shell. I rescued my poor pet, who seemed completely exhausted, and, conscience-stricken, loosed the string and gave him his liberty. A last glance revealed Bird paddling downstream. He will surely be a well-travelled turtle by the time he reaches the sunny south for which he so boldly headed.

The scene on the river seemed very charming after our hot and dusty ride across the arid plain. Masses of wild roses in full bloom glowed against the soft green background of willows. Birds had woven a hanging nest over the water, and the little mother sat demurely on the eggs, while her mate swung on a slender perch and fairly burst his throat with song. They reminded me of some wrens a few miles back who had built their nest in an abandoned mailbox, but I suppose they could scarcely belong to the same species. In the rippling water beneath, fish of many sizes darted to and fro, while a fitful breeze set the silvery foliage to glimmering.

Reluctantly we said farewell to river and birds and roses and, skimming over a long bridge, entered a sleepy little town. Here we loaded the wheel to the limit with groceries, for the country grew wilder each day.

The weather was fine and we were able to camp out in accordance with our original plans. Still, we thought it best to follow the railroad as closely as possible in the event of more rain and muddy roads.

While boiling our cocoa in a lonely spot, our attention was attracted by the fine soldierly figure of a man who stood on the railroad embankment about fifty feet away, gazing down at us. He was dressed in khaki, *sombrero*, and leggings, and seemed preternaturally tall, silhouetted on the dull red evening sky.

"Hello, comrade," called Dan. "Want a bite to eat?"

The man strode down the bank and approached our fire. He was tall indeed, with the slim waist and long limbs of a track athlete. His smooth, deeply-tanned skin set off his bright blue eyes and white teeth to advantage as a real Tipperary smile curved his humorous lips. As he removed his hat, a thatch of white hair added an incongruous touch to his appearance.

Squatting on his haunches like one accustomed to that posture, he explained that he had just eaten a hearty meal, but accepted a cup of cocoa to keep us company. After listening to an account of our experiences, he stated that he was an ex-soldier, now walking from San Francisco to New York on a wager. He had made the trip from east to west in ninety days and was bent on returning in ten weeks. So far, he had made good time and felt confident of winning. With scant regard for the property of the railroad company, he insisted on carrying a great pile of old ties to a secluded spot and there started a bonfire. When I considered the forty-odd miles that he had covered on foot that day, I marvelled at the man. When the fire was blazing brightly, we settled ourselves on the windward side for a real talk-feast.

His most exciting adventure on this trip had occurred far out on the desert when he had been accosted by three tramps, who demanded the canteen of water that he carried on his shoulder. He unslung it with the intention of sharing the precious fluid, but one attempted to snatch it from his hand. As they struggled, another approached and struck him from the rear with a rock. With a sudden sidelong leap, he wrenched himself free, and swinging the canteen by the strap with all his force, let the first man have it full in the forehead. The fellow went down without a groan, and with a backhand motion, the soldier brought the canteen up and around, striking the second tramp on the point of the jaw. His companions out of commission, the third man took to his heels, while our hero gathered up the first hobo, who still lay unconscious, and with the aid of the second carried him to the railroad track and there flagged a passing freight, which took the two tramps to the next town.

As the evening advanced, the Irishman entertained us with descriptions of the many strange corners of the world that he had visited in the service of Uncle Sam, and told wild yarns of his experiences in the Philippines and in China during the Boxer rebellion. After a last creepy story of a looted temple and a dead Chinese priest, who came to life while the foreign devils were holding high carnival, and walking into their midst in his grave clothes, caused them to drop their spoils and flee, we stretched ourselves beside the glowing coals and slept.

The sharp cold of early morning awakened me, and heaping the ashes high with dry wood, I kindled a fire and started breakfast. Our soldier friend lay with head on knapsack, and in the deep relaxation of sleep the harsh footprints of the years disappeared and his face looked pure and boyish in the soft light of dawn. As he whimpered with cold and weariness, I could scarcely restrain myself from easing his head with a motherly touch, but contented myself with covering him with our blankets. Breakfast concluded, we prepared to follow our diverging paths. The soldier wrote a note to a pal at the military reservation at Cheyenne, commending us to his care. Then, as we said goodbye, he thrust the battered canteen into my hands.

"Your need is to come, but mine is ended. Keep it in remembrance of me."

He lifted his hat and was gone.

77

## CHAPTER ELEVEN

# Aboard a Modern Prairie Schooner

Dates are a thing of the past along with newspapers, street cars, electric lights, the hope of a speedy arrival in California, and last, but not least, our faithful companion, the stout, green tandem. And, it came about thus:

We had reached a country of great level stretches, with grazing cattle and raw looking farms, of infrequent water and distant ranges of bare, blue mountains. Following a barbed wire fence, our road turned at right angles to the north, whereas the way should have been open straight into the west where a more fertile region was blazoned forth in masses of green and long strips of yellow.

We stopped at a rude cabin which crouched, mouse-like, at the turn in the road, to fill the canteen. A woman, withered and sun-browned and worn by pathetically futile efforts to maintain a home in an unfriendly land, answered my knock. She informed us that the fenced range that blocked our path was part of a great holding to the south, which projected a long tentacle to enfold a source of lifegiving water far to the north. Thus, we needs must make a great detour to reach the point to the west of us where the highway again took up its march toward the setting sun.

This strip, it appeared, was but a scant three miles in width, and we were at once filled with the idea of walking across instead of riding so far around. After some manoeuvring, we succeeded in crowding the wheel beneath the barbed strands and set off across the prairie, which was almost as hard and bare as the county road. We had not gone far when a group of cattle caught sight of us and moved up to inspect the strange intruders. These were followed by others, which seemed a signal to hundreds. Soon a dense mass was tagging at our heels and spreading out to right and left, while in the distance still more could be seen lumbering up to join the herd. A peculiar prickling sensation began to manifest itself in the region of my scalp.

"Dear me, I do wish your sweater was blue instead of red," I observed nervously to Dan. "I believe it is making these cattle angry. Do you suppose they really would attack us?"

"No, of course not. They are perfectly harmless. They don't know what to make of us, that's all, and their curiosity urges them up to take a good look."

"Nevertheless, I noticed that he was quickening his pace. As for myself, I scanned the distance to the boundary fence with anxious eyes. The cattle, which at first had maintained a respectful distance, now began to crowd closer.

"Please, Dan," I urged, "take off that sweater and hide it till we get out of this pasture. I don't like the sight of so many cows a little bit."

"Rats, Ethel, don't be a coward. Who's afraid of a few cows?"

He turned to wave his hat at the advancing animals, stepped into a prairie dog burrow and came heavily to the ground. As he regained his feet, his features twisted in pain and he caught at the handle bars.

"Gee whiz," he grunted, "I gave my ankle a beastly wrench. It hurts like the devil."

Visions of dislocations, sprains, of incapacitation in this Godforsaken spot, flashed before my brain as I sank to my knees to learn the extent of the injury, the cattle for a moment forgotten. I unlaced the shoe, and after a careful examination was delighted to find that it was nothing worse than a sprain which would doubtless be well in a few days.

"I'll take the wheel and you sit down while I unpack the emergency kit and get out the bandages," I remarked, rising to my feet, "I'll just put on a ——" The words froze on my lips. We stood in a ring of cattle less than two hundred feet in diameter. They stood shoulder to shoulder, heads down, noses to the ground, blowing, snorting, pawing, while here and there some young bull would advance a step with tossing head, then pause While the herd moved in to join him. Dan broke in on my immobility.

"We can't stop to bother with my ankle now," he muttered. "We must make tracks out of here as fast as the Lord'll let us."

He hobbled on a few steps, leaning on the tandem. At once the animals in the rear moved forward, while those in front set up a peculiar moaning bellow, which seemed to enrage the whole herd. The air vibrated with their bawling. To my affrighted eyes the whole plain seemed a solid mass of reddish backs and tossing heads. Fragments of what I had read and heard of western cattle came to my mind. They would attack a man on foot—a person on horseback was safe——

"Get into your saddle, quick," I cried. "It's our only chance."

I steadied the bicycle with a firm hand. "Just get on. I'll start it."

Dan seated himself and grasped the handle bars, while with straining muscles I bent desperately to the task of getting the heavy load in motion. The tyres seemed glued to the rough, uneven surface of the prairie, and when at last with sobbing breath I was able to leap into the front saddle, we were almost on the horns of a heavy animal that blocked the way. But to hesitate meant death, so with a blood curdling yell I headed full at his nose. He crowded aside, I swerved, and we passed between the rows of cattle with room so scant that we almost brushed the hairy flanks. I could hear the thunder of hoofs as the herd got into motion behind us.

The protecting fence seemed very far away. Bushes slapped at us in passing. The difference between riding on even a poor road and pedalling over this unsurfaced plain, level as it was, became increasingly evident. And how to cross the fence to safety with a crippled man and a laden wheel, even though we survived that long, was a problem. The front wheel struck a sharp, projecting snag and air hissed from the flattening tire. An instant later the rear tire also gave way, but we pedalled desperately on, bumping along on the rims, which each moment threatened to let us down.

We were nearing the western boundary when I heard a shout and glancing to the right saw a man on horseback tearing down the road in our direction. He began swinging his hat and shooting in the air, and as the wheel struck the fence, almost throwing me to the ground, his horse reared to a stop directly before us. To help Dan through, slip under myself and drag the wheel to safety was the work of a moment and I was free to watch the herd as they swerved away to the south.

"Gosh all hemlock, that was a close shave," gasped the cowboy. "How in Sam Hill did you all get into such a scrape?"

As I started to explain, he noticed that Dan was lame. He leaped from the saddle and in a trice had loaded Dan onto the horse. Then, giving me a hand with the wheel, started briskly in the direction of a thrifty-looking farm.

We halted at last beneath a tree at the edge of the road. Dan let himself down from his perch, and upon my firm assurance that we would be all right, our rescuer resumed his interrupted journey. I kindled a fire, brought water from a well, then sought the house, which stood well back from the road, to secure the loan of a deep bucket. A timid little woman accommodated me without demur; then followed curiously into camp. At once I treated Dan's ankle with a prolonged hot bath, followed by a careful massage and the application of arnica-soaked bandages.

The little woman followed every motion with the keenest interest, and discovering that I was a doctor, burst into a detailed account of an accident that had befallen her young son. He had fallen from a tree and sprained his wrist, which remained somewhat stiff. Would I be so kind as to examine it and see what was wrong? This I agreed to do before leaving, but for the present decided to make camp for the night, rest, and calm my quivering nerves.

Next morning Dan was able to get to work on the wheel, replacing the ruined tires with extras purchased in Kearney for some such emergency. Again, we rested during the heat of the day, and resolved to resume the journey next morning.

The tandem was packed for the road when the farmer's wife came hurrying out to remind me of my promise regarding her boy. We entered the farmyard, which swarmed with hogs of all sizes, and were led to an enclosed shed where I shut in the wheel for safe keeping while we entered the house.

But the lad was nowhere to be found. After an hour of searching, the mother, assisted by an older brother, dragged the patient, struggling and howling, from his hiding place in the attic; then held him while I discovered a slight displacement of one of the small bones of the wrist. This I reduced after considerable trouble, due to the boy's unruly temper, and bandaged the arm as the clock struck eleven. The mother then insisted that we stay to dinner and as Dan was still rather in need of rest, we accepted gratefully.

The head of the house, a great, burly, red-haired farmer, came in with the oldest son, a perfect chip off the old block, and we sat down to a repast of fried salt pork, fried potatoes, fried onions, hot biscuits and coffee.

The meal concluded, the whole family went out to see us off. As I rounded the corner of the shed, I noticed the door which I had latched so carefully, standing open. Then what a sight met my eyes!

The wheel lay flat on the floor, groceries, bedding and equipment scattered all about, while a shoving, grunting, struggling mass of hogs rooted, trampled and fought over it. Chains were broken, tyres torn from the wheels, spokes out, skirt guard bent and twisted, while through and over all was cocoa, sugar, coffee, plumbago, clothing, oil and pieces of the repair kit.

"Haw, haw," roared the farmer, delighted with the novel sight. Them hawgs sure have made a mash on that there bicycle."

"Ya, hah. I fixed 'em, I fixed 'em," shrieked my erstwhile patient, jumping about in glee. The little woman burst into tears.

Dan seized a heavy single-tree, which stood in a corner, and laid about him fiercely, sending the squealing drove pell-mell from the building. Before the farmer could stay his hand, he had laid low with a broken back a fine young boar. A few moments later a sow showed evidences of internal trouble, was taken with convulsions, and while we were gathering up the almost hopeless wreck, laid down and died, much to the grief of friend farmer, whose mirth was turned to mourning. Dan declared that the sow had swallowed his razor and wanted to hold an autopsy on the remains, but was forced to let the cause of death stand as acute indigestion.

The owner of the hogs cursed bitterly as we started to drag the poor old wheel back to our little camp, where Dan spent a day and a half endeavouring to repair it. But the case was hopeless. The good green tandem would never take the open road again.

The world seemed desolate that night as we sat beside our dying campfire discussing the situation. The mournful call of some night bird through the vast silence waked melancholy echoes in my lonely heart. The wind, moaning across the barren plains, spoke of darkness, inchoate, overwhelming. The stars seemed to stare coldly down upon the whirling mote to which we poor humans cling so doggedly. A gleam from a lifted window of the farmhouse only added to my feeling of isolation.

I visioned the thousands of family groups gathered round the evening lamps, enjoying the cosy comforts of home, the sense of peace and security that springs from a recognised place in society, the feeling of love and protection, the intimate companionship, and opportunity for service,—the mother with her sewing, the father with magazine or paper, the children with school books or toys—all unwitting, unheeding, uncaring, utterly indifferent to the fate of the thousands who roam the highways even as we, having no place to lay their heads. These, outcast, abandoned, wretched, are exiles from a land of plenty through no fault of their own—their only roof, the threatening vault of heaven, their only couch, the bare cold ground, their evening lamp some solitary campfire. Their naked souls shudder in the relentless blast of endless ostracism.

Our little hoard of silver was running low. We knew by experience that no work was to be had in this inhospitable land. Our only hope lay in pressing forward.

Early next morning we cooked a meagre breakfast, packed such articles as were worth saving into two bundles, swung these on our shoulders and were off. We had covered perhaps eight miles and Dan was beginning to complain of his ankle when in the distance we sighted a little settlement strung out along the railroad track. As we approached, I took both bundles and turned toward the railroad station to wait while Dan searched for work.

As I crossed the right-of-way my attention was attracted by a man seated on the ground, his back against a telegraph pole. As I walked past, he raised his hat and spoke.

"I would advise you to stay away from the depot, madam. The station agent is having a little dispute with a couple of drunken cowboys. It is scarcely the place for a lady."

"It is kind of you to warn me," I replied. "It was my intention to wait there for my husband, but we can scarcely miss one another in this town."

The stranger sprang to his feet. "Permit me to offer you my telegraph pole," he exclaimed with a winning smile. Lifting one of the blanket rolls, he placed it for a seat, and as I settled myself, sank down on the other bundle and entered into conversation.

He was a man on the sunny side of forty, tall, slender, but possessed of evident strength. His mouth was at once humorous and stern, his nose, high-arched with sensitive nostrils, gave him a cold, patrician air, which one forgot when he spoke. Then white teeth flashed from his sunbrowned face, and his eyes, of a peculiarly intense reddish-brown, twinkled roguishly. Never had I listened to a more musical human voice. With the utmost tact he led me to tell of our experiences. Soon he was in possession of the salient features of our journey.

"I am a sort of Ishmaelite myself," he declared. "I take my home with me. I pay no rent, no interest, no taxes. I do no worrying. I make no plans. I dream no dreams. I enjoy all in the way of good living that a human animal can hope for. When this civilisation is tottering to its fall, I shall be safe in a mountain resort known to me alone, prepared to round out my days in peace and comfort."

"Too bad that such a nice appearing man should be so crazy," I said to myself as he ceased speaking. As though in answer to my thought he burst out laughing.

"Oh, I'm not as crazy as I sound. At any rate, I'm mighty practical about it, as I shall soon demonstrate to you. My modem prairie schooner, a home on wheels, will be along presently, and then I hope to initiate you into a rational method of living in an insane world. Yonder the caravan approaches."

Following his gaze, I saw a team of mules hitched to a long, broad, light spring wagon with a black cover like a heavy automobile top, driven by a large fair woman, dressed in a yellow duster. Close behind a young man followed with a team of horses attached to a smaller wagon or buckboard.

My acquaintance stepped to the side of the road and hailed the woman, who halted at the edge of the right-of-way. After a brief conversation, she turned the mules and moved off across the track. The man turned as Dan approached and introduced himself at once.

"My name is Adams—Frank Adams," said he, "and I have been having a chat with your good wife. As a consequence, there is a matter of business, a little proposition that I would like to put, up to you. But this is no place to talk. Besides, the hour grows late and we must make preparations for the night. I have directed my outfit to a camping place in a grove of trees that I located this morning and I should be very much pleased to have the two of you come over with me and enjoy a real open-air dinner. Afterwards we'll make ourselves comfortable and go fully into my plan, which I have every reason to believe will result in pleasure and financial benefit to us all."

Dan seemed favourably impressed by the stranger's frank address. Besides, there was nothing to hope for in our present situation. So, he picked up a bundle, our friend shouldered the other, and we were off for the camping ground.

As we entered the clump of trees, my eye was caught by a small chicken coop with slatted bottom, which was suspended beneath the rear end of the wagon bed. Our guide stepped forward and swung open the door. Three fine young Plymouth Rock hens, who had been eagerly awaiting this opportunity, fluttered out and began to peck and scratch vigorously.

"This simple arrangement ensures a few fresh eggs for emergencies," Mr. Adams informed me. "These hens are very tame and are quite accustomed to this mode of living. Now and then, as today, we get a couple of fryers, and sometimes a nice fat hen for roasting, which we confine in the rear compartment until wanted. Thus, we are seldom at a loss for fresh meat. Just step around to the front and I'll show you the cooking arrangements."

At the front of the wagon we found the woman actively engaged in preparations for supper. Our acquaintance informed her of our situation in a few crisp sentences and without waiting for a formal introduction she took up the task of enlightening us in the art of scientific camping. She directed our attention to the dashboard which pivoted in the centre on a horizontal axis to form a support or worktable that could be used for dining purposes if necessary. A hood, which telescoped under the front edge of the wagon cover, could be pushed forward on such occasions, and by rolling down the curtains, perfect protection could be secured from wind and rain.

As we gazed, the young man brought a pail of fresh water and set it in a metal ring which was clamped to a front upright. The back of the seat was made in two parts, and to the back of the left-hand one—formed of sheet metal—a gasoline stove with oven attachment was fastened. The upright back revolved in such a way that the stove faced the rear when the seat was occupied, but could be turned to the front for cooking purposes. The housewife—campwife would be the better term in this case—could sit in comfort in the right-hand seat and secure everything required from the racks or from the boxes on the bed of the wagon. With competent hands she opened the oven door and withdrew a pan of cookies which flooded the air with a rich, spicy odour. These she replaced with a pan of biscuits, then produced a large skillet of broiling chicken from beneath the spreading burner which heated the oven. A few deft touches and the savoury pieces went back for further browning.

"I generally make most of my preparations while travelling," she informed me. "The mules are so gentle that they amble along without much driving and everything is so convenient that I can cook without stepping from the rig. Even the water is handy." She pointed to a heavy canvas bag, beaded with moisture, which hung on the outside wall.

The side walls within were fitted with ingenious racks like a kitchen cabinet, and a little to the rear and close against the roof I discerned the wire springs of a suspended bed.

"Yes," our host explained, in answer to my question. "The top framework is of metal, made extra strong with a block and tackle arrangement for hoisting the bed as soon as it is made each morning.

The mattress and springs were made to order and are very light. By disposing of it in this fashion we gain free access to our stores which, as you see, fill the bottom of the wagon. The horse feed is in the rear, our clothing lies in the centre, and the food supplies occupy the front. We have lived entirely out of doors, summer and winter, for two years now, and have suffered practically no inconvenience from bad weather."

"I wouldn't move into a house again for anything," his wife exclaimed. "You have no idea what a pleasant life this is. Housework is reduced to almost nothing, we get a chance to see the country and are as free as air."

"Don't you find it rather crowded at times?" I asked.

"Oh, no. Every few days we make a regular camp where we stay for a day or two. Then I get out the portable oven, make a wood fire, bake bread and cake, cook meat and vegetables, wash the clothes, and plan for the next jump."

Our host went to the rear, lifted off the flat top of a fibre trunk, unfolded a set of legs and set it up as a table. Then he lifted out the seat from the second wagon, unloaded three folding camp chairs and proceeded to set the table with white enamel dished.

Meanwhile, the young man, Peter Bates, had come in from caring for the livestock, and was introduced. We all sat down to broiled chicken, boiled potatoes warmed in gravy, hot biscuits and honey, stewed fruit, cookies and tea. The food was delicious.

"What do you think of the cooking?" enquired our host, serving us a second helping of chicken. "Not many places where you can get meals like this. We live on the fat of the land the whole year round, don't we, honey-drips?"

"You're quite right. That's just what we do. And nothing to worry us, either," responded his wife.

Mine host produced a bottle of port, while Bates brought out cigars. They greeted our pleasant refusal to indulge with uplifted brows, and when Dan passed by the perfectos as well Mr. Adams remarked: "And not even a cigarette? You are a Puritan, if I may be pardoned for saying so. Well, maybe we can do business in spite of handicaps." He paused to light a cigar, then lounged back in the wagon seat.

"I'm a sort of sublimated pedlar. I travel from town to town selling a couple of styles of window signs, which our young friend Pete here, puts up for me. Then, to ensure continuous action, I take orders for a special lamp and for handy tools—combinations, you know—in the country districts. Thus, I am never out of a job. The lamp orders are filled by a mail order house in Chicago, as are the ones for tools, so that I carry nothing but a sample. The signs consist of letters which are pasted on the inner side of the window glass. . . . You've seen them many times.

"Peter wants to quit us and push on to Cheyenne, and while I am perfectly competent to put up the orders, I dislike to do so. Why work, when I can profit from the labour of others? And that is where you come in. I'll get the orders and pay you so much for each sign that you put up. In fact, I'll even do better. If you are able to pick up an order here and there, I'll sell you the supplies for ten *per cent* above cost to me. The work is easy. Any mechanical man with a true eye can manage with a little instruction and a day or two of experience."

"Oh, yes," young Bates broke in, "I've always been a clerk, but I had no difficulty in getting the hang of this thing. I wanted to go to Cheyenne, and this gave me a fine chance to see the country and make a little dough on the side."

"A man with your experience and training should have no trouble at all in making two or three dollars a day," the boss continued. "And it should be mostly velvet. Honey-drips has a little side line of her own. She carries a few toilet accessories to sell to the ladies. In the country districts the housewives are only too glad to have an opportunity to get such things in exchange for butter, eggs, poultry, vegetables, or even bread and canned fruit. We can always use the stuff some way and it cuts the living expenses to almost nothing. I get horse feed in exchange for tools and lamps, and often I can let the animals graze for a day at a time. Now your wife can get a supply of these female fixings for ten *per cent* above cost and make most of your living. After you have played the game for a month or two and find you like it, I'll fix up that second wagon like this one here. We use it now for trips off the main line where we don't want to take the heavy outfit.

"That's the gist of the plan. Now, how does the scheme strike you?"

"I'd be glad enough to get a couple of dollars a day over our living," replied Dan. "What do you think about it, Ethel?"

"I believe it would be an excellent thing for the present, at least. Of course, I won't be satisfied till we get back to California, but we should be able to save money enough to make the trip comfortably in a few months if we manage carefully."

"Well, so far as getting to California is concerned," observed Mr.

Adams, "we expect to arrive there about the middle of next December. We will work the territory between here and Cheyenne, then swing down across Colorado, pass through Arizona in November, and work California in the winter months. Then if you have not come to love this life, as I think you will, you can leave us and return to the old grubby existence."

"Now, that will be splendid," I cried enthusiastically. "We'll not only reach home, but we'll see the country and save some money for a fresh start—we'll need all we can save before we get on our feet again, I'm afraid."

"Very well, then, good people. We'll consider the matter settled. You can camp here tonight and begin to learn the ropes the first thing in the morning."

The conversation turned on the day's work and I gathered a fair idea of the usual activities. Mr. Adams would take the light team and with Mr. Bates push ahead, leaving Mrs. Adams to pursue a leisurely course with the mules. The men struck the first little store they came to, or if the country was very sparsely settled, they stopped at a farm. If they secured a sign order from the store-keeper. Bates remained to place it, depending on Mrs. Adams to pick him up as she passed. Meanwhile, Mr. Adams drove on to solicit more orders, search out a suitable camping place, and otherwise prepare for the coming of his party. This particular morning Adams had left the light team with Bates, who was busy with a sign, and had caught a ride in a passing buggy to the little town where I had met him. Each day's programme was the spontaneous result of immediate needs.

As we rose to say goodnight, Mrs. Adams produced milk, eggs and whiskey, and they prepared a customary night cap. I was startled by the enormous draught of liquor poured out by our employer, who, noting my surprise, remarked apologetically, "I've been a frightful sufferer from insomnia for a number of years. That was one of the reasons which led me to adopt this mode of living, but even the open air has failed to relieve me. I've tried vigorous exercise, long walks, hot food and drink on retiring, medicines—everything—and I've found my only relief in these stiff jolts of whiskey. At times I am compelled to get up in the night and find the bottle. But I never become intoxicated."

"I should think that sort of thing would ruin your digestion."

"Well, I take certain precautions. I always take my evening dram in the form of an eggnog, and if I need a drink in the night, I take a large cup of milk first, which seems to prevent any untoward effects."

We made camp at the far side of the grove and were up bright and early, ready for the day's work with the "California outfit," as we dubbed the new caravan. The three men set out with the buckboard, while Mrs. Adams and I broke camp. After everything was packed and the mules hitched to the wagon, my companion got out a few handfuls of chicken feed and soon had the hens nicely settled for the day's journey. Once the mules were in the main road and headed in the right direction, she slipped the lines into a patent clutch and began to unpack her wares.

I was glad to find the goods of excellent quality and reasonable in price. She gave me a few talking points for each article, told me how much cash I should demand or about how much I could expect in trade. Trading, she observed, was an art in itself and worthy of much study. Stock was replenished by frequent orders to Chicago, the goods being consigned to the larger towns along the route. Thus, she would find a fresh supply awaiting her at Sydney, Nebraska, and would there place an order to be shipped to Cheyenne, Wyoming.

I had familiarised myself with the most important details when we approached a good-sized farmhouse.

"Come in and watch me work this time, and at the next place you can try it yourself," she remarked, swinging the mules into the driveway.

A weary-looking woman opened the door at our knock and brightened with interest when she learned of our errand. She led the way to the closely shut parlour, and flung open the old-fashioned blinds as Mrs. Adams prepared her goods for inspection. After long consideration she laid down the case with a sigh.

"I'd just love to buy some of these things, but I haven't a cent in the house. My husband is working way over in the back lot and anyhow I'd hate to bother him."

"Now, maybe you'd like to trade for what you want. I would be glad to get some good, smooth potatoes or nice fresh vegetables if you have any to spare."

"Oh, could I do that?" Her voice was eager as a child's. "Come right into the kitchen and see what you would like."

Inside of half an hour we were back in the wagon with a fine assortment of vegetables. In fact, it seemed to me that we had much the best of the bargain. In answer to some such observation, Mrs. Adams chuckled.

"When I saw how that woman had been trained, I led her right along. She has no idea of the value of money or of produce either. How can she, when her husband never allows her a cent of spending money? The kind of women who must always beg for every calico dress and pair of shoes, go wild when they have a chance to trade for themselves. You should do as much business as possible with them—take anything they have—get flour or sugar if there is nothing else on hand. String 'em along and you can get a wagon load of groceries for a dollar's worth of goods."

Privately registering a determination to do nothing of the kind, I observed, "I should think their husbands would find out about that sort of thing and make trouble."

"Don't worry, we'll be well out of the way before they could find out anything about the business."

"I wasn't thinking about you and me, but about the farmer's wife. Seems to me she has troubles enough without our adding to her burdens."

"Now, you got to learn the first principles of this business, and the main thing is to look out for number one. Skin the other woman every chance you get. Lots of times they'll stick you and by minding your own business, you'll come out about even in the end. And you needn't think there is anything new in a wife's selling the groceries out of the house to get a few nickels to spend for herself. Why, when I lived in—" She stopped abruptly, then resumed.

"Most grocerymen have cases of women who make a habit of padding the bills to get a few dollars returned on the sly. It's all in the game, and you've got to play your end of it."

"Well, I can't say I like that kind of a game," I declared decidedly. "I hope the day will come soon when men and women will develop a new psychology along those lines. The first thing that should be settled after a couple become engaged is the money question. They should have a definite understanding as to how the money is to be spent after marriage, and the girl should see to it that she never drifts into a position where she must plead with some man for what rightfully belongs to her."

"That sounds very pretty, my dear, but most girls are glad enough to catch a man without taking chances by arguing over money matters—they're too scared of being old maids."

"That's mostly the fault of their training or, I should say, lack of training. So long as they are led to consider marriage the whole end and aim of life, I suppose they'll go on getting into situations where they are compelled to cheat and steal and lie to secure a few paltry nickels. If I had a daughter, I should see that she was fully equipped to become a self-supporting, self-respecting member of society, a woman who would not look upon marriage as the only possible solution of life's problems."

Mrs. Adams rolled her eyes in horror. "Good gracious, woman, you talk like one of these here suffragettes. If I had a girl that talked like that, I'd disown her. Why, you want to break up the home!"

"If financial independence for women means breaking up the home, then let it be broken. Poverty and the economic dependence of woman on man is the curse of the whole sex relation. It extends from the society matron who caresses and fawns upon a husband whom she loathes in order to wheedle him into the gift of a diamond necklace, a new mansion or other extravagance, through all the middle class women who lie and cheat and steal the household goods to get spending money, on down to the daughters of the poor who are forced to sell their bodies in order to exist.

"We frown upon European marriages, but expect our own girls to make good matches, marry for a home, do anything to catch a man. Faugh, the thought makes me ill. If we support the American idea of matrimony, then we must admit that the only proper basis for marriage is love. If we are to have free men, we must have free women who refuse to sell themselves for a home, social position, or material gain in any form whatsoever. We must adopt a single standard of morals, and abolish prostitution, both within and without the marriage relation."

"Why—why, you—I'm surprised at you," stuttered my companion. "I never heard a woman speak such words before. Such talk is indecent, that's what it is, indecent."

"The truth is often considered indecent, I believe, especially the naked truth. Like the human body, it needs to be concealed by a peek-a-boo waist of prudery and licentiousness."

"Stop, stop, not another word. . . . Such language is positively shocking . . . not fit for a decent woman to listen to."

At this point in this most shocking conversation, the mules headed for a wretched two-room shack that stood a little away from the road. To me the place appeared too poverty-stricken for hope of business, but our driver let the mules have their way.

A frowsy woman was carrying two heavy pails of water from a well near which stood a cesspool, a ramshackle shed for stock and a great heap of refuse. The dooryard swarmed with dogs, hogs and children. A sallow girl, gathering corncobs for the fire, loosed her loaded petticoat and dashed forward to greet us. Mrs. Adams seized her sample case and leaving the mules to their own devices, scrambled from the wagon. I followed meekly.

The farmer's wife set down her dripping burden, wiped her hands on her tattered apron and proffered us a brimming dipper. Thirsty as I was, I felt impelled to decline—the well's environment did not appeal to my taste. No sooner were we within the house, than Mrs. Adams opened negotiations for a side of bacon.

"We've got some extry bacon, but I dunno about sparin' none. My old man's aiming to take some into town to trade in a day or two and I dunno what he'd say if I let go of a side."

"Oh, Maw," broke in the oldest girl, who had been examining our display with longing eyes, "never mind what Paw says. If he trades the side meat, he'll just get drunk on the money. He always does."

"You shut your mouth and don't go talking about your Paw." The mother gave the girl a sharp slap on the ear as she spoke.

The child's face crimsoned. "I don't care. It ain't right. We don't ever do anything but work, work, work, and Paw, he never works. Then everything goes for hateful old booze. It ain't right."

"Now, now, Mandy, you orta treat your Paw with respect. I can't see what's getting into the young ones these days, especially the girls. Mandy here, bellered her head off cause we let Jeffie, that's our oldest, stop last winter with my brother Jed to go to school. She thought she orta gone too."

"Jeff's had two years more in school now than I've had, and still I'm ahead of him."

"hat's all the more reason why you orta stay home and work. Jeffie's a boy and needs schoolin', while you're a—"

"You're quite right," Mrs. Adams interrupted; "a girl don't need much book learning. She wants to learn to cook and sew and take good care of her house so she can make some man a good wife."

"Yes, so she can plough and harrow and husk corn and carry swill to the hogs while her man goes to town and gets drunk. I hate men. I hate men." The girl's eyes blazed.

"Get out that door, you ungrateful hussy, or I'll give you a good lambasting." The child burst into tears as her mother pursued her from the untidy living room. "I can't see what's got into the child. She's always been such a comfort to me—worked since she was knee high to a duck. Seems like she's dead set on going to school, but I can't spare her. Why this spring, she and I put in eighty acres of corn with our own hands, besides milking seven cows and all the other work. I've only got the one boy; he's the oldest in the family. I aim he should have an education, but Jeffie hates school. Mandy can learn as much in eight weeks scattered through the winter term as he can in a year, but the spite of it is she's only a girl and don't need schoolin'."

"You're very wise to keep her with you. A woman's place is in the home. Now, don't you think it would be a good idea to trade me that bacon? It'll make the girl contented to get these things she wants and she'll forget all about that fool notion of going to school. She needs stuff like this to attract the boys. You make the trade and then figure out some way of pulling the wool over the old man's eyes."

"Well, maybe I can manage some way. I orta get something for the poor child, I suppose. Paw'll raise Cain, but he does that anyhow. Now, what'll you let me have for a good fat side of bacon?"

Leaving the two women to conclude the bargain, I stepped outside and sought Mandy. The poor girl seemed only too glad to find a sympathetic soul to confide in.

She was sixteen years old, she said, and although her opportunities for study had been so limited, she had managed to keep up with her classes by studying every spare moment. For the past two years her teacher had taken a special interest in her and had advised and helped her in every possible way. She had a great ambition. It was to become a school teacher and thus be able to help her mother and younger sisters.

"Toots is past fourteen and strong for her age," she concluded, "and May is twelve. They could help Maw out if I was gone. If I could only have Jeff's chance—just have some place to live while I went to school. But Maw won't hear of it. I just don't know what to do. It's not for me alone, it's all the little ones. Paw gets worse all the time, and Jeff's got no ambition. I got to succeed to save the family." She squared her wiry little shoulders as though to support the world.

"Sometimes people are willing to take a good, strong girl and let her earn her board and keep while she goes to school by working mornings and nights and holidays. It's a pretty hard way to live. A girl must be a servant and never gets any fun. Would you want to do that?"

Mandy stretched out her browned and calloused hands. "Do you see those paws? I've milked cows and curried mules and ploughed and suckered corn, to say nothing of washing dishes and packing wood and water and such like, all without any hope at all. Give me a chance to earn an education and I'll work these fingers to the bone and be glad to do it."

"Well, I can't promise you anything definite, but I meet lots of people and I'll see what I can do. If I do find a place, how'll I let you know?"

"I'll give you the address of Mrs. Cummings. That's where my teacher boarded. You can send a letter there for me and she'll see that I get it safely. Oh, if you'll only get me a chance!"

"Are you sure you have the courage to leave your home in the face of the opposition of your father and mother and go away alone to work in some stranger's kitchen? You're under age, too, you know, and if your parents can find you, they can force you to return. You'll have to cut yourself off from them for two whole years."

"Yes, I can do it. I swear to you, I will do it—cross my heart and hope to die. I wouldn't leave my mother, if I didn't feel sure it's for her own good. I can do so much for her when I get to be a teacher. You'll try to get me a chance, won't you?"

I promised to do my best.

As Mrs. Adams came out of the door with her side of bacon, Mandy dashed inside, and returned in a few moments with a piece of paper which she slipped into my hand.

"Here's the address," she whispered. "You won't forget, will you? Please, please, don't forget."

With a few reassuring words I bade her goodbye and took my place in the wagon.

"That good-for-nothing hussy of a girl will come to a bad end, you mark my words," Mrs. Adams said spitefully, as I turned to wave my hand to the plucky little figure standing in the dust of the roadside, "but I suppose you think she's real cute, running down her poor old father."

We jogged along in silence for some time, then, as we approached a prosperous-looking farm, my employer suggested that I try my hand at the game. With sinking heart, I dragged my reluctant feet up the path, but was surprised and reassured by the warmth of my reception. Unlike the city dweller, the average country woman rather welcomes the call of a peddler. I was fortunate in more ways than one, for my customer had money and made a large selection, so that I was enabled to pay for my goods and retain sixty-five cents to jingle in my pocket.

For the rest of the day, we took turns at the farmhouses and by night I had quite a supply of food, which represented clear profit, as I had paid for the toilet articles in produce. Dan and I had determined to attend to our own culinary operations instead of boarding with Mrs. Adams, as had been suggested. We felt that we could save more money, and while our table was not elaborate, it satisfied our needs very nicely.

About five o'clock we overtook the men, and following their direction, soon arrived at the camping place.

The evening meal concluded, Dan and I were sitting beside our little fire, comparing the day's experiences, when Mr. Adams strolled over and threw himself down beside us. After some desultory conversation, he plunged into a philosophical discussion.

"Have you ever made a study of Nietzsche?" he demanded.

"I've tried to read him, but with little success," I replied. "His philosophy is so revolting to me, that I can scarcely pass an unbiassed judgment on him."

"You surprise me. I consider Friedrich Wilhelm Nietzsche the greatest genius and the most profound philosopher that the world has yet produced. His work is so free from sentimental mush, his attitude is so clearly scientific, he shows none of the weakness that comes from . . ."

"Oh, Frankie, love, come quick. I need you." It was the voice of our friend's fair partner. He rose slowly to his feet and bade us goodnight.

"I have a hunch that Honey-drips does not care for philosophy," observed Dan, as we rose to turn in for the night.

The next few days were uneventful. Mr. Bates took a train for Cheyenne, leaving Dan to handle the sign orders alone. We had accumulated an abundant supply of farm produce of all kinds, in fact, we were overstocked in some lines, so that Mr. Adams suggested a change of programme. Instead of riding behind the mule team, I now go with the men in the buckboard, and while Mr. Adams solicits sign orders, and Dan puts them up, I canvass the towns where my goods sell for cash.

The drives seem but half as long as before, thanks to the superior speed of the horses and the pleasant banter of Mr. Adams, who is a most interesting conversationalist.

The man is a wonderful study. He often starts to speak of some personal experience and breaks off in the middle of the first sentence. He never has given me the least hint of his earlier life, but I feel sure that he is a college man. There must be some mystery in his life. I spoke of my beliefs to Dan.

He replied, "The only mystery that I see is that he is falling in love with you, and that's not much of a mystery either. Honey-drips sees how the wind blows and loves you like a rattlesnake."

I indignantly denied the allegation, for Mr. Adams' conduct had been exemplary. But Dan refused to retract his unjust words, so I determined to keep my opinions to myself.

CHAPTER TWELVE

# July 12th, 1908, Sydney, Nebraska

We had worked a small town a half day's drive east of Sydney, where pressing business awaited Mr. Adams' immediate attention. Dan had a number of sign orders to fill and Mrs. Adams some culinary duties to perform, so it came about that Mr. Adams and I drove ahead with the buckboard, leaving the others to finish their tasks and follow.

We rose early and began our journey as the rose and opal tints of dawn were disappearing in the mounting flood of sunlight. The air was cool and bracing and the horses cavorted with delight as we spun past the scattering outposts of the village and took the white, winding road across the western plain.

Mr. Adams set me down at the edge of town and headed for the express and telegraph office, while I prepared for peddling. He was out of sight before I realised that we had not touched the lunch that was in the buckboard, although it was after one o'clock. I hadn't a cent with me, for I had put all the money available into an order for special goods, which Mr. Adams was going to send east. Making change might prove awkward at first, but I could only do my best. I selected the most prosperous street and set resolutely to work.

At the first three houses the inmates refused to open the door, although I could see them peering at me from within.

"Nothing today," exclaimed the fourth housewife before I could open my mouth.

I was growing very thirsty and as I walked up a flower-bordered path to a vine-covered veranda, I decided to ask for a drink of water without mentioning my wares. A sharp-nosed woman answered my ring.

"Please, madam, could I trouble you for a drink of water?" I asked.

"You can't play any of your tricks on me," she replied spitefully, slamming the door in my face.

As I walked slowly through the yard, I saw a pleasant-faced young Swedish girl at work on the back porch of the large house next door.

"She'll surely give me a drink," I said to myself. She greeted me with a smile as I made known my wants and, in a moment,, I was quenching the thirst which had grown unendurable. As I set down the glass, she noted my sample case.

"You bane sell someting?" she enquired with a wide smile.

With eager hands she fell upon the toilet articles as I opened the case.

"Yaw, yaw," she cried. "I bane want someting long, long tam. Youst wait. I got money."

She disappeared into the house.

I was laying out her selections when a harsh voice startled me.

"How dare you sneak into my home and take up the time of my maids? Leave this house instantly."

I whirled around, too amazed to speak. A large, pompous woman was standing in the inner doorway, motioning me out with a be-ringed hand.

"But—but madam," I stammered, "your maid wants to buy some of these articles. She has gone to get the money."

"I'll not have you cheating my servants. Go away from here."

The girl appeared at that moment, but her mistress blocked the door.

"Hulda, you stay right where you are. Shame on you, wasting valuable time on a tricky pedlar. What do you suppose I pay you wages for?"

"Oh, mam. I ban long tam want . . ."

"That will do. That will do. I don't want any of your saucy talk. You are paid to do the housework, so get at it." She turned on me.

"Get off these premises at once. You may be able to swindle these ignorant foreigners, but you can't impose on me. Go now, or I'll call the constable. The very idea, crowding yourself right into people's homes, talking to their servants, impudent . . ."

She was still raving as I passed out of hearing. The day was very warm. I was dusty and tired and hungry. Aimlessly I followed the street till it terminated in a country road and finally sank down by the roadside, too weary and disheartened to think clearly.

I was roused by the sound of pattering hoofs and glancing up, saw a team of grey Indian ponies, attached to a light buckboard, come scampering around a curve. They shied sharply at sight of my recumbent figure, reared and tried to break into a run. Their driver drew them in with masterly skill, and circling through the weeds and brush, returned to learn the cause of the fracas. She was a tall, strong woman, with an aquiline nose and iron grey hair. The smile with which she greeted me as I approached the wagon was very winning.

"Is there something the matter? Are you ill or hurt?" she inquired, leaning toward me with kindling eyes.

"No, just tired and a bit blue, I guess. It didn't seem worthwhile to walk anymore, so I dropped right down here."

"Pardon me, but aren't you a stranger to these parts? I don't recall seeing you before. In these little towns we generally know everyone, at least by sight."

"Yes, I arrived only a couple of hours ago, but I know this town pretty well already."

She searched my face as though seeking the true meaning of my words; then her eyes fell on my sample case, which was still clutched in my left hand.

"Oh, you are selling something," she exclaimed. "What is it, books?"

"No, not books. And I'm not selling anything either—not in this town."

"Oh, so that's it. You must have started on the wrong street. Suppose you jump in with me and ride out to the house. Maybe it will change your luck."

I hesitated for a moment, my usual faith in human nature somewhat shaken by recent experiences.

"Come on, now. Jump in. I'll bring you back to wherever you want to go, whenever you are ready."

I walked around the wagon and clambered in. The ponies bounded forward, and away we flew, winding up among low, rolling hills, until we came to a small house perched on the side of a knoll. Care of the team had occupied my companion's attention to the exclusion of conversation until we had entered the house. Then, as she set out a substantial lunch—afternoon tea, she termed it—we began to get acquainted.

Mrs. Holiday's home was in Cheyenne, but her husband owned this large stock ranch, which led them to make frequent visits to Sydney.

As evening approached, she declared her intention of driving into town after Dan and keeping the two of us as long as our business permitted us to remain in the neighbourhood. Leaving me to devour a tableful of newspapers and late magazines, the first I had seen in months, she sped away with her frisky team and returned with Dan, who had grown quite accustomed to my peculiar way of making myself at home in unusual places. As they drove into the yard, Mr. Holiday rode in from the range and we all were soon on a most friendly footing.

Mr. Adams had already left a couple of sign orders with Dan to put up the next morning, but instead of going into town with him to resume my interrupted labours as a pedlar, I decided to take a day off to wash and mend our clothing and incidentally starch my crumpled courage by an interchange of confidences with my hostess, who possessed a peculiarly invigorating temperament.

Her early years had been full of privations and severe struggles to gain an education. She had become a high school teacher, but her health failed, forcing her to seek the high altitudes of the Rockies. Here she had met and married Mr. Holiday, a well-to-do cattle man, and they had built a home in Cheyenne. One child—a girl—was born to them, but she had died some two years previously. Since her death the mother had been almost mad with loneliness, finding her chief consolation in mothering the calves and colts and other young creatures of the range.

She was greatly interested in the history of our experiences, and as I was telling her the story of Mandy of the cornfields, she suddenly leaned forward with sparkling eyes.

Give me the address of that Mrs. Cummings. I'm going back there and if she is half the gritty little heroine that you make her out to be, I'll bring her home with me and see that she gets the best education that money can buy. Maybe I'll take one or two of the other children, too."

"But . . . but maybe their mother will object," I faltered.

"It won't do her a bit of good if she does," Mrs. Holiday replied firmly. "I always get what I go after. You know, when I saw you beside the road yesterday, I felt impelled to take you home with me. I believe in that kind of instinct—intuition—fate—call it what you will. That little Mandy will be my girl. I can teach her so much. It will be like renewing my youth. Of course, she'll go to school in Cheyenne, too, and later to college if she likes. Oh, I'll get her—rest assured of that. It's mostly a question of money, anyway."

I handed over the address without another word. Yes, it would be largely a question of money with that drunken father and ignorant mother, and it would be a wonderful opportunity for Mandy.

The workings of fate are marvellous to contemplate. If that old harridan of a woman had not ordered me from her house, I would not have wandered out into the country and met Mrs. Holiday. Then Mandy would not have had her chance. Thus, the harridan woman is clearly seen to be but an instrument of a benign Providence. Should she be censured for an act that results in so much good? I put the question to my companion, who laughed as I told her the story.

"You were unfortunate in that you began operations in the fashionable quarter of our fair city. I know the woman you describe. She is the shining light of local clubdom, the greatest society leader here. She would be highly insulted at the idea of serving as an instrument of Fate. Why, she would not be the servant of the Almighty himself—if she can't boss the job, she won't play."

"It must be rather hard on the maid," I observed.

"Well, she's notorious for the way she handles her servants. She gets these green foreigners fresh from the old country, and keeps them penned in her kitchen so long as they will endure it. They are taught to cook and wash and all that, but she pays next to nothing, and does her best to prevent their learning decent English or mingling with their kind. She is a fine person to talk of swindling ignorant foreigners. A worse exploiter of unfortunate servant girls it would be difficult to find.

"But tomorrow I'll take you into another part of town, over where the human people live, and probably you will do quite well."

She was a good prophet, for I have succeeded in clearing nearly five dollars during the last few days. It will be with keen regret that I leave my newfound friend tomorrow morning and take the road again with the California outfit.

CHAPTER THIRTEEN

# July 23rd, Cheyenne, Wyoming

Alas, for our dreams of a comfortable journey home; alas for our expectation of seeing the country; alas, too, for our hopes of saving money for a fresh start in the world. We face mountains and desert with nothing but a grim determination to win or die.

After we left Sydney, Mrs. Adams abandoned herself to a mounting jealousy, which became increasingly evident to us all. The hours that I was forced to spend with her behind the ambling mules, were torture. She took advantage of every opportunity to annoy and humiliate me, so that every atom of my patience and control was needed to avoid a scene. But my best efforts availed nothing with the woman. We had been travelling through a very sparsely settled region some twenty-five or thirty miles east of Cheyenne when the affair came to a climax.

About eleven o'clock I left Mrs. Adams waiting in the country road while I called at a farm house, which stood some distance away in a clump of trees. She had refused to drive in as usual, but had ordered me to go in and trade for or purchase some fresh eggs. When I reached the house no one was at home, and after considerable search in the outbuildings, I returned empty handed to the road, only to find the wagon gone. Dust was rising in the distance and I could just see the black wagon top as the mules pulled slowly over a rise.

My blood was boiling as I set off down the road at a jog trot, expecting to overtake the slow-going mules in the first mile or so. I was within hailing distance of the team when Mrs. Adams glanced back, whipped the animals into a lively trot, and with an insulting gesture coolly outdistanced me.

"Very well," I said to myself, steadying my pace. "I'll walk no further than the first water. Then I'll rest until night. Dan will come into camp and miss me. He'll take the buckboard and start hunting. And when we finally come up with that woman there will be something doing."

But water is scarce in that country, and at last I sat down in the sparse shade of a clump of bushes to wait for a rescue. It came much sooner than I expected, for it was not more than three o'clock when I was roused from a light doze by a cheerful halloo and sprang up to see Mr. Adams reining in the horses. He leaped down in a jiffy, brought out the oozing canvas bag of water that he always carried in this desert country and handed me a delicious draught.

"Get right into the rig, and I'll unpack your lunch," he exclaimed solicitously, assisting me over the wheel. "I only learned of this infernal outrage by accident. I landed a rather unusual order this morning and, leaving your husband on the job to sketch the preliminaries, drove back to meet the wagon and rush along the necessary supplies. What was my surprise to find you missing. My wife and I had a beautiful row while I was putting up this lunch and starting back to look for you. She's gone ahead now, to take that new lot of letters to your husband."

He had turned the team around as he spoke and was driving rapidly along the western track. Then I looked up from my meal in surprise, for he had swung into a narrow trail leading away to the north.

"What's the idea?" I inquired. "Aren't you taking the wrong turning?"

"There is a little spring up here a mile or so where we'll stop to feed and water the horses. They've been jogging pretty steadily since early this morning."

It was true. The poor beasts were in need of food and water, and I was glad when we drew up at a tiny stream, which flowed through the bottom of a ravine, where we could enjoy the protecting shade of a few straggling willows. Mr. Adams unharnessed the sweat-stained animals, allowed them a swallow or two of water and spread a flake of baled hay for them to munch until cool enough to eat their grain. I had settled myself beneath a tree and had just finished my lunch when he threw himself down beside me.

"Ethel," he began, "you are too fine a woman for the kind of life you are leading. I love you, dear. Won't you let me take you away and give you all the beautiful things that belong to you?"

I gazed at him a moment in silence. "Aren't you forgetting yourself, Mr. Adams?" I inquired coldly. "How about your wife?"

"Oh, that woman. She is not my wife, and she has no hold on me whatever. Why she was running an assignation house in Detroit when I picked her up. Let her go back where she came from."

"And you can live with a woman for more than two years, share the burdens of the road, eat at the same campfire, travel with her as your wife, and then dismiss her with a wave of the hand? You may consider yourself free perhaps, but I am a married woman and, besides, I love my husband."

"You think you love him, no doubt, and maybe you do—now. But who knows how long that love will last? You yourself admit that love is the only legitimate basis for marriage. Your love for your husband may die tomorrow as the love of thousands of other women has done. Love is free as the wind, it comes and goes without reason, without warning, without restraint.

"Now, I am rich, I flatter myself that I know the world. I will aid you to a divorce and obtain one myself. After marriage we will travel, visit Florence, Naples, drink in all the myriad beauties of the Old World. If you have ambitions, I will help you to achieve. I will gratify your tastes for music, art, literature; I will free those wonderful impulses that throb beneath that calm exterior—those sensuous instincts to which your lout of a husband is so totally oblivious."

I sprang to my feet. "That will be all, if you please. Don't say another word."

I busied myself with the horses. He placed their grain, then drew close to me.

"My God, Ethel. I love you, girl, love you, do you hear? Give me just a little chance, won't you?"

He caught my hand and pressed it to his lips. I wrenched it away roughly, and looked about in desperation. The long shadows of late afternoon lay among the hills; the country was wild and rugged—not a human habitation in sight. I was absolutely alone with this maniac. I turned with resolute mien.

"See here, my friend. If you love me even half as much as you say you do, you will cease your insulting proposals, hitch up this team and take me back to civilisation. You will make me hate you, if you keep on as you are doing."

He stood motionless, staring at me with sombre eyes. Then, as I began to place the harness on the horses, he came to my assistance, and together we watered them and hitched them to the buckboard.

We drove home in silence and reached camp just as Dan came whistling down the road. It was plain that my husband knew nothing of my desertion by Mrs. Adams that morning, and I was in no condition to tell him anything coherent. I stood like a wooden Indian as he seized me around the waist with a bearlike hug.

"Good news," he cried. "Today's work brings our credit with the old man up to an even fifty dollars. Not so bad for a poor hobo, is it, now?"

He caught sight of my face and became all sympathy. "Why, sweetheart, what's the matter? Are you sick?"

"N-no, not sick exactly," I faltered, with lips that persisted in quivering a trifle.

"Well, you look awfully queer, some way. Has that old cat been bothering you again?"

"Yes," I murmured. "She's pretty mean, and it's been so hot, and I—oh, I guess I'm about played out."

He gently led me to a spot as far removed from the Adams' camp as possible, made a couple of trips to the wagons and brought back our bedding, a few cooking utensils and some food for supper. Then he induced me to lie down, while he built a fire and prepared the meal.

"Poor little girl," he murmured. "I know all this is mighty rough on you, but if I can only keep on as I've been doing for the past three weeks, it won't be so very long till we can ride the cushions home in comfort. Meantime, leave the old cat alone as much as possible, and try not to take the situation too seriously."

It seemed that I had scarcely fallen asleep when I was awakened by a consciousness of something wrong. The night was dark, but judging from the stars, it was about midnight. What was it that had aroused me? I lay still and listened.

There came a tinkling of trace chains from the other side of the big cattle pen where the Adams' camp lay. Pshaw, it was only one of the mules, nosing around the camp in search of fruit parings, as he often did. I lay back reassured and dozed once more.

Again, that premonition came; that peculiar instinct that thrills one into vivid wakefulness in the midst of quiet slumber. Again, I sat up with a start. Again, I heard mysterious noises from the direction of the other camp. I took my husband by the arm.

"Dan, Dan," I hissed. "Wake up. I hear something."

He grunted, groaned, stretched himself and sat up. "What's the matter, Ethel?" he muttered sleepily.

"I don't know what it is, but I feel sure there is something wrong. This is the second time I've waked up feeling this way."

"Something wrong! What do you mean? What's wrong?"

"That's just it. I don't know what it is, but there is something the matter at the Adams' camp."

"I don't hear anything—you must have been dreaming— Don't you feel well? I'll get you a drink of water." He jumped up and searched around for a cup.

"What's the matter, folks? Did the noise disturb you?" It was the cheerful voice of Mr. Adams.

"Oh, Ethel's got a notion that the bugaboos are after her," answered Dan,

"She heard that mule, I suppose. Jack tried to get into the grain as usual and got tangled in the harness. I just finished straightening him out."

"Anything I can do to help you, old man?" Dan called.

"No, thank you. Everything is all right now. Go back to bylo land and never mind if you hear me fussing around. I'm going to take a high-ball."

Once more we lay down, and this time I slept soundly. I was awakened by a shout from Dan, who had risen and dressed without disturbing me. The sun was well up, but the camping ground was unaccountably silent. There was no sound of cackling hens, or of stamping, munching horses and mules; no smoke rose from the other side of the cattle pen.

"Ethel, Ethel," Dan was calling. "Come here, quick."

I wrapped a blanket about me and ran to him, then stopped in consternation.

The California outfit was gone.

Gone also were our odds and ends of equipment, saved from the wreck of the wheel, my emergency case, a change of clothing, all the groceries and provisions that I had worked so hard to accumulate, and last, but not least, gone were the fifty dollars, left in Mr. Adams' hands for safe keeping, over which we had been rejoicing the night before.

Dan was stamping about like a madman shouting, "I'll kill the ——— I'll get the law on him."

He followed the wagon tracks to the main road, but it was impossible to tell in which direction they had gone. As he returned, he picked up the old battered canteen, given me by the ex-soldier as a keepsake, which had evidently slipped from the wagon as it jolted over the uneven ground.

Together we wandered back to our little camp. We still had our blankets, a few cooking utensils, a partly used box of cocoa, a little sugar, part of a can of sweetened condensed milk, and a few scrappy remains of the evening meal.

After making an unsatisfactory breakfast, we cast up accounts to determine our line of action. I had nearly five dollars in silver in a concealed pocket in my clothing, and Dan had a few dollars also. We were camped near the loading pen of a large cattle corral placed beside a lonely railroad siding. We had no means of knowing where Adams had gone; no way of pursuing him. We had no idea where to find the sheriff of that county or other officer of the law.

If we should succeed in capturing the thieves, what sort of a case could we make against them? We had no written agreement—not the scratch of a pen to show that they owed us anything at all. And possession is nine points of the law. Then, how could we live while waiting for results from the slow-moving legal machinery? The case looked hopeless from every angle.

I told Dan about Mrs. Adams' conduct the day before and something of the affair with the man. He read me quite a lecture and then advised me to forget the whole episode as quickly as possible. We had but one object in life—to reach California as soon as fate would let us. We must dismiss the California outfit from our minds—not speak of it again. But one road lay open to us. We must have recourse to a "side-door Pullman."

Bundles on backs, we struck out for a water tank, there to await the coming of a freight. A long string of coal cars pulled in and stopped for water. Dan's request for a ride to Cheyenne was granted with the proviso that we drop off before we reached the city. The brakeman spoke to the engineer, who agreed to take advantage of a steep grade a few miles east of town to slow down sufficiently for us to jump in safety, adding that this would be our only chance, as trains always ran down the further slope into the city at a high speed. We were forced to ride in a gondola, which is a fairly warm place in a blazing sun. Mile after mile we rode, and at last were warned of the approach to the hill. Crouching at the end of the car, we waited for the speed to slacken.

Suddenly I noticed that the speed was increasing instead of diminishing, and a glance ahead showed the engineer waving his arms frantically. The brakeman bounded into the car.

"My God!" he yelled. "The super's on behind and Buck daren't slow down. We're over the hill. You'll be pinched in Cheyenne, sure, and we'll get a sixty-day layoff, if we don't all get the bounce."

"We must jump for it, Dan," I said. 'There is no other way. And we'll have to be quick about it, too."

Gathering my skirts in one hand, I clung to the side of the car with the other and leaned far out and down. Dan begged me not to try it, but followed my lead when he saw that I was determined to go. The earth reeled by at a frightful speed, the wind lashed my face, the heavy freight lurched from side to side with crash and roar, gathering momentum with every turn of the wheels.

For a moment my courage failed and I hung motionless. Then with a violent outward thrust of hand and arm, I made a sidelong leap. My feet struck the gravelled path at the side of the rails with a thud, and catching my stride, I ran clear. Dan was not so fortunate, but rolled headlong down the embankment, landing in a clump of brush. In an instant I reached his side and found him unhurt, but pale as a ghost from the strain. Together we darted into the tall bushes and sank down, just as the caboose swept by, with a man, evidently the superintendent referred to by the brakeman, standing on the rear platform beside the conductor.

We were still a couple of miles from town, so, adjusting our packs, we set off down the hot and dusty road. We had not walked far when a teamster gave us a lift to our destination.

The only possible camping place was beside a small stream in a group of trees at the south side of the town. While I made camp, Dan went into Cheyenne. About dusk he returned, whistling cheerfully, with the welcome news of a job in the morning. He had also made a trip to the reservation and delivered the note sent by our wayside acquaintance to his friend. This man sent us a little brown tent, made in two pieces with folding supports for convenience in carrying. It is called a "dog tent" by the soldiers and formed a valuable addition to our equipment. It shelters two persons comfortably and is so light that I could carry half besides my usual load without serious inconvenience. For a week now I have had leisure to wash and mend our clothes and purchase a few necessities for the coming struggle with deserts and mountains. Work is too scarce and wages too low to tempt us to remain here in the hope of accumulating enough to take us home in proper fashion.

## CHAPTER FOURTEEN

# July 24th, Cheyenne, Wyoming

Dan came in last evening quite disturbed over his failure to collect his wages on the completion of the work. He worked very cheap for this contractor, who seems to employ many floaters, and now he is refused the little money that is due him. He went uptown this morning, and returned about four o'clock enraged and disheartened. It seems that his employer makes a business of hiring men who drift into town, at as low a wage as possible; then beats them out of the money altogether, if he can. At times some unfortunate, whose spirit is not yet broken, threatens violence, in which case a trip to jail and a month on the chain-gang curb, if not cure, his desire for justice.

When Dan hinted at reprisals, legal or otherwise, it was suggested that the Cheyenne climate was wont to prove unhealthy for such as he, so it would be well for him to seek new fields while the going was good. Inasmuch as we have no standing in this community, besides possessing less than three dollars in cash, which would not go far toward lawyer's fees or bail money, it would seem that this advice, bitter as it is, should be followed.

## CHAPTER FIFTEEN

# August 2nd, Laramie, Wyoming

A faint sunset glow illumined the dry, brown plain as we approached the grade west of Cheyenne. A pungent odour rose from under foot as we trailed through the low brush, and as we approached the track, the rails set up a low humming that steadily increased in pitch and volume. A glaring eye appeared in the distance. I had never attempted to board a train in rapid motion and was more or less ignorant of ladders, hand holds and other details of car construction, and the idea of leaping on the roaring mass that came thundering through the semidarkness appalled me. Nearer and nearer drew the engine. The fierce glow of the furnace, as the fireman laboured to fill the insatiable maw, gleamed red upon the gravelled track. Black smoke rolled from the stack and hung low in the quiet air. With laboured pants, like an exhausted leviathan, the great machine lurched past.

Dan caught my hand and we ran beside the track. Car after car clanked by. The hammering wheels seemed hungry for a victim. My eyes visioned the ghastly death of an unknown man, whose life had been ground out but a scant half hour before we had discovered the mangled remains. I saw myself, hampered with clinging skirts and weighted with a heavy bundle, clinging, slipping, falling between the ravening wheels, and a deadly nausea seized me. With a half-stifled cry, I turned down the embankment. Dan pulled and exhorted in vain.

"It's no use," I said doggedly. "I just can't do it."

The tail-lights of the caboose faded from view.

'Well, I'll be darned," said Dan. "I never knew you were a coward."

"I don't care if I am. It's better than being chopped to pieces under that train. I feel sure I should have gone under if I had made the attempt."

"Nonsense," he replied. "Now we're in a nice fix. We can't stay here. We can't walk across that wilderness. And we can't catch a freight in the railroad yard on account of Jeff Farr. First time I ever saw you show the white feather."

"Just you wait till morning and we'll see who'll show the white feather. I'm going to walk right into that yard, and Jeff Farr or no Jeff Farr, I'll board the first west-bound freight that pulls out."

Jeff Fair, as all the hoboes know, is an officer, especially dreaded because of his drastic methods of handling vagrants, who makes his headquarters at Cheyenne. We had heard of him repeatedly, for his fame had spread even beyond Omaha, and his mere name was sufficient to strike fear in the stoutest heart.

In a disgruntled mood, we plunged into the bushes, and without attempting to make camp, threw ourselves on the ground and slept. At dawn we ate a cold lunch and turned back toward Cheyenne.

At the west entrance of the railroad yard, a watchman stopped us. I pleaded our cause to such good effect that he turned his back and gazed into space as we scurried past. Two long strings of boxcars stood as though ready for the road, and as we approached, a brakeman clambered from the top of the nearest and spoke to me. He had noted the behaviour of the detective, so as soon as I explained the situation he motioned to the second string and told us that it was a west-bound train, already searched and passed by the detectives, and now waiting, under the guard of our friend the watchman, for engine and crew.

Ducking across the track, we examined the long line of cars, but each was shut and sealed. In the middle of the train stood several gondolas, and in lieu of nothing better, we boarded one. Crouching down, we waited for the start with every nerve at high tension. A pair of hands grasped the edge of the *gondola*. "Jeff Farr," thought I with a shudder. A man's head appeared above the brim. With staring eyes, he glared at us for a moment, then, with an inarticulate grunt, dropped to the ground. The brakeman who had directed our movements engaged him in conversation. Another pair of hands came over the other side of the car. Again, a vision of revolvers, handcuffs, courtroom and jail flashed through my mind. Again, a man's head appeared.

"Well, I'll be blowed—a woman!" he gasped, and disappeared from view.

Then a third man appeared. He evidently, knew what to expect, for he stared at us with a friendly grin.

"The boys said they was a woman up here, but I thought they was kidding me. Say, you folks got nerve—sticking your head into the lion's mouth like this. Ever hear of Jeff Farr?"

"It'll take something a whole lot worse than Jeff Farr to keep me in this Godforsaken hole of a Cheyenne," I replied.

"They said you had grit. Hope you get through all right," he answered, as a jolt announced the arrival of the engine.

"Off brakes," whistled the engineer. With gasps of relief we saw the buildings glide past, for we knew we were safe for the present.

At the second station out an empty box car was picked up and the crew transferred us into that. The strict laws against riding freights caused us to keep every opening closed. There was no ventilation, and as the sun climbed higher, we suffered severely from thirst, for in the excitement of departure we had neglected to fill the canteen. Shortly after noon the train stopped and we heard voices near at hand. The door was shoved open and a man's head appeared.

"You can't ride in there. Come out at once."

We leaped to the ground.

"Clear out as fast as you know how. I don't want to run you in, but if anybody comes along, I'll have to, and that may mean a month in jail."

After our Wood River experience, a word was sufficient to put us in motion, and as we struck off across the tracks, I glanced back and saw that we were in the town of Laramie.

This little city stands in the midst of a barren plain, ringed about by distant mountain range. Trees are scarce, and what few there are evidently belong to doting owners, so that it is difficult for travellers of our persuasion to find shelter from the broiling sun. On the south side of town, a narrow-gauge railroad meanders off across the flat, grey plain, and near it we found a few discouraged trees in an abandoned rhubarb field. We made camp, set up the tent and cooked a much-appreciated meal. As night came on mosquitoes swarmed about and we had recourse to a great smudge in front of the tent. About sundown I saw a tall, gaunt man walking slowly toward an abandoned freight car that stood on a rusty spur of the dinky railroad. As I watched his listless movements my professional interest was aroused, for I took him to be some unfortunate from the east in search of health.

Next morning, we went up town, Dan to hunt for work and I to buy some much-needed provisions. Dan was lucky enough to secure immediate employment on some construction work at the Wyoming State University, located a short distance north of town.

I learned from a neighbour that no use was now being made of the pie-plant that grew on the railroad property, so I helped myself to a fine cooking. Forced to abstain from fruit and vegetables so long, the rhubarb made an especial appeal to our palates. I also discovered a large patch of a wild plant, which, as a child, I had often gathered for my mother. She called it "lamb's quarter," and held the young and tender shoots in high esteem for greens. I now pulled a large panful and we found them a pleasant addition to our menu. As I worked, I again saw the invalid, and that night the poor fellow was sitting on a pile of ties with his head in his hands when Dan came home from work. He looked so desperately lonely and miserable that I asked Dan to go over and talk to him and see if there was anything we could do to help. In a few minutes Dan came back.

"The man is not sick. He's hungry," he said.

"Hungry!" I cried. "If that is all that ails him, he must be starving to look as he does. Go and invite him here for supper."

Dan returned with the ragged, pallid stranger, whose emaciated face was almost covered by a heavy brown beard. He took a seat on an old stump and ate what was offered him in silence. After the meal he filled the water bucket, carried dried dung to replenish the smudge, then set off toward the boxcar without a word.

Next morning, he sat on the ties as before. Again, Dan called him over, and again he ate in silence, but on leaving he doffed his scarecrow hat.

"Thank you very much," he muttered.

That evening he appeared without waiting to be summoned and as he drank his cocoa, I saw Dan choking with suppressed emotion. No sooner had the man gone, after attending to the chores as before, when Dan burst out.

"Did you see what that chap did? He picked up the salt instead of the sugar (we keep both in cocoa cans) and put a heaping spoonful in his cocoa, and blessed if he didn't drink the unspeakable mess without a quiver."

Next day our peculiar visitor came in rather early and stood awkwardly about, fumbling with his hat. Then with a shy, sidelong movement, he laid a fifty cent piece on our pine box table, and bolted away like a scared rabbit. A half hour later he came hesitatingly back, and prompted by Dan's questions, explained that he had spent most of the day chopping wood, for which work he had received the fifty cents.

We had dubbed him Larabo for want of a better name, as a convenient abbreviation of Laramie Hobo, and that night he spent the evening beside our fire. Emboldened by our acceptance of his pitiful offering and encouraged by tactful questions, he told us his story.

He was born in Angel's Camp, California, some twenty-three years ago, and was one of those unfortunate children whose father must remain unknown and whose mother died at his birth, leaving him to the care of her sisters in shame. The lad grew up untrained and uneducated, despised by the children of decent parents; and as he developed into a rugged, raw-boned youth, took up the work of a gold miner. He was not lacking in ambition, and saved his money with some vague idea of escaping the sins of his parents by migrating to parts unknown and establishing himself in some business.

At the age of twenty-one he had several hundred dollars in the savings bank, and set out for the east to better his condition. Farm life attracted him, so he hired out to a dairyman. In course of a year he became very expert and, having saved his wages carefully, in the fall of 1907 determined to start a dairy of his own. He rented a small farm, laid in a good stock of hay and arranged to buy a herd of dairy cattle. His idea was to make as large an initial payment as possible, giving his note for the balance and depending on cream checks to pay off the indebtedness.

The farmer from whom he was purchasing the cows took him to a money lender to arrange for the loan. When Larabo came to sign he discovered that the note ran but six months, and since winter was coming on with the inevitable drop in cream production, he doubted his ability to meet the note when due. The banker assured him that the note could be renewed without trouble, if necessary, and advised him that this short term note was in his favour, since it would enable him to pay off some of the debt in the spring and secure the remainder with a new note if desired, thus effecting a saving in interest. Thus persuaded, Larabo signed.

All winter long he fed and tended the cattle most faithfully and they did well, but as he had anticipated, the receipts from the creamery were insufficient to meet the note. When he asked for the promised renewal, the banker declared he could not do it, the times were too hard, money was scarce, some banks had issued script. If he failed to pay the debt, he would be sold out. The green, ignorant boy did his utmost to raise the necessary cash, but money was tight, as the banker had said, and a month later hay, equipment, cattle and savings were swept away.

Penniless and discouraged, he started to beat his way to the gold mines of the west. He was brutally slugged at Cheyenne, and at Laramie was arrested and given thirty days in jail. On his release he obtained work as a dishwasher in a restaurant and there remained until he had saved twenty dollars. On his way to the station to take a train for the west he met an officer, who took his money and ran him in. The judge remembered his face and gave him a sixty-day sentence.

During this period, he brooded over his experiences and on his release sought out the man who had arrested and robbed him and administered a beating. He was once more arrested and clubbed and sentenced as a habitual offender. When his term expired, the chief of police ordered him to stay away from the business section of town under penalty of immediate arrest, and all officers, train crews and detectives were warned against him. Twice he walked miles along the western track and caught a freight, only to be beaten and thrown off. He was too feeble from abuse and confinement to cross the mountain wastes on foot, and at last resigned himself to slow starvation in the rotting freight car. For five weeks he had averaged but one meal a day, earned by doing odd jobs around the outskirts of town, and his wonderful endurance had almost reached its limit when we took him in.

Daily he has come to the camp for breakfast and supper, and has revealed his gratitude for our attentions by many little helpful acts and a dumb show of affection like a faithful dog.

Yesterday afternoon dense black clouds blew up while I was doing some marketing, and before I could reach camp the most severe hailstorm of my experience struck the town. I took shelter in the doorway of a cottage to escape the fearful pelting, but a woman appeared and sharply bade me be gone. I then stopped under a cow shed, but a man came from a nearby house and threatened me with arrest. Buffeted by the slashing hailstones, I struggled on to camp, only to find our little tent blown flat and covered with limbs torn from the trees by the storm.

The clouds passed as quickly as they had come. The sun shone with dazzling brilliance but little warmth; the sky resumed its wonderful transparent blue; and in the rarefied atmosphere the distant mountain peaks loomed clear and sharp with a deceptive aspect of proximity.

Despite the flood of golden sunshine, the ground was still concealed by a liberal coating of hailstones as night fell.

I had done all I could to make things endurable when Dan came in from work, but he thought it best to sleep in some barn on account of the intense cold. After seeking permission at four or five houses and meeting with curt refusals and even threats, we returned to camp and found Larabo feeding a rousing fire and busily scraping a spot clear of ice. Here we set up the tent and spread our thin blankets on the ground, while a cutting wind swept across the valley and threatened to tear our shelter from its fastenings.

Dan's work was finished, so as soon as we had thawed out and eaten breakfast this morning, he went to town to get a time table and see if something could be done for poor Larabo. We have decided to take a passenger train to the first small station west of here, so I packed our baggage for the journey while Larabo looked on disconsolately.

Suddenly he whirled about and took to his heels and, glancing around, I saw a well-dressed man approaching through the rhubarb field. He came directly to me and began to talk about the recent storm. This led to some conversation concerning the University and I told him that Dan had been working there. His eyes fell on Larabo, who was moving restlessly about some hundred yards away.

"You should not allow that disreputable tramp to hang around your camp," the stranger said. "People complain that you are harbouring hoboes and criminals, and it is giving you a bad reputation."

His words loosed the flood of seething indignation that had been gathering strength with each succeeding day. I described the heartless treatment accorded us by the townspeople; I told the story of Larabo, and concluded with a scathing arraignment and denunciation of the Chief of Police who permitted such outrages. As I paused for breath the stranger broke in.

"I feel sure that the things of which you complain are mostly due to lack of understanding," said he. "Take this Chief of Police now. He is really not such a bad fellow. His intentions are good. Fact is, I'm the chief. Some of our good people have been complaining and calling this a tramp roost, and have asked me to have you arrested or run out of town."

"You don't look like the heartless brute that I had pictured, and I am glad indeed to meet you," I responded, "for now I feel sure that you will take poor Larabo up town and protect him while he is earning enough money to get away."

With that I invited the chief to have a seat on a stump and we talked with mutual benefit and pleasure until Dan returned. The men were introduced and Dan explained that he had secured work with room and board for Larabo with a Socialist family, who would treat him kindly and vouch for his good behaviour. All that was necessary was for the chief to grant permission for him to remain in town and furnish protection from official thugs.

Larabo was summoned and came reluctantly. I bade him and the chief goodbye as Dan went with them to see our protege settled in his new quarters. When Dan gets back, we, too, will bid *adieu* to the rhubarb field and go our way with a satisfied feeling of work well done.

## CHAPTER SIXTEEN

# August 9th, Ogden, Utah

One more step taken, and a nice long one, too. We left the passenger train that took us out of Laramie at the inevitable water tank. The first freight that passed we made no attempt to board, for excellent reasons. A number of hoboes were lounging about, and when this freight pulled in the crowd separated, some running one way and some another.

As we walked down the siding loud sounds of altercation arose and a hobo came tearing up the path with a brakeman swinging a pick handle one short jump behind. The tramp dodged under the train and disappeared. A few yards further on another trainman with a heavy chain in his hands was making vicious cuts at a slender boy, who dodged nimbly around and over the cars, now here, now there. It seemed an inauspicious moment to make the acquaintance of the train crew, so we returned to the welcome shade of the water tank.

Evening came. We cooked our simple meal and prepared for the journey. It was perhaps nine o'clock when the heavy vibration of the roadbed announced the coming of another freight. We crouched in the bushes at the side of the track. The train jarred to a halt and in the light from the fire box we could see the hose being let down to the engine tank.

Silently we drew near and made a hurried inspection of the rolling stock. Only one car was open. This was a *gondola* loaded with some massive, black machinery. We swung our bundles over the edge and scrambled in ourselves. Pieces of machinery were heaped in a confused mass, but in one end two broad, curving bars of metal like huge springs fitted together in such a way as to form an elliptical enclosure. Hastily we opened a bundle and extracted an oilcloth covered blanket. Bundles, hats and canteen were stowed beneath a projection. Then we wedged ourselves into the oblong space that scarcely afforded room for our bodies and tucked the black covering neatly over us. Hardly were we down when a "shack," as the hoboes call the trainmen, approached over the top of the train and with lantern in hand leaped from one piece of machinery to another, narrowly missing our bodies as he passed.

Dan fell asleep almost immediately, but I was not so fortunate. My head and shoulders rested on a heavy piece of metal which vibrated and bounded up and down with the violent jarring of the train. Crowded as we were in the constricted space, I had no opportunity to change my position, so could only submit to the constant pounding with fortitude. At times it seemed that I could no longer endure the concussion at the base of the skull, which set up a violent headache, and also, I was in fear that a shift of the great mass of metal might pin us down and perhaps crush us. But moving was out of the question, for the trainmen were constantly passing with lanterns and pick handles, and woe to the unlucky hobo who crossed their path.

The night wore away, and as the first grey streaks of dawn showed in the sky the train entered a division point. Several men engaged in conversation at the side of the car in which we lay concealed.

"Got any 'boes aboard this trip, Bill?" inquired a heavy voice.

"Well, I've got a suspicion that we may have. When we stopped for water just this side of Laramie, I thought I saw a couple scooting along the side. But we haven't been able to locate anybody. Better see what you can raise."

The next instant a man vaulted onto the end of the car and sat on the edge, with feet dangling a scant twelve inches above my head. Dan was sound asleep, and I was in deadly fear lest he waken suddenly and make some move or sound. The intruder carried a lantern, which shone palely in the growing light.

"Here, Joe, gimme that lantern a second. I want to take a look in that refrigerator car."

The seated detective passed the light to his mate, then leisurely placed his foot within an inch of my right ear, and stepping over our heads, made his way across the car. His pal peered into the open ventilator in the ice chest of the car ahead, and a moment later both men jumped to the ground to greet the new crew.

"All right, boys. No 'boes this morning. She's all ready to take out."

The engineer sounded the welcome signal and we entered a new division. It was broad daylight before I saw a trainman, and then a brakie appeared, coming over the tops from the rear. With a cautious motion I pulled the blanket over Dan, who still slept, and drew a fold across my own face.

The brakeman advanced with a cheerful whistle, and his heel rang sharply on the iron projection at Dan's shoulder, who threw out both arms and raised up with a cry. As Dan sat up, the brakie sat down with exceeding swiftness. The two men glared at one another and it would be difficult to say which had the blanker expression—Dan, who had been so rudely startled out of his sound sleep, or the brakeman, who had witnessed the apparition of a man rising out of apparently solid metal.

The sight of their gaping mouths and bulging eyes proved too much for my risibles and stretching out my cramped arms, I burst into peals of laughter. My unexpected appearance seemed the one thing needed to complete the utter mental disorganisation of the unfortunate trainman. He was too far gone to speak, but gulped and gasped like a dying fish. Dan and I gradually eased our stiffened bodies out of our iron cradle, and by degrees the brakeman's wits returned. I at once got to work and soon had his promise to leave us unmolested.

But we were not to remain so for long. The conductor himself came over the top—a new thing in our experience—and kindly, but firmly, told us to get off at the next stop.

Thus, we found ourselves in the edge of a fair-sized railroad yard, the name of which we made no attempt to learn, but contented ourselves with seeking a quiet spot where we could cook a meal and rest. The back of my head, neck and shoulders was bruised black from the hours of pommelling, and I was glad to snatch a few hours of restless sleep. Dan prepared and packed a box of food, filled the canteen and made ready for the night's adventures.

Just at dark we entered the railroad yard as a freight rolled in from the east, Dan told me to wait while he reconnoitred. Hardly had he gone when A man appeared at my side as though he had risen out of the ground. He held a pocket flash in one hand and a club in the other.

"What are you doing here?" he demanded sternly.

"Waiting for my husband," I said.

Lifting the flash, he examined me from head to foot. Reaching forward, he tapped the box of lunch under my arm with his billy.

"What have you got in that box?" he inquired.

"Grub," I replied.

"So bo! A box of grub and a roll of blankets. You look like a woman hobo."

I admitted the charge and declared my intention of taking the west-bound freight. "And I suppose you are a detective hired to prevent that very thing," I concluded.

"You've struck it," he answered. "That's . . . "

He leaned forward and stiffened like a pointer dog in the presence of a flock of quail. With wonderful dexterity he slipped the flash in his pocket and drew a revolver, then moved forward with the sinuous grace of a panther and as silently as a shadow. I heard the footsteps of several men approaching across the yard.

"Halt!" barked the detective. "Throw up your hands. Keep 'em high now, and face the east. Now, beat it."

I heard the sound of running feet, punctuated by dull thuds as the detective belaboured the heads and shoulders of the fleeing men with his billy,

"Fo Gawd's sake, don't. Boss. Oh, Gawd. You're killin' me." It was the pleading voice of a Negro, who seemed to be bearing the brunt of the clubbing.

In a few minutes the detective came back, panting. My blood was boiling.

"You great big brute, you," I began. "Why don't you jump somebody who has a decent chance, if you must act like a devil?"

"You've got your nerve, young lady, talking to me like that. Don't you know I can run you and your old man in if I want to?"

"Oh, I suppose you could. But what makes you want to be so cruel? You don't look like a brute."

"Well, maybe I am too rough, though that is what I'm hired to be. Besides, some yeggs broke into a building in a little town up the line about a year ago, and when me and my mate tried to run them in, they shot my pal dead and winged me in the shoulder. Since then I club all hoboes on general principles."

Just then I recognised Dan's step as he came up the yard. The detective made a forward movement, but I seized him by the arm.

"That's my husband coming, and you better let him alone. If you start clubbing him, I'll fix you, pistol or no pistol."

"Let go. I'll not hurt him."

He bounded forward, and intercepting Dan, questioned him closely. Then ordering him to remain where he was, he returned and questioned me. Then he summoned Dan.

"Well, people," he said, as Dan came up. "I guess I'll take a chance on you. If the conductor don't get wise and make a kick, I'll not see you when you get aboard that cattle car yonder. So long."

Hurrying over, we climbed in just as the train pulled out. As I peered through the slats in the front of the car, I saw a hobo make a running leap into the *gondola* immediately in front of us. A soft footfall sounded on the roof of our car and the detective leaped down beside the hobo, who scrambled madly up the end of the boxcar ahead. The men reached the roof almost together and for a moment seemed etched against the sky. The officer made a mighty swing with his billy at the tramp's head. There was a crack like a revolver shot, and the hobo pitched from the top of the rapidly moving car and rolled head over heels down the twenty-foot embankment. Sickened, I clung to the bars while the train rushed on.

The floor of the car was covered with filth, so that sitting or reclining was out of the question. To add to our discomfort a storm blew up and the cold wind and rain beat between the slats and chilled us to the bone. As we slowed at a siding a low, mournful sound came to our ears, and we found ourselves beside a great cattle train. The poor animals moaned and bellowed in the sleety blast. Some were down, and I could easily picture their experiences of long hours without food and water, exposure to the broiling heat of the noonday sun in the crowded cars, followed by the night's cold wind and rain.

We were completely exhausted when morning came, and crawled weakly out when a brakeman ordered us off the train. Throwing ourselves in the shade of boxcars that stood on a lonely siding, we were instantly asleep. The sound of voices wakened me and, sitting up, I saw a dozen hoboes scattered about. Some were east and some westbound, but all agreed that this particular division was the deuce to cross.

A freight rolled in and some boarded her, but did not linger long. With shouts and curses, the train crew plied pick handles and chains, and every man was beaten off.

Some two hours later another freight hove in sight and we concealed ourselves in the high brush beside the track. The crew united to drive the crowd of hoboes down the line, and as the chase swept past, we hastened to examine the unguarded cars. In the middle of the train stood three cattle cars loaded with ninety-pound steel rails. These were piled in sloping tiers on each side, leaving a runway down the centre of the car.

"Here's a good place, Dan. We'll lie down in there."

"Good heavens, girl," he cried aghast. "If those heavy rails should shift in swinging around these mountain curves, there wouldn't be enough of us left to hold a funeral over."

"I'm not particular about my funeral, if it should come to that. I'd rather trust the rails than the detectives. Come on, I'm going in."

Opening the end door, I piled in and lay down in the little runway. On either side the sloping heaps of rails rose high above my head. Dan closed the door and lay down also.

The trainmen were too busy with the hoboes to disturb us, or they considered the rail cars too dangerous for the most daring adventurer, for we were left in peace.

The rails grated and chafed as we rocked along. I took a look at Dan, who grew a trifle white about the lips when the rails shifted a little. I was full of content as I realised that we were making good progress, and laid my head on the bundle and slept.

It was night and Dan was shaking me and whispering in my ear when I wakened. Staggering up, I gazed about, bewildered. Taking my hand, Dan led me out of the car, which stood on a siding, and across the tracks away from the lighted street of a town.

"This is an awfully tough town," he said softly. "The rail cars were cut out here, and I went for fresh water. I never saw so much drunkenness or so many toughs in my life. We must get away before morning if we possibly can."

A distant whistle announced the approach of an engine. A long train of tank cars clanked to a standstill. We advanced hopefully, but not a car was open. The yard was dark and we chose a tank car close behind the engine. A narrow ledge projected in front, and on this we perched—feet dangling and backs close pressed against the end of the great cylinder. The engineer and brakeman sauntered up and paused close by. The brakie carried a lantern in one hand and rested the other not two feet from my side. There they stood and talked while we almost ceased breathing. But the deep shadow of the tank concealed us, and they separated, leaving us undiscovered.

Then began the wildest ride of my career. That engineer seemed speeding to the bedside of a dying friend, or perchance, to some sweetheart who awaited his coming. The crest of the mountain range was past and the train shot like a meteor round shouldering hills and through the steep ravines. The tank car leaped and plunged like a thing of life, threatening to leave the rails at each sharp turn of the road. Balancing perilously, we clung like limpets to the narrow shelf, while a wild thrill, born of the rapid motion through the mountain fastnesses with the night wind fanning my face, drove all fear from my mind. I could have shouted with pure delight and felt that I need only will it and my soul would part company with all material things to soar to meet the stars that blazed overhead.

The first flush of dawn brightened the sky as the lights of a good sized town appeared ahead. We gathered ourselves up for the leap. The train slowed and entered a long railroad yard. A group of men, lanterns in hand, stood at one side of the track, and as they caught sight of us, they set up a shout and raced for the train. A dozen cars swept past before they were able to board it, and we saw them moving forward around the awkward tank cars. A single glance identified them.

"We'll have to jump quick before the brutes get any nearer," I cried.

The train was still moving at a lively clip as we leaped off. Catching our stride, we raced for the sagebrush on the right. The officers set up another racket, but apparently considered a chase hopeless.

Circling widely, we came to a squat building on the outskirts of town. From within rose a hum of machinery and in the doorway stood the stalwart figure of a young man. He hailed us merrily.

"Hello, there! Where are you going in such a hurry?"

We explained our plight, and he was good enough to come to our aid.

We entered the power plant and watched the youth fetch out water, soap and towels for our convenience. Catching sight of myself in a mirror, I uttered a cry of surprise. Coated with dust as I was from the long ride so close to the engine, I more nearly resembled a negress than a white woman. While we removed the stains of travel, the boy placed coffee pot and frying pan on a small stove in a corner and soon spread a savoury meal on the pine table. While we ate, he explained that he had the night shift at the plant and slept in the building during the day. He had a reputation for feeding every hobo who came along. Consequently, the officers might come there to look for us. Besides, the day man was not so charitable, so it would be well for us to be out of sight before he arrived.

Leading the way to his little cubby hole of a room, he pulled the bed out from the wall so that it stood almost across the doorway, and spread some quilts on the floor behind it. Tossing our bundles out of sight, he suggested that we lie down and remain as quiet as possible.

We were scarcely hidden when the day man arrived. Our friend complained of a sick headache and said he had moved his bed to get more fresh air. He had darkened the room as much as possible and now threw himself down and feigned sleep. Three men approached the door.

"Say, Frank," one began, "a couple of hoboes came up this way and we want 'em. You better come across now and tell us where they went. We're getting tired of the way you run a tramp roost up here."

'Well, you've got your nerve, I must say. Can't a fellow get any rest from you fee-chasing scavengers? Here I go to bed with a sick headache, and no sooner do I fall asleep than you come chasing hoboes and wake me up again. If you want any information, why in hell don't you talk to Harry? Ask him if he's seen any tramps."

"Sorry if you're sick, old man," answered one of the officers soothingly. "We didn't mean to disturb you."

"Cut the bunk," growled another. "I want to know if you saw these bums?"

"No, I haven't seen any bums," shouted Frank savagely. "Furthermore, I want you pussy-footed bulls to clear out of here. I'm sick, and I want to sleep."

He whirled over with his back to the door. The officers stood about uncertainly for a few minutes and then we heard them tramping about the building. When all was quiet, Frank thrust his head over the edge of the bed.

"How was that for a stiff bluff?" he chuckled. "Your Uncle Ezra is right there with the goods, ain't he, what? See any bums? No, of course not. The only bums I ever see are those bulls that hang around the station. And now that the fly cops have flitted, tell us the sad story of your young lives."

So, I took up the familiar tale and the lad listened with bated breath and sparkling eyes while I led him step by step across the country. On conclusion he told me of himself. He was a student in a technical school, utilising his vacation to gain practical experience in his specialty of electricity and earn money for the coming term.

As I lay prone on the floor, the intense pain of my bruised spine eased a trifle, and lulled by the hum of the generators, I fell asleep. Night had fallen when I awoke and both men were gone. I found them chatting busily, while Dan repacked our bundles for the journey and Frank broiled a large steak over the coals.

"Fill up, sweet friends, fill up," quoth he, carving a huge slab of meat. "Ways are long, the steak is fleeting, and the jail is not your goal. At least, we hope that it doesn't prove to be. So, eat and be merry, for tomorrow you may be in Granger."

Nothing loath, we fell to with great gusto, and while we ate, discussed the best method of getting out of town. We decided to take a passenger to the first stop, as at Laramie.

As we started to the train, our host seized his hat and made ready to accompany us.

"I'll just let the buzzers look after themselves while I give you the benefit of my powerful protection up town. Those bulls won't be so liable to run you in because you're walking the streets without a thousand dollars in your pockets if I am by to testify to your noble characters. Then I know most of the boys who run out of here and I may be able to fix it so the freight crew will pick you up without any trouble."

Thus, we bought our tickets and said goodbye to our young friend while the officers glowered from a distance.

Once more we got out at a barren flag station, but we hadn't long to wait. As the freight stopped, a brakeman leaped down and came directly to us.

"All right, folks, we'll give you a lift and pass you over the next division if we can. Get in that boxcar over there."

In we crawled and rode in comfort the night through. Early next morning, as the train sped through a desolate wilderness, another brakeman climbed into the car.

"How do you do?" he began, "We heard about you from the boys back there, and we'll see you as close to Ogden as we can. But you'll have to leave this car, as it'll be dropped next stop, and the only place for you is in an empty fruit car way up near the head of the train. You'll have to go over the top while she's spinning. Do you think you can make it?" looking at me anxiously.

"Sure," I answered boldly, my tone implying that I had walked the tops of moving freights since the age of three.

Strapping our bundles to our backs, we started. I confess to a peculiar sensation in the pit of my stomach as I trod the narrow plank nailed along the apex of the roofs, and jumped from car to car, while the train rocked heavily along, lurching around the curves, and the wild landscape rotated past on either side. But after the first few minutes the feeling passed and I was able to conclude the journey with all the *sang-froid* of an old hand.

"After today, I'll be expecting to meet women brakies most any

126

time. You'd make a swell member of the Union," volunteered our guide, as we settled ourselves in the fruit car.

The day passed and the night. About four in the morning another brakeman appeared and roused us.

"We will stop at Uintah about sunrise," he said. "You will have to go back to the rear of the train, and be ready to drop off as the train slows down for the station. Get away as quickly as you can, for if you are discovered riding on this train, the whole bunch of us may spend a month in jail."

So, I took another stroll along the swaying roofs and climbed onto the rear platform of the caboose. As the train began slowing for Uintah, we slipped off and bolted away from the track.

After many miles of wilderness, the fertile valley looked very beautiful to our tired eyes. Accustomed from childhood to an abundance of fresh fruit the year round, the restricted diet of recent months has told on me. Now berry vines, fruit orchards and vineyards reminded me of home, and we determined to buy a little fruit, fresh from the garden.

Passing up a tree-bordered roadway, we came upon a long, low farmhouse, squatted at east upon a terraced hillside, the brown of its unpainted wooden frame blending with the russet hues of tree trunks and knotted loops of trailing grape vines. A fluffy maltese kitten with arching back scampered with sidelong leaps to meet us, then frolicked up a tree. Two dogs set up a racket and a winsome, dark-eyed girl came to the door. I asked for ten cents worth of raspberries. With a charming smile she led the way to the roomy kitchen, and taking down a bright tin pail, placed it in my hands with instructions to go right into the patch and help ourselves to what we wanted. We busied ourselves among the tall, green canes, and as the scent of flowers and fruit came to my nostrils, it seemed that I had been transported to the beautiful spot where I was born.

"At last I can realise that I am nearing home," said I, turning to Dan.

On our return to the kitchen with the luscious red berries, the laughing maid met us, and set out dishes, spoons, sugar and a great pitcher of yellow cream. And what a feast we had! Our hostess informed us that the first passenger train that stopped at their little station did not come through till nearly one o'clock, so while Dan roamed about the ranch, the little woman and I sat on the long veranda and got acquainted.

With shy head hanging and many a blush, she said she had been married but four months. Her husband, who was a Mormon, was then at one of his other ranches, where he stopped for weeks at a time. I surmised that she was not his first wife, but warned by her attitude, forbore to question. She told me of her limited opportunities and narrow horizon. With wistful eyes she listened to my descriptions of large cities. She herself had never been further than Ogden, and only twice to that metropolis. The furnishings of the house were crude in the extreme, and she confided to me her longing for curtains such as she had once seen in Ogden, and hoped to have a strip of carpet for the parlour floor some time.

Suddenly she flung herself on her knees at my side and buried her face in my lap, while great sobs shook the slender body. She was all alone she said, all, all alone, and she was afraid. Her mother had eleven children and was always too overworked to listen to her daughter's nonsense, as she called it. I gently raised the child—she was but sixteen years of age—to my lap, and with tender words and petting calmed the storm of sobs. When she could listen, I advised her as best I could, and wrote a set of instructions to guide her in the coming hours of need. Poor little wild rose. I dread to think of what the future holds for her, so sensitive, so frail.

Once more we took a train and soon landed in Ogden. Turning to the left, we crossed the river and came to a large cottonwood grove. Here we pitched camp and Dan took up the never-ending search for work. Last night he came home with a big watermelon and the welcome news that he was to start work on Monday morning. So, for a few days at least I am free to rest and sew.

CHAPTER SEVENTEEN

# August 22nd, On the Sacramento River

Well, little book, my entries are almost finished, for the business of building a new niche in the world with nothing but our bare hands will leave scant time for keeping a diary.

Dan had several days' work in Ogden. Then we took a passenger to the first stop west as usual and there boarded a freight. We had not gone far when a trainman thrust his head into the car in which we were riding, and failing to see me huddled in a corner, accosted Dan.

"Hello, Jack. What are you riding on?"

"A union card," replied Dan, following the accepted formula, and pulling the card from his pocket for inspection.

"And what else?" queried the brakeman.

"A dollar," said Dan.

"Not enough, Jacko. It's two dollars or nothing on this division. Cough up."

So, Dan gave him the two dollars and the train moved out.

On the edge of the Great Salt Lake the freight stopped again and another brakeman leaped into the car. He gaped in amazement at sight of me, then turned to Dan, "You'll have to come through old sport. This kind of baggage is worth a five spot. Come across now, or you'll have to swim the lake."

"Here, Dan," I broke in sharply, as he hesitated. "Don't you give those petty grafters another penny. Let's get out."

The trainman turned on us threateningly, but one good look sufficed, so we were left undisturbed beside the track. We had heard more than once of trainmen who not only took money from hoboes, but also relieved them of Ingersoll, knife, or any little trinket they happened to have about them, but this was our first experience with the breed.

With our bundles for pillows we slept through the night, and awakened at dawn when another freight stopped for a last drink before crossing the lake. We piled into a *gondola* just as the train gathered speed and felt that we would at least cross the lake in safety. We had not gone a mile when a trainman leaped in beside us.

"What are you riding on, friends?" he inquired.

"A union card," said Dan.

"And what else?"

"Not another blamed thing," Dan answered determinedly.

"Well, that don't listen very good to me," the fellow growled. "Where did you come from and where are you going?"

While we gave him a sketch of our experiences and reasons for riding freights, he drew a stub of a pencil from his pocket and began scrawling on the back of a timetable.

"Loan me your knife a minute, old man," he said to Dan.

Dan passed over the knife, a very fine one that I had given him the first Christmas after our marriage, and the brakeman sharpened his pencil.

"Well, so long," said he, turning on his heel, and starting to slip Dan's knife into his pocket.

I seized his arm like a flash and wrested the knife from his hand before he could recover from the unexpected assault.

"No, you don't. Oh, no you don't," I hissed furiously. "That's my knife and I propose to keep it."

"Why, you little hell-cat, you." He burst into a laugh. "I didn't mean to steal your knife. Gee, she's some scrapper," turning to Dan. "Wouldn't mind having a pal like that myself."

With another laugh he made his way to the rear of the train.

A half hour had passed when we were amazed to see him coming over the top with a coffee pot in one hand and a pan in the other.

"Thought maybe you might be hungry," he said with an embarrassed laugh, as he set the pan of boiled meat and doughnuts on the bottom of the car. As he bolted toward the head of the train, we attacked the food with ravenous appetites.

We were so engaged when a man leaped from the boxcar behind, landing in the *gondola* with a clatter. I looked up into the amazed face of the conductor.

"Good Lord!" he ejaculated. "Well, good Lord, so this is what old

Tight-wad was up to. What have you done to him anyhow? Hypnotised him?"

"What are you talking about?" asked Dan.

"Why, that front brakeman of mine. He's the meanest cuss on this division, bar none. He'll hold up a 'bo and pry the gold out of his teeth. I noticed him skirmishing around in the caboose a while back, and he acted so blamed mysterious that I had to come up front and see what in blazes he was up to. Well, I'll be jim swiggled if ever I expected to see old Tight-wad pulling any charitable stunts."

The conductor proceeded to ply us with the usual questions, which we answered to his entire satisfaction.

"There's an empty refrigerator car up ahead," he declared, "that is billed straight through to Sacto. She's locked all right, but the ventilator in one of the ice chests is sealed open, and you can slide in there and lie snug till you land in Sacramento."

Swallowing the last drops of coffee, we followed him over the tops to the fruit car. Sure enough, the little door that covered the hatch at the end of the car stood open, the support bound with the lead seal, which must never be broken except by the proper officials.

Gathering my skirts closely about my ankles, I slid into the opening feet first, and catching the edges with my hands, swung inside the ice chest and let go. Dan followed, and we found ourselves in peculiar surroundings. The floor of the cubby-hole was formed of scantlings laid on their edges, with wide interstices for drainage. There was scarcely room to move and the only light entered the little opening high above our heads. As I gazed upward, I felt caught in a trap. We curled down on the grating and resigned ourselves to fate.

As the sun climbed the sky the heat increased, and it was then that we noticed that our canteen was empty. Nobody came near. We dared not show ourselves. So, the day passed in great discomfort. Night fell and we slept fitfully. Morning came and again the sun blazed down on the desert wastes and the tortures of thirst became intense.

We had been twenty-four hours without food or water when Dan decided to risk a reconnoitre. Taking the canteen, he swung himself up to the hatch and thrust out his head and shoulders. A brakeman came on the run. After considerable parlour he took the canteen and promised to fetch us water at the first stop. But the afternoon wore away and he failed to appear. We were almost insane from thirst and heat when at last he lowered the dripping canteen into our prison.

In Winnemucca the car was shunted back and forth for an hour, but at nightfall we were off on the long climb to the summit. I climbed hand over hand to the hatchway, and after a cautious survey of the surroundings, drew myself out and perched on the roof of the car. The Overland Limited shot past, the roof covered with the crouching forms of hoboes, thick as barnacles on an old pier. The desolate expanse of desert seemed full of mystery, as the long train, dotted here and there with lanterns, crawled like a gigantic snake up the steep grade.

Far ahead two engines coughed and laboured, the black smoke rolling in great billows from their stacks. As I realised that we were nearing the boundary of California a great contentment filled my soul. Thus, I revelled in thoughts of home, while the cool night wind fanned my face and the Big Dipper swung across the northern sky and the speeding wheels clanked a cheerful refrain.

Early next morning the brakeman made us a visit and said we would be in Sparks before noon, where we must make another change.

Just outside the city limits we dropped off, and as guests of the trainmen were soon eating our first restaurant meal for months. About two o'clock we wandered to the outskirts of town, for it was useless to attempt to catch a freight in daylight. We came to an irrigating ditch lined with a tall growth of weeds, and slipping off our footgear, were soon paddling about like a couple of kids in the swift running water. Late in the day we cooked and ate a meal, took a farewell wash in the stream and returned to the railroad yard. Word had gone forth not to molest us, so we boarded the night freight without difficulty. The only available place was a cattle car loaded high with lumber. The end door was unlocked and there was quite a space between the piles of boards and the roof of the car. I settled myself in a corner with back against the siding, and Dan lay at my feet.

It was pitch dark when the train clanked throng the streets of Reno. As we drew slowly out of town, dim forms appeared, and hoboes began piling into the car through both doors. In the darkness I could sense the presence of a large number of men. Two lads curled down at my right, their voices proclaiming their youthfulness. On the left two hoboes lay so close that I could have touched them. They had come from a long ride on a limited passenger and were completely exhausted. A group of men in the far end of the car began smoking, and as each match flared, some face would stand out in bold relief. They talked with perfect comradeship, and though they were totally unaware of the presence of a woman, there was little to complain of in their conversation. In fact, I can truthfully say that I heard more profane language in one year's attendance at Medical College than on this entire trip.

At the first stop out of Reno still more men came aboard. A trainman came to the far door with a lantern, but one look sufficed and he returned no more. At Truckee the car was switched to a siding.

"Beat it, boys, here come the bulls!" shouted a hobo.

Like dry peas out of a pod, the hoboes scattered out of that car and fled in all directions as officers flung open the door at our side and emptied their revolvers into the interior. We remained motionless as the bullets thudded into the wood, and in a few minutes looked out to see the detectives chasing the fleeing hoboes across the yards.

"Now is our chance," whispered Dan. "Make for the round-house yonder."

We dived within the yawning portal and crouched within the engine pit. The place seemed empty and we sat in silence for a time. What to do we did not know. It was impossible to remain where we were for long; discovery meant a trip to jail and a month on the chain-gang for Dan. The town lies in a mountain fastness with snow-sheds protecting the tracks, so that foot travel was out of the question, and our money was almost gone. While we studied the problem, a long freight came through without stopping. We ran out to the main track and the first thing that caught my eye was the familiar old refrigerator car with the open hatch in which we had already ridden so many miles.

"Quick, quick!" I cried. "We must catch that train."

The engine had cleared the yard and was gathering headway with each turn of the wheels. Racing madly beside the track, I made a desperate lunge and caught a hand rod. My arms seemed torn from their sockets as my body was snapped into a horizontal position by the speeding train. A moment I clung, unable to move, then with a fierce scramble, I found my footing and clambered to the top of the car. Dan had landed on the car behind and together we started for the head of the train.

A brakeman appeared on the top of a boxcar. At sight of a woman coolly parading the roof of the freight, his jaw dropped and he started so violently as to make me fear for his safety. We stopped on a flat car and gave him a brief explanation, then hurried forward and swung ourselves into the familiar ice chest, for we were nearing the snow-sheds.

The trainman soon joined us. He told a long story about some division official who was death on hoboes, and who made a practice of travelling up and down the line and pouncing on the train crews at unexpected places in hope of catching them in some infraction of the rules, which would enable him to indulge in his love of discipline. This martinet took a special delight in harrying the men, and would suspend an *employé* for sixty days on the smallest pretext, or deprive a man of his credits for the slightest infraction of some unimportant rule.

"He's a Company pet, who was born with the big head and then bitten by the efficiency bug," our companion concluded, "and if he should catch a woman on this freight it would be as much as all our jobs are worth."

At that moment a man thrust his head into the manhole and called the brakeman out. He ascended quickly and his place was taken by the other, who proved to be the conductor. Dan started to speak, but was interrupted.

"Let the woman talk. I'll get the truth from her."

So, I began the old, old story, and after a bit secured permission to ride as close to Sacramento as we dared. We were well outside the snow-sheds when the conductor left us, and I settled down with the thought that the worst was over.

As the train pulled out of a station the light was cut off abruptly and a young man in a business suit bounced into the ice chest. As he landed, I looked up and caught sight of the horrified face of the brakeman leaning over the manhole.

"Who put you in here? How much did you pay that brakeman to let you ride?" he demanded fiercely.

"Why, we haven't paid anybody—we haven't seen any brakeman. We just got in when the train slowed up back there a ways; and we took good care not to see any brakeman or let any brakeman see us," I answered innocently.

"But what are you doing here, and where are you going?"

"Oh, we came up from Sacramento for a little camping trip. My husband thought he could get a little work in the mountains, but he couldn't find any, and we spent most of our money, and then started to walk home. This old freight came crawling along, and there wasn't anybody on the far side of the track, so just for a lark we slipped in here."

"So, you're sure your husband didn't pay the brakeman for the chance, are you?"

"You bet I am. Do you suppose anybody would pay good money for riding in this old hole? Besides, we haven't any money. I couldn't see anything wrong about riding, exactly. But, of course, we didn't want the trainmen to see us. I was afraid they might not like it, and I'm dead sure nobody but you knows we're here."

The brakeman's face appeared for an instant in the manhole above, then disappeared from view. "You're not going to put us off, way out here, are you?" I asked pleadingly. "It's awful hard to walk clear down to Sacramento this hot weather, and carry these heavy bundles. It didn't cost the railroad company anything for us to ride here. We ain't doing any harm."

The young man's face softened a trifle and he launched into a long dissertation on the evils of jumping trains, the hobo menace, and kindred topics, to all of which I listened with wide eyes and bated breath. The train drew into a station and out again, while he was thus absorbed, and he made no move to put us off. I was drawing him on with deft questions and flattering attention when the brakeman's head appeared once more.

"What in blazes is all this?" he bawled. "Hey, you bums, come out of there."

Our kind instructor cast a startled look aloft. "Why, hello, Condon," he called ingratiatingly. "You are on the job, I see. But these people don't happen to be bums. Everything is all right. I'll assume the responsibility, so just trot along and leave us alone."

He resumed his pompous attitude and took up the delightful task of enlightening me on the importance of his position, which he declared was extremely difficult to fill. I gathered that the destinies of the entire railroad system rested on his narrow shoulders; that he was the original efficiency expert; and that all other *employés* of the Company, from train boy to superintendent, were a lot of mutts, if not worse, and were it not for his constant supervision and stern discipline, the division would just naturally go to the bow-wows. The miles slipped by as I drank in this information with greedy ears. His chest expanded like a pouter pigeon and his hat band seemed to stretch visibly.

The three of us were standing in one end of the restricted space when once more the daylight was cut off and the conductor slid down beside us. Completely ignoring our existence, he turned a cold and hostile eye upon our companion.

"Sir," he began stiffly, "I have been informed by a member of my

135

crew that a high official of this division has taken it upon himself not alone to disregard the strict rules of this company regarding the carrying of passengers on freight trains, but has arrogated to himself the control and management of those directly responsible to me. Such a situation is unprecedented, sir, and I hereby make formal protest against its continuance."

While he was speaking, I saw the shadow of a man pass the opening overhead.

"But, my dear man," stammered the "high official," wholly taken aback. "How can you make such statements? I had absolutely no intention—no such intentions at all. How can you make such a charge?"

"The facts, sir, speak for themselves. My brakeman discovers his superior closeted in the ice chest of a refrigerator car with a young woman and an unknown man. When he endeavours to exercise that authority with which he is vested by the rules of this company and requests the said young woman and unknown man to leave the train at once, you, my dear sir, impose the force of your superior station, and taking all responsibility upon yourself order him to 'trot along.' I claim that such conduct destroys efficiency and is fatal to discipline."

Our young entertainer seemed at a loss for a reply; then he plunged into a long explanation of our presence and his intentions regarding us. The conductor listened with an air of undiminished coldness.

"Very well, sir," he said shortly, at the close of the harangue. "Your conduct is, of course, highly irregular, but I shall make no report of it—at least not at present," fixing the unfortunate "high official" with a piercing glance. "As to your er—guests, I shall leave the matter of their disposition entirely in your hands, since you have assumed the responsibility."

The conductor swung himself out of the ice box while the young man turned his harassed gaze upon us.

"You better get off at Auburn," he said weakly. "Climb out as soon as the train stops, so nobody will see you."

As he clambered slowly out, the general impression was that of a man about three sizes smaller than the one who had entered.

We left the car the instant the train stopped at Auburn, but as we hastened away, we were hailed with loud shouts by the train crew, who followed us on the run, headed by the brakeman. We stopped behind a row of boxcars as they joined us. With whoops and howls they slapped one another on the back, danced about, doubled up and fairly rolled on the ground in convulsions of laughter.

"Say, didn't our old man hand that fellow some chunks of language? Say now; didn't he?" gasped the brakeman when he could speak.

"He passed it out like a regular dictionary. Just the same kind of dope that Little Tom-tit has been feeding us on so long," sputtered the fireman, who it seems had left the engine on the way down to join the gleeful circle about the manhole while the circus was going on within.

"Well, I guess I punctured his tyre, all right," vouchsafed the conductor. "Guess he'll go a little easy on efficiency and discipline with this crew for a while."

"I wouldn't have missed that performance for five hundred dollars," broke in the rear brakeman. "It was the richest thing I ever heard."

"You should have heard Miss Innocence here stringing him along when he first came aboard. Her eyes kept a-glowing bigger and bigger, and his chest kept a-swelling and a-swelling, till I thought I'd bust. Oh, he was a wonderful man, all right, all right."

"Well, boys," remarked the conductor, whipping off his cap. "You all admit you enjoyed a good show, that would have had a very different ending if it hadn't been for the quick wit of this gritty lady. Chip in now, and pay for your reserved seats."

Money rattled into the cap and despite our protestations the conductor forced it into Dan's hands. With quip and jest the men bade us goodbye, and we passed over to the main street in search of a restaurant. Our hunger appeased, we marched boldly to the station and took a passenger train to Sacramento, where we made connection with the river boat for San Francisco.

So now I sit on the deck of the steamer and watch the green and fertile country glide past. From time to time a signal flutters on the bank, the boat swings over and the crew rapidly loads great boxes of plums, luscious peaches, early pears, and crates of seedless grapes. Here comes a man with a truckload of magnificent Burbank plums. I once read of the little plum with the enormous pit, from which the California wizard evolved this beautiful fruit. He did not attempt to change the nature of the plum to that of some transcendental fruit. He simply modified the environment so that the inherent qualities of the plum might develop. Would that the environment of the little children of the slums and sweat shops, to whom the meanest cull that lies in yonder orchard would be a gracious treat, might be so modified as to give their essentially beautiful, natural qualities an opportunity for healthy, normal growth.

I give a sigh of contentment and happiness as I realise that the hazardous journey is ended. And now I realise another fact. For weeks I have been free from colds or cough; my digestion is superior to that of an ostrich; a ten-mile jaunt with twenty pounds of baggage on my back would be mere child's play. A more healthy human specimen than myself it would be hard to find, so I feel free to dismiss the spectre of tuberculosis along with the other horrors of the slums.

But physical benefit is not the greatest gain. A change has taken place in my psychology. My belief in the inherent kindliness and unselfishness of the human heart has been strengthened. In cases of cruelty I recognise an outside influence or pressure that warps natural instincts. Toward the trainmen especially I am deeply grateful. When one realises the risks, they ran to aid a couple of outcasts, and the kindness and consideration so often manifested, a wonderful appreciation of their sterling manhood is born. Never again will I think it necessary to change human nature before we can improve social conditions. I am conscious of a deeper human sympathy; a wider vision; a greater understanding of the problems of the underdog and a closer sense of fellowship with him. I feel that I am learning the divine lesson of human unity, which is rooted in the Fatherhood of God and manifests itself as the Brotherhood of Man.

# From North Carolina to Southern California Without a Ticket and How I Did It Giving My Exciting Experiences as a "Hobo"

"Good-bye, brother. If I never return again, be good to mother."

# Contents

# Preface

After a good deal of persuasion upon the part of my relatives and immediate circle of friends, I have decided to write an account of a few of the many adventures and dangers that befell me while making my way, practically without a penny, from Tarboro, North Carolina, to Tucson, Arizona; and thence to the stricken city of San Francisco, Cal., and other points of interest throughout the West, including New Orleans, Dallas, Texas, Fort Worth, El Paso, Dalhart, Texas, Alamagorda, New Mexico, Juarez, Old Mexico, Bisbee, Arizona, Los Angeles, California, San Pedro, California, Searchlight, Nevada, Denver, Colorado, and more than a hundred other points of interest, coming back home on a telegraphed ticket, *via* Chicago, Cincinnati, and Richmond, Virginia.

The book bears no relation to fiction, as the reader will discover before reading many of its pages. The writer, believing it will be more interesting, will unreservedly show up all his faults and mistakes along the trip, as well as his good qualities. There is nothing in the book pertaining to the supernatural, nor is it of a highly sensational character, but the writer believes it will prove more than interesting to the intelligent mind. It is a true story from real life that every boy in America can read and profit thereby. The book is a record of facts and incidents, which were written down in shorthand, and transcribed at different stages of the journey by the author. The story is backed by the indisputable evidence of testimonials and correct addresses of the most prominent people with whom the writer came in contact. This book demonstrates the value of physical culture and education to the American youth as the author believes no other work upon the market has yet done. The writer graduated at the Massey Business College, Richmond, Va., in bookkeeping, etc.

Feeling the need of rest and recreation after several years of hard study at school, and being a great sufferer from asthma, the author, hearing of the dry and beneficial climate of Arizona and New Mexico to those who have weak lungs, decided almost immediately after leaving school at Richmond, Va., to go to Tucson, Ariz., and personally verify these reports, and probably settle there permanently himself.

The author, John Peele, of Tarboro, N. C, is just nineteen years of age, and though he had knocked about the world considerably prior to the opening of this story, he had heretofore always held a ticket to his destination. And now, dear readers, follow him patiently and he will attempt to show you how he turned the trick of getting West without a ticket. Trusting the book may be of value to mothers in restraining their wayward sons to stay at home, however humble it may be, I beg to subscribe myself, sincerely, the author,

John Peele.

## $50.00 Reward. $50.00

I am a poor man, but if the Negro, who twice saved my life by catching me while standing up on the end of a loaded flat-car fast asleep, and preventing my falling between the wheels of a rapidly moving freight train about ten or fifteen miles from the town of Woodbine, Fla., on a certain night in May in the year 1906, and who afterwards accompanied me forty-nine miles on a hand-car to Jacksonville, can prove his identity, by telling me what happened when we parted on the railroad in the suburbs of that city, and will communicate his intelligence to John Peele, Tarboro, N. C, he will receive the sum of fifty dollars ($50.00).

John Peele.

### TESTIMONIALS

San Pedro, Cal

John Peele was employed by us as a clerk in the Angelus Hotel.
Jennings & White

Searchlight, Nev.

John Peele was in my employ here for some time, first as porter, then as bartender in the Searchlight Hotel.

I hereby give Mr. Peele the privilege of printing this testimonial, both in his book and in the newspaper columns, advertising the book.

Fred. Ullman.

John:—Whenever you come out West again, you can get another job. You are all right.                                    U.

144

Chipley, Fla.

This is to certify that John Peele, being pulled down in this town from under the boiler of a morning passenger train bound for Pensacola, Fla., was employed by me at my brick yard.

J. D. Hall.

JOHN R. PEELE.

# CHAPTER 1
# Off for California

The details of my former life will not be given here, but as I stood waiting on the depot platform at Tarboro, N. C, with my brother Joe, who had come to bid me goodbye, one fine day in early May, in the year 1906, I could, at least, say that no other chap of my acquaintance could name any more varied occupations in which he had been engaged than I could.

I had been grocery clerk for my people at Tarboro; water boy at the age of 14 at the Buffalo Lithia Springs in Virginia, where I made scores of friends from all parts of the country; dry-goods salesman for Chas. Broadway Rouss, New York City; waiter in a Coney Island restaurant; bell-boy in the Fifth Avenue Hotel, New York City; waiter in Buffalo, N.Y., where I had gone to be treated by the famous Dr. R. V. Pierce for asthma; traveling agent through the South for Jas. M. Davis, New York, with stereoscopic views, at which I cleared over $400.00 in one summer's canvass, nearly ruining my vocal organs; Bible agent through the country for J. S. Peele & Co.; stenographer, bookkeeper, and scores of other things I engaged in, too numerous to mention.

The train, which was to mark the beginning of more adventures, hardships and trials than I, at that time, could possibly imagine, pulled into the station at Tarboro, N. C, and bidding my brother goodbye, I got aboard.

I had four dollars in money, several letters of recommendation, and a ticket. Among the letters was a note of commendation, kindly given me by Mr. John F. Shackelford, of the Bank of Tarboro, and another one, equally as highly appreciated, from Mr. Frank Powell, the editor of the *Tarboro Southerner*. The ticket was labelled Wilmington, N. C, and had been purchased merely as a blind to my parents, who were unaware of the fact that I had come home from school "flat-broke," and as a consequence, of course, unable to purchase my fare to the West.

Parting with my mother affected me no little, for it was my intention not to return home for several years.

Tarboro was soon left behind, however, and now other and graver thoughts began to take possession of me. What was I to do in Wilmington with only four dollars? And how was I to get out of the town anyway, unless I purchased another ticket?

During all of my travels, I had never yet beaten the railroad company out of a penny, and just how I was going to board a train without being caught and locked up was the question.

Little did I think at that time how expert and bold I was to become at this kind of thing before reaching far off Tucson, Arizona.

The train pulled under the shed at Wilmington just after dark. It was with great reluctance I got out of my seat; in fact, all the other passengers had alighted when I got my bundles together.

I would have sworn that there was a big, blue-coated officer waiting to put handcuffs on me the moment I stepped from the car platform, but no such thing happened. Instead, the whole train was deserted and the porter informed me that I had better hurry, if I wanted to get through the exit before it closed.

Regaining courage, I hurried along in the direction the other passengers had taken, and a few moments later emerged on Front Street, Wilmington's busiest thoroughfare.

I was by no means a stranger to Wilmington, and, therefore, had little trouble in finding a good place at which to put up, without going to an expensive hotel.

Leaving my few belongings behind, I started out afterwards to retrace my steps back to the depot and railroad yards for the purpose of obtaining any information I could regarding the schedule of the trains.

About midway the bridge, which connects the depot with Front Street, I noticed two Negro men engaged in watching the trains shift in and out of the yards. I at once decided that here was an opportunity to start the ball rolling, and accordingly approached them and told them where I wanted to go. In return they informed me that they were not trainmen, as I had supposed, but were employed on the steamboat *Perdy*.

The name of their captain was Archie Marine, they said, and added that he was a good, free-hearted sort of a man, and might be able to help me get down the coast on a boat. One of them offered to conduct me to the *Perdy's* wharf, and a short time later we were on board.

The engineer of the boat was the only man on board when we

arrived, and he informed me that the captain hadn't shown up since late in the afternoon.

A significant twinkle of the eye accompanied this remark, and not being altogether blind, I concluded that the *Perdy's* captain was in some respects the same as all other sea-faring men.

"Do you know where he generally holds forth when on shore?" I asked.

"No, but probably some of the crew on shore can tell you, if you can find them," he replied.

Disappointed, I made my way up town again.

Entering a drug store, and calling for a directory, I soon found Marine's residence address, and a half hour later I had reached his home.

Several children met me at the door, and in response to my query, summoned their mother, a very pleasant-faced woman, as I recall her, who at once seemed to know that I was in trouble.

She gave me explicit directions how to find her husband.

"Please tell him to come home at once, if you find him," she said. It was after 11 o'clock when I bade the lady goodnight.

After losing all this time, I was determined to find Marine now, if I had to traverse every street in Wilmington.

Having canvassed views in the town, I had no trouble in finding the section the lady had directed me to.

The place I entered was a kind of half grocery store and half saloon—the saloon, of course, being in the rear.

On entering, my attention was directed to a party of four men, evidently seamen, judging from their language, who were in the front part of the store engaged in a conversation that could easily have been heard a block away.

At last, I felt sure I had cornered my man.

It has always been my belief that I was especially blessed with the knack of making friends with a stranger, and this talent, which is the only one I think I ever possessed, had certainly had ample opportunity in my varied life to develop into an art.

"Hello, mates!" I sang out, approaching the quartet with a smile— what wonders a smile will work when used right—"I'm looking for Archie Marine, fellows. Do you know where he is tonight?"

Immediately one of the men stepped forward.

"My name is Marine," he said, "What's up?"

He had a pleasant way of speaking, and it was soon apparent that he embodied all the good qualities which the two Negros on Front

149

Street bridge had invested him with.

"It's something important. Marine; come with me and I'll tell you."

Without a word the man turned his back upon the jolly companions with whom he had been lately carousing, and together we left the place.

We went two blocks up the street, and here, under the shelter of a drug store, I told him I wanted to get as far down the coast as Jacksonville, Fla.

He said he thought he could help me do so.

"The boats no longer run from here to Georgetown, S. C.," he said, "but there's a boat from Wilmington to Southport, N. C, daily for seventy-five cents, and you can easily walk across the sands from Southport to Georgetown in a day and a half. You'll not be lonesome," he added, "for there are houses every few miles, and I'll write you a note to a friend of mine in Georgetown, who'll take you to Charleston, S. C, and another note to the engineer who runs between Charleston and Jacksonville."

This was great! I was to get nearly a thousand miles on my journey without incurring the risk of beating a train. The mere contemplation of beating a train seemed to stir up all the animosity in my nature towards all train officials.

What! I, John R. Peele, the boy who had always been so careful at home about washing his face and keeping his clothes brushed, attempt to hide on a train, and beat his fare?

No, I was to preserve my dignity and travel like a gentleman on a large steamboat to Jacksonville, and then other means would surely present themselves, as probably another boat ran from Jacksonville to Galveston, Texas.

Splendid idea! Why the trip was going to prove easy—a regular "cinch," and I could afford to laugh at the train people now, and that for a good long time, too, but alas! my joy was short-lived, for I was soon to learn the truth of the old adage: "The best laid plans ofttimes go astray."

We entered the drug store, and Marine, after much effort, composed the notes, which he wrote down in my memorandum book.

The following is a reproduction of one of them, *verbatim*, taken from the same little book, which I yet own:

Engineer,

Mr. J. Dunn wil you bee kind enough to help my yung friend

150

over to J. and let me hear from you oblige.

Archie Marine.

I was also given a letter of introduction to his brother, William Marine, who is a very popular Jacksonville citizen, and who is superintendent of the Clyde Line Docks in that city.

The author desires to publicly thank Mr. Marine through this book for that service, and feels confident, had he ever reached Georgetown, the notes would undoubtedly have been of much assistance.

At 2 p. m. the following day I boarded the boat for Southport, and knowing how I was to travel on leaving home, I had only brought along one suit of clothes, which I had on.

It was a nice fitting khaki suit, with prominent brass buttons, and seemed to be the very thing for the wear and tear of a long journey. It was a home-guard suit, though I was no home-guard, and had never been one, but purchased the suit just before leaving home.

Now, as the reader may not be aware. Southport is a favourite camping resort of North Carolina's home guards, and as luck would have it, there was a company encamped there at this particular time.

Up to this time I had paid no heed to what I was wearing, but it was soon obvious that I was attracting unusual attention.

There were three or four men in blue uniforms on the boat, who seemed to give me their whole attention, for everywhere I went on the boat they would follow me and begin their whisperings, and it was fast becoming a nuisance, when, finally, one of them stepped up to me and asked:

"Are you a home guard?"

"I am not," I replied civilly, realising my clothes warranted the question.

"The reason I asked," he said, "there has been a desertion in one of the companies lately, and the description of the deserter fits you. If you were to land there now and suddenly make off across the sands towards Georgetown—I had informed him of my intention—you would quite likely be overtaken and held three or four days for identification," he said.

Having never been a home guard, I did not know whether the man was playing a practical joke on me or was telling the truth, but I did not want to be detained there for several days, and I was inclined to believe what he said was the truth. However, I did not betray this fact.

Instead, I laughed and remarked that I was not afraid; but all three of the men stoutly maintained that they had tried to do me a favour, and seeing that I appeared to take it as a joke, one of the men finally got angry and wished me all sorts of bad things, and said he hoped I would be arrested as soon as the boat landed.

The cabin was filled with passengers, and soon it was the topic of conversation, and some thought I would be held, while others took the opposite side.

Sitting almost in front of me was a well-dressed man, whom, I noticed, had taken no part in the conversation, and he, catching my eye for a moment, winked at me and arose and left the cabin.

Soon after I followed him to a deserted part of the boat.

"I am a Philadelphia drummer," he said, "and don't know which side to stand on, but if you will go to the engine room, I will follow soon with a sample grip of cheap clothing, and you may pick out a cheap suit free of charge, if you will cut the buttons off your khaki coat and give them to me, and I readily agreed and the change was soon effected.

Whether I was the victim of a practical joke or not, I have never learned, but if so, I was ahead of the game in the clothing by a long sight, for I had selected a good, warm suit.

And now the strangest part of all, I had decided not to land in Southport.

It was seventy-two miles to Georgetown, and bad walking in the sand, I was told.

The more I thought of it, the sicker I became, and now what was I to do? Turn tramp?

Never!

Beating the trains would be infinitely preferable, and I would go back to Wilmington and do so.

The boat landed and discharged the passengers, when, to everyone's surprise, I remained on board, and just what they thought I am unable to say.

Quite likely the Philadelphia drummer thought the joke was on him, for I had told him I was so eager to get to Georgetown.

Passengers returning to the city now filed on, and in a short time the boat cast off and headed for Wilmington.

On the return trip I noticed I was charged twenty-five cents more than when coming down, and I supposed the home guards were allowed this discount. We landed in Wilmington just after dark.

My lodging, breakfast and dinner had deprived me of seventy-five cents, and the trip to Southport had cost $1.25, which left me the sum of $2.00, but I had no occasion to regret my trip down the river, for as a result I was now wearing an early spring suit.

All of my fond hopes of reaching Jacksonville easily were now cast to the ground.

Gathering up my bundles and the khaki suit, I made my way on shore.

## CHAPTER 2

# The First Blush of Shame

It would be hard to describe my feelings as I started up town. I was hungry and ate a good supper, though I felt like crying as the cashier took my twenty-five cents, for I had never been penniless in a strange town in my life, and now my stock of nerve was weighed exactly by just what money I had left; but the worst thing that hindered my progress, I was heartily ashamed of what I was going to attempt to do.

Arriving at Market Square, I experienced no difficulty shortly afterwards in striking an acquaintance with a rather shabbily dressed young man, who seemed to know all about the trains.

Finding that I was eager to leave at once, he remarked:

"You have just about fifteen minutes to leave Wilmington on a freight train tonight. The last freight train pulls out at 8:15 tonight, and it is now 8 o'clock."

Luckily what little baggage I owned was with me, and in another moment, I was rapidly walking to the place named. I quickly saw this wouldn't do, though, for it was nearly a mile to the depot, and turning into a residence street, I broke into a run.

Panting for breath I reached the railroad yards.

There was no sign of a train pulling out, nor was there one making up, and so far as I could see there was not the slightest evidence of life about the yards, and it began to look like another practical joke had been played on me.

Just across the tracks at this point are a good many small tenement houses, for the most part occupied by Negro people, who are employed by the railroad company.

Calling out one of the occupants of these houses, I asked him if the 8:15 freight had gone.

"The schedule's been changed, and there ain't no 8:15 freight," said the Negro. "The last night freight for Florence left about an hour ago."

To reach Jacksonville, I would have to go through Florence, S. C, and Savannah, Ga.

"If you'll go to Hilton Bridge tomorrow evening," said the Negro, "you might be able to catch a passenger train that passes about 3 p. m. on Sundays."

Hilton Bridge spans the Cape Fear River near this point, and all trains are required by the law to slow up before crossing.

For this information the man received a buttonless khaki suit.

The next morning was Sunday, and after paying my lodging I had but $1.35.

Hardship was certainly beginning to stare me in the face at an early stage of the trip.

Oh! how I wished now I had stayed at home, where my every wish had been gratified by tender, loving hands, but it was too late! My pride was up in arms, and I would see the game through to the bitter end.

On this day I ate neither breakfast nor dinner, and early in the afternoon I repaired to the bridge to wait.

The man who runs a small "pop shop" on the Wilmington side of the bridge amused me with stories of the many young men he had seen beat their way from this point, and I got him to tell me just how the others had done, and was becoming quite brave, till he began describing how he had seen one man miss his footing, and showed me the spot where the cars had run over both legs.

The train was coming! And the supreme test of the trip was at hand.

I took up a position at the curve, which is about two hundred yards from the bridge.

The engineer bestowed a quick glance at me as he passed, then his gaze wandered ahead.

Grabbing up the two bundles, which were hidden behind a telegraph pole, I made a quick dash forward and succeeded in boarding the first coach from the engine, commonly known as the "blind baggage."

I didn't stop on the car platform, as is usually done, but crawled to the top of the tender, which was well loaded with coal.

As near as possible I made things comfortable by placing the largest lumps of coal out of reach, thus enabling me to partly conceal myself by lying down.

Exultation was now mingled with excitement.

I had just begun to congratulate myself when, to my dismay, I noted that the train was slackening speed. A moment later it stopped.

Footsteps now sounded, hurriedly approaching the engine.

I lay quite still, almost afraid to breathe, as the conductor and porter came up.

"Come down from there! Come down!" cried the conductor.

I raised up intending to ask him to let me go.

"Come down, quick!" he cried. "Tramps and hobos are not allowed on this train."

This was quite enough for John Reginald Peele, and without any more ado he crawled down.

My first impulse was to knock out my insulter with a lump of hard coal, but better judgment prevailed, and I soon reached the ground by his side.

After all, I reasoned, he was only performing his duty in putting me down, and he was fully justified in calling me a tramp and a hobo, for I was not only acting both these parts very well, but was now looking the part.

Before boarding the train, I had been spotlessly clean. Now my hands were black, my white collar soiled, and my new clothes nearly ruined.

This was the picture I presented to a score or more of curious passengers, who had poked their heads out of the car windows to ascertain the cause of the delay.

In deep shame I hung my head, and it seemed that every one of those passengers had recognized me. This was mere fancy, of course, for I was then over a hundred miles from home. At any rate, there was one thing certain. I had been left and the train was now belching forth black smoke far up the road.

Those who had witnessed my defeat from the "pop shop" on the other side were now eagerly awaiting me as I recrossed the bridge, and they were ready with sympathy as I told them how I had been put down.

"That train goes to Charlotte, anyway," said the storekeeper. "I think the next one, which is due in about twenty minutes, is the Florence train."

A good many men will live half their life in a place and yet never know the exact time a certain train is due, nor where it is bound, and I would have to rely on my own luck, for it was quickly apparent that he was one of the class who are never profoundly sure of anything.

"Come down quick!" he cried. "Tramps and hobos are not
allowed on this train."

Had I gone to Charlotte I would have been taken completely out of my way, at the very outset, causing all kinds of trouble, and this served a good deal to show me the exact size of the job I had undertaken.

Most of my fear had now vanished. No real harm had resulted in my first attempt at beating a train, and the tinge of excitement had proven quite fascinating.

Of course, the local authorities of the hundreds of towns I must pass through had to be considered, and indeed this was now my greatest fear, for, in a good many towns, as the reader is perhaps aware, a man caught beating a train suffers the penalty of from one to twelve months hard labour on the county roads.

A second train was coming; and now was the time for me to make good!

This time I boarded the train without exciting suspicion. A repetition of my former antics quickly followed, and I was soon lying flat upon the coal, gripping the top of the tender now, though, for my uncomfortable bed of coal had suddenly assumed the motion of a cradle, as the result of the train's sudden increase of speed.

Wilmington rapidly receded from view, and with a feeling of joy, savoured with suppressed excitement, I closed my eyes for a moment.

Where I was going and what I would do when I got there were thoughts that chased through my brain.

I tried to picture far off Arizona, with its mountains and barren deserts, and wondered if it would cure or benefit my asthma—I would go direct to Solomonsville, Arizona, where our State Treasurer, Lacy, had been cured.

Suddenly I sat up.

"What a fool I am," I muttered. "Sitting here in plain view, to be arrested at the first station we stop."

In a few moments I had dug out a large hole in the coal and crawled into it, placing the largest lumps around the edge of the opening to help shield me from view.

Everything went well until about dark, when we reached the small town of Chadbourn, N. C, fifty-seven miles from Wilmington.

Here the man at the pump house, which is located close to the depot, had seen an uncovered foot, and called the conductor's attention to it.

The conductor, who was a good sort of a man, had discovered my presence on the train long before reaching Chadbourn, and so had others of the train's crew. The man in the baggage car was even taking care of my bundles, which he had allowed me to deposit in a corner of the car.

Unaware of the fact that I had been discovered, I lay perfectly still, afraid to move hand or foot, and it seemed to me the train would never start.

Several people approached the engine, including a policeman of the town and the conductor.

"Come down off that coal pile," cried the conductor.

There was no mistaking the command, and I crawled down.

If I was a sight before, I was a whole show now, for I was smutty from head to foot.

"I didn't know he was up there," said the conductor.

Inwardly I thanked the conductor, whom I knew had been trying to help me along.

"I'll take charge of this young man," said the policeman.

"Please get my things," I said. "I hid them in the baggage car."

"I'll take charge of this young man," said the policeman.

CHAPTER 3

# Snatched From Death

Two-score people had seen me pulled down from the tender, and were now watching the result of my sudden discomfiture with interest, and with a look of deep humiliation and embarrassment—for the most part assumed—for my vanity had materially suffered in that fifty-seven mile ride, I now stood in the presence of the policeman.

Apparently, I could not even look up at the cruel, cold-staring crowd of country folks that thickly gathered around me.

Evidently the policeman was touched, and unaware of the fact that I was playing on his sympathy, he questioned me as to where I lived, where I was going, etc., all of which I answered in a straightforward manner, adding that I was going West to cure the asthma, and that I had letters of recommendation.

I had several other letters of this kind in my pocket, but remembering that home reference is said to be the best, I selected only two from the bunch—those of Mr. John Shackelford and Mr. Frank Powell, and here I must beg their pardon, most humbly, for using their kind notes of praise like this, and am sure they'll forgive me, for I was in a tight box.

After reading the two papers over carefully, he slowly remarked, with a puzzled look on his face:

"Look here! it's against my rule, but I'm going to let you go this time. Just scoot down that track, now, and remember," he added, as I started through the increasing throng, "if you return, I shall run you in."

There was nothing to do but walk, and I started down the tracks, walking—I knew not where.

My scheme had worked and I was free, but far from being in a happy frame of mind.

A small hand-mirror showed me a face that frightened me with its blackness, and my hands were in even a worse condition.

"Oh, if my people could only see me now!" I mused.

A sudden recollection quickened my pace—in the terms of the law I was a vagrant, and what, if the Chadbourn official should change his mind about letting me go. This was a phase of the case I had not considered before, being a vagrant, and darkness had settled down, and I had been silently walking along the pathway of the track for some time, when my melancholy musings were suddenly put to flight. A quarter of a mile ahead a light was shining. "Some farmhouse built near the railroad," I speculated; "wonder if they'll give me shelter." Drawing nearer, I discovered my mistake. The light was issuing from the windows of a small store.

A large railroad board in front of the place told me I had reached the town of Grice—containing three or four small dwellings, one store and a town pump; the place is hardly on the map, though it was a boon to me just now.

On entering the store, I was surprised to find a good number of people trading, notwithstanding the fact it was Sunday.

Several Negros were in the place, and calling one of them outside, we headed for the pump.

"Been hoboing?" asked the Negro, beginning to pump water for me to wash.

"Yes," I replied, not relishing his familiarity, "I'm going down to Florida."

Now it's a fact, though not generally known, that between South Carolina and Florida, both being warm sections, a good many of the Negro gentry are continually traveling back and forth the year round, but very little, if any, of this migration reaches up to North Carolina or Virginia.

"I'm going South myself tonight," said the Negro. "Can't I go along with you?"

My ablutions ceased.

"Say that over again, my man. Did you want to go with me, you say?"

He was a large, powerfully built fellow, with a face calculated to give a timid man chills, and that the suggestion frightened me, I must admit, for suppose he attacked me during the night, thinking I had money with me. Creepy sensations began to steal over me, and yet it will be better than being alone, I thought.

"I know the ropes pretty well, young feller," he added.

This settled it, for I did not know the "ropes," as he expressed it.

"You may go with me," I said.

I was dying for some kind of companionship, and being the possessor of unusually good strength myself, as a result of years of physical culture, I saw no serious cause for fearing my formidable looking companion, providing I could keep awake during the night, so, purchasing a bite to eat at the store and some smoking tobacco for my Negro friend, we began to discuss a plan of action.

"We'll have to go back to Chadbourn and lay for a late freight tonight," said he, "for the trains seldom stop in Grice."

I was afraid the authorities of the town would nab me, but he only laughed at my timidity.

We left Grice about 8 p. m. and set out for Chadbourn, some three miles off. We had gone perhaps a mile on the return journey when I observed another Negro leading up a close rear. I didn't like this for a cent, however I kept quiet, and our dusky follower soon came up quite close.

My grandfather. Dr. Hicks, of Rocky Mount, N. C, famous for his writings and adventures of Civil War life, has many a time illustrated to me where stratagem is better than strength.

On one occasion, when he was a young man, he was proceeding along a lonely country road. It was nearly dark and several miles to the nearest house, and in those days, houses were scarce and the people were more lawless, and, suddenly, a thick set, fierce looking man, holding a stout cudgel in his hand, emerged from the dense woods, which were on either side of the road, and began quickly to overtake him. That my grandfather was pretty well scared can well be imagined, but being a ventriloquist and full of tricks, he soon dispatched his enemy. Glancing into the woods nearby, he shouted: "Come on Jim!" then using his powers of ventriloquism, a hoarse voice close at hand seemed to say, "All right, be there in a minute."

The next moment the man who had been following him plunged deep into the forest and grandfather was left to proceed alone.

That these two men were in collusion and had designs on robbing me I now felt convinced.

Our late addition had drawn up dangerously close.

It was pitch dark, and evidently, he was unaware I had discovered his presence in the party, and the other fellow was exerting himself about this time to keep me entertained with stories of "hobo" life.

It was up to me to use stratagem, and use it quick!

"Confound the luck!" I exclaimed, "I forgot those pistol balls back at the store, but it is all right, Bill"—Bill was the name he had called himself at the pump—"my little Iver Johnson is full loaded, and good for at least five brakemen. Ha I ha! ha! they had better let us go through to Florence, I guess."

Most Negros are afraid of a gun in a white man's hand, and these were no exceptions.

The third man was not long in speaking out, and as if he had just joined us.

"Howdy, gentlemen," was the expressive salutation, "going over to Chadbourn?"

"Yes," I retorted.

"We's gwyne down to Florida," supplemented Bill.

"Dat's strange, I'se gwyne dat way myself," muttered the Negro, "let me go too."

"We don't own de roads," shrewdly observed the man named Bill.

"Well, I'll go den," declared the newcomer, and thus they arranged it to suit themselves, and I said nothing, though I mentally concluded to shift them both at the first opportunity.

One at a time we filed across the main street of Chadbourn an hour later, and, undiscovered, made our way to a large pile of railroad ties some two hundred yards from the depot.

The Negros, unconcerned, stretched out full length upon the timber, and their heavy snoring soon denoted that they had passed into the land of dreams, but their lively trombone music quickly became disgusting, forcing me to seek another pile of the timber for rest.

My thoughts drifted back several years to the scores of positions and hundreds of places I had been in, but none ranked so low as this; and again, thoughts of the warm, comfortable home I had left stole over me.

About midnight my reveries were disturbed by the laboured puffing of a heavy laden freight train, which had just begun to ascend the long grade outside of Chadbourn.

My companions were awakened and had silently joined me in the darkness. The train had pulled up the grade now and the cars had attained a dangerous speed.

As the engine dashed by, my companions came near knocking me down in their greedy endeavour to secure the handles of the first two cars from the engine.

With the throttle open a car's length is a serious matter to the man on the ground, but I caught the third car safely and climbed aboard.

Chadbourn was left like a flash, and a few moments later we went hurling through Grice like a shot out of a gun.

The train was a through freight, and we were bound for Florence.

Crawling back on my hands and knees through the darkness several car lengths, I found an empty coal car. In this car I would be shielded from most of the cold wind, which was blowing at a terrific rate over the top of the train.

Carefully descending to the car and peering over the edge I was surprised to find another passenger, a mild looking *mulatto*, who, upon finding that I was not a brakeman, as he at first had supposed, became quite sociable.

"I'm also bound for Jacksonville," said he, "and we'll go along together."

The proposal suited me to a T, as he added that he was an expert at the business, having been over the same road several times before, and knew every move to make to avoid being "nabbed."

The other two men now got into the car, at which the *mulatto* immediately drew off to the opposite end.

"Two together is safer," he said, as I joined him.

A drizzling rain set in and we were left to ourselves.

"What have you got there?" he asked, some hours later, stumbling against my paper bundles.

"Medicine and clothes," I retorted. He laughed.

"You'll never get to Jacksonville with all that truck," he said. "You'd better get clear of it."

So far, my baggage had been a source of constant annoyance, and I, therefore, readily agreed to part with it.

It had ceased raining now, and the dim light in the east told of the near approach of day.

The lights of Florence could be seen faintly gleaming in the distance as we rapidly drew near, and there was no time to lose, so throwing off coat, shoes and hat, I quickly tore open both bundles, and out in a heap rolled shirts, collars, socks, photographs, cough syrup, quick asthma cures—but space forbids naming all the things.

The bundles had been carefully packed by a loving mother, who had thoughtfully placed in one of them a small Bible. I felt better as I placed the little book in an inside pocket, and I would read it and daily pray to God to take me safely through the long journey before me.

My next move was to astonish the Negro at the number of shirts and socks I got into.

"Put on all you can and be quick," I exclaimed, in answer to his questioning gaze.

He needed no second invitation, and I now began to stuff my pockets with the smaller things, again inviting him to follow suit. About the first thing he grabbed up was a $1.50 razor, which I politely deprived him of.

Within a few minutes the train slackened speed and pulled into the yards.

Quickly alighting and bidding me to follow, the Negro made off from the tracks at full speed.

At first, I thought he was running away with my things, but the wisdom of the move was soon apparent, for at a safe distance, he pointed out to me two slow moving lights going up and down both sides of the train we had just deserted.

"Spotters," he whispered, breathing heavily.

I realised then just how green I was at the profession of hoboing. Undoubtedly, I would have again been picked up, and this time it might not have gone so easily with me as at Chadbourn.

For nearly an hour we walked about the streets of Florence looking for a restaurant, but it was yet too early for them to open, and, disappointed, we returned to the railroad yards.

Two or three trains were beginning to pull out when we arrived.

Plunging between two long freights, and walking rapidly, my companion began to scan the car doors.

"In here," he presently whispered, drawing up before an empty car. "This is the Junction train, and will leave in a few minutes."

Afraid of going wrong and being pretty well frightened, I hesitated.

"What Junction? Are you sure this is the right train?" I questioned, fearing the cars might be made up for Atlanta or Columbia.

His reply was to furtively glance up and down the tracks, and the next instant he had vanished through the half open door. Greatly frightened, I followed.

Quickly and silently, we closed the door, leaving us in impenetrable darkness.

It was not long before an engine bumped against the cars, and shortly after we pulled out.

The day dawned beautiful and clear, and being warm, we opened the car door to enjoy the sunshine.

We had gone some fifty or sixty miles down the road, perhaps, when the *mulatto* declared his intention of getting out to buy something to eat.

"You had better stay in here," I called, but the next moment he was gone.

To my dismay a few minutes later the train slowly began to move off, then faster and faster.

Downhearted, I sat down in the end of the car alone. The wheels began to roar and sing with increasing speed. Once more I cast a last despairing glance at the door. Suddenly a hand was thrust into the opening! In a flash it had disappeared.

Rushing to the door and looking out I was horrified to see the man who had lately left me lying helpless, stretched upon the ground.

No doubt, in jumping he had miscalculated the position of the rod under the door, and as a result of the misstep, had been thrown from the car with considerable force.

Being unusually intelligent, and of a quiet kind of disposition, I had taken quite a fancy to the fellow by this time, and it was with a sigh of genuine relief I noted he had not been run over.

Struggling to his feet with one hand pressed against his head, he waved to me for a moment and then slowly staggered off the pathway of the track.

The man who had claimed to be an "expert" was left, and I was soon miles away, but such is life.

Going back into the car, and being exhausted from hunger, I soon fell asleep.

My last conscious thought was a desire to wake up in Savannah, Ga.

Two hours later it would be time to change trains at Charleston Junction for Savannah, but being blissfully ignorant of this fact, my slumbers were undisturbed.

I slept long and sound—then with a start awoke.

The car was no longer moving. I listened intently for a brakeman, but the grave-like silence was unbroken. Darkness had long since settled down. Now fully awake and being of a logical turn of mind, I began to speculate. Evidently, we had run into Savannah late at night and were now in the train yards. Noiselessly I tiptoed to the door—imitating my late companion—and with great caution poked my head out.

The moon was just rising from behind a distant cloud-bank.

Surely my hunger must be causing some horrible nightmare, and directly in front of me was a large cabbage patch—the largest I had

"Surely my hunger must be causing some horrible nightmare—'

ever seen, in fact.

Countless thousands of cabbages were growing on every hand, and as far as the eye could reach large nice ones they were, too, some of them growing so close to the railroad track as to be almost under my feet.

I had eaten but once since my arrival in Wilmington Saturday night from Southport, and it was now Monday night.

I ceased to remember I was trying to reach Savannah, nor did I speculate long as to the reality of the vision before me.

Springing from the car door into the patch, I sat down before one of the largest of the vegetables and had eaten nearly half of it when I heard some one approaching.

With a guilty start I sprang to the railroad track.

Now would be a good time to locate my position.

The man soon came up.

"Hello! my friend, how far is it to Savannah?" I asked.

"About 150 miles, sir," said the man looking at me curiously.

The truth dawned upon me instantly, while sleeping I had been switched off on the wrong road.

The man started down the track.

"Say, hold on there a minute!" I cried. "How far is it to Charleston Junction?"

"Forty-seven miles," replied the man.

"Well, how far is it to the next town, then?"

The fellow's short answers were exasperating in the extreme.

"Three miles," he hollered, fast getting out of ear shot.

I must confess I completely lost temper.

Making a trumpet of my hands, I shouted:

"I say, you escaped lunatic, what is the name of the town?"

"Meggetts," came back the faint reply, and the man passed out of range.

The solution of the problem was now easy. Not knowing I must change trains at Charleston Junction, I had been carried forty-seven miles out of my way down a branch road.

Twenty-four empty box-cars had been side-tracked to be loaded with cabbage, and I had been in one of the cars.

After an hour's walk, I arrived at Meggetts. It was near 11 p. m., though all the stores, five, I think, were open.

Appeasing my hunger at a small restaurant in the place, I had just $1.05 of the original $4.00 I had left home with.

Upon inquiry, I found that a freight would leave Meggetts at 2 a. m. that night bound for the North.

The train was loaded with early vegetables, and I was told would make a short stay at the Junction.

Eighteen Negro men, whose homes were in Charleston, boarded the train that night when I did. The men had been sent down from Charleston to help load the train.

The brakemen, whose instructions were to let the men ride free kept to themselves on the train, and without stop we ran back to the Junction. The men clamoured down and were soon walking the remaining few miles to their homes.

There are several tracks at Charleston Junction, but before departing the men showed me the track leading to Savannah.

About daylight a freight pulled upon this track and came to a short standstill.

Once more I was fortunate in finding an empty car, and getting into it unobserved.

I was not absolutely sure the Negros had not deceived me, but then a man beating the roads has got to take all kinds of chances, and I was fast learning the fact.

At noon that day I arrived safely in Savannah, that is to say, I arrived within a mile of the town proper, where I ran the risk of breaking my neck by jumping off, but that was much better than being pulled into the yards in broad open daylight to be arrested.

There is one thing peculiar about Savannah, which can't fail to impress a stranger on his first visit. For the size of the town, I think it contains three times as many Negro people as any other city in the United States.

That afternoon I found the time to read a chapter in the little Bible my mother had given me. I shall always believe it was the work of a kind Providence that sent me upon the streets of Savannah that night in quest of someone to go with me to Jacksonville. Luckily for me this time too, as subsequent events will prove.

It was past midnight. Again, my conveyance was a freight train; this time bound for Jacksonville, Fla., and again I had a Negro for a traveling companion.

We boarded the freight one mile from the city limits at a slow-down crossing. There was no empty car to get into and the only other place was on the end of a loaded flat-car, where we were shielded somewhat from the cold winds blowing over the train.

The rain was coming down in a steady downpour, and had been for two hours or more.

We were still standing close together on the end of the car, and had entered Northern Florida, and lying or sitting down in the rain would have been courting death of cold. There was nothing to do but stand up and take our medicine quietly. The cold winds had chilled us to the very marrow.

Weak and faint from the loss of food and sleep, and from the high nervous strain I had been subjected to, I was fast becoming insensible.

I forgot that I was standing on the end of a wildly rocking flat-car rushing through inky darkness at the rate of forty miles an hour. The danger seemed fading away now, and I imagined I was home again resting in my own comfortable bed. The limit of human endurance had been reached, and poor, exhausted nature gave up the battle.

Slowly my eyes closed. "It will be for just one sweet moment, just one," I promised, and the next instant I was fast asleep.

Two rough hands reached out and encircled me about the waist just as I was toppling between the swift running cars, and drew me back to safety.

"Good God! young feller, don't trifle wid your life like dat," exclaimed the frightened Negro.

In a vague way I realised my danger and promised to do better, but I was too sleepy to be much frightened, and inside of a half an hour I had again closed my eyes, promising not to go to sleep, but the promise was broken, and once more I was indebted to the faithful Negro man for saving my life.

It was now breaking day and the train was slackening speed. The next stop was Woodbine, Fla.

Here the conductor discovered us and we were put off.

It was not long before the stores opened up. There are but two or three stores in Woodbine, though one of them is a very large one. It was in this store we got something to eat.

A young lady waited on us, who informed me that Jacksonville was forty-nine miles away.

Guessing our intention, she remarked: "You can't walk it, for twelve miles from here is a long trestle, which is patrolled by a man with a Winchester rifle. He is in the employ of the government and it's his duty to see that no one crosses over on foot. Every twelve hours he is relieved by a man who watches the bridge at night."

"When is the next freight due?" I asked.

"Good God! young feller, don't trifle wid your life like dat,"
exclaimed the frightened darky.

"Tomorrow morning," was the reply, "it's the same one you just got off."

Things were beginning to assume a gloomy aspect.

"Is there a ferry?" I asked, brightening up.

"There was so little travel the ferry was abandoned over a year ago," replied the young lady.

"Well, goodbye; if there is no other way, we'll have it to swim."

We had gone probably a mile down the track and had begun to look out for a place to put in a few hours' sleep, when looking back, I was overjoyed to discover a hand-car rapidly overtaking us.

Stepping into the middle of the track I signalled the car to stop.

"Hello, captain! we want to help you peddle that car across the bridge. Do you go that far?"

"Yes, I'm the track inspector, and go as far as Jacksonville," was the reply.

"Let us go?" I questioned.

"I don't know; I need two more men, but white men, as a rule, are no good peddling these cars on a long run," was the retort.

"I'm as strong as either of the two men now propelling you, sir," and, to prove the assertion, I rolled up my sleeve.

The man's eyes opened wide in astonishment, for notwithstanding I'm an asthma sufferer, his gaze rested on an arm that had undergone five years of hard physical culture training.

"You may go," he said, "and I'm glad to get you."

We passed the man with the Winchester rifle safely, and at 3 p. m. I got off in the suburbs of Jacksonville, parting with the Negro, who is the right owner of the reward offered in the front pages of this book, and whom the track inspector had engaged for railroad work at $1.00 per day.

It was nearly two miles down town, and being fatigued from my recent exertions, I invested five cents in a street car ride.

The car was full of gaily dressed people, white being the prominent colour, all of whom seemed bent upon some kind of pleasure, judging from their happy faces.

Race prejudice is strong here. Half the car was devoted to the white passengers and the other half to the Negro, and is rigidly enforced.

The gay costumes on the streets, and the brisk, business-like air of the people, next attracted my attention. Nearly all of the streets are broad and well paved, and some of the business blocks remind one

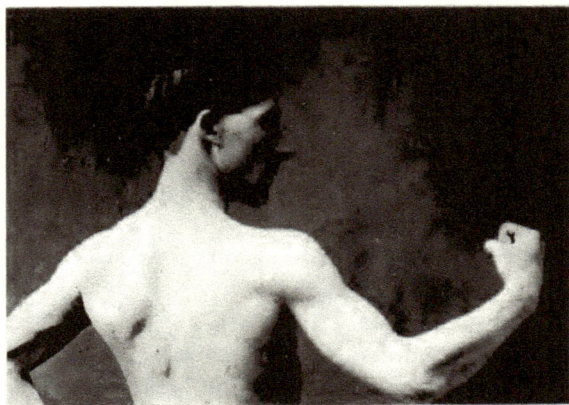

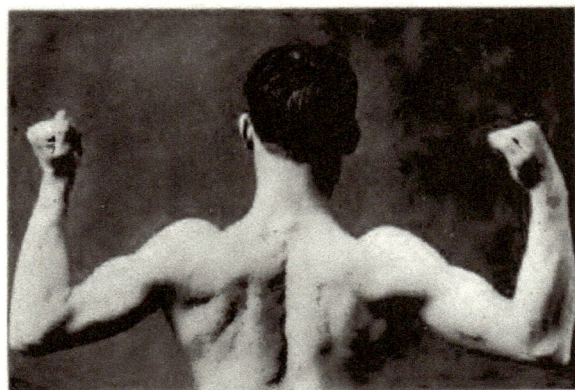

John Peele

of Baltimore, Md. The whole scene was an entire surprise to me. But what impressed me more than all else was the long line of beautiful palms, extending quite close on either side of the street car line.

## CHAPTER 4

# Stranded in New Orleans

I left the car at a point near the Clyde Line docks, and shortly after succeeded in finding William Marine—Archie Marine's brother—who informed me that the boats were no longer running between Jacksonville and Gulf points.

"There's but one way I could help you, young fellow. If you desire, I'll get you on a boat, as a cook's assistant, that will take you to New York City, from which point you might be able to work your way to San Francisco on an ocean liner."

"I thank you, but will risk working my way overland," I replied, and left the wharf.

Sometime during the afternoon, I smeared nearly a whole bottle of Vaseline upon my face and neck, which had begun to burn like fire, as a result of my exposure to the sun while peddling the hand-car.

At 9 p. m. that night I made my way to the Union Depot. Some five or six passenger trains were under the shed. A man in the crowd pointed out to me the train he thought was bound for New Orleans.

Five minutes later I was in the express car.

A pleasant looking young man, I should say about twenty-two years of age, was checking off the express, assisted by an older gentleman.

"Does this train go to New Orleans?" I asked, lowering my voice to a whisper.

"No, it goes to Montgomery," replied the young man, eyeing me closely for a moment, and then turning to his work.

"May I go with you to Montgomery?" I whispered.

The young man again glanced at me, but vouchsafed no reply.

Though not well known, it's no less a fact that most roads of the United States today employ numerous detectives—known as 'spotters'—who travel over the road in various disguises, and whose business it is to discover any employee of the road assisting some poor chap to beat the train.

Sometimes the detective thus employed dresses himself like a tramp or hobo and appeals to the engineer, baggageman or conductor to help him get to a certain point.

Woe be unto the kind-hearted employee who does help him, for a few days later he is discharged almost without notice.

Later on, he finds that his goodness of heart was bestowed upon a railroad detective. Those who understand this can more easily appreciate my present difficulty.

Desperate diseases require desperate remedies; and I hereby admit that I told the express messenger a falsehood.

There was little time to lose. Every moment the express packages were being hurled through the door, and the train would soon be ready to depart on its long four hundred mile journey.

"I can show positive proof, in the way of letters, etc., that I'm no 'spotter,'" I whispered. "For Heaven's sake don't refuse, old man. My parents formerly lived in North Carolina, as the heading of this reference shows, but years ago they moved to Texas, and I went to New York. My parents are poor and I'm their only support. Having been robbed in New York and learning by letter that my mother is near death's door, I've decided to work my way to her. Pardon me saying it; you look to be a pretty square sort of fellow. Please don't refuse the chap who stands before you down and out this time."

The work of checking up had been finished, and the elderly man, after whispering something in the young express messenger's ear, crawled out of the car door to the ground.

A moment later the door shut with a bang.

I had succeeded, and five minutes later was again traveling up the road without a ticket.

I've confessed to telling a lie, and I must now confess to having acted the part of a fool.

I had been sleeping on some express packages in the forward end of the car, and upon awakening glanced at my watch. It was 4 a. m.

Throughout the night the train had been running at a high rate of speed and I figured we ought to be somewhere near Montgomery.

It'll be a great joke to tell him where my home really is, and to let him know how I fooled him, for being near Montgomery, he'll hardly trouble to put me down anyway now, I reasoned, and without thinking, I gave him the whole story of just how neatly I had deceived him.

Instantly the young man's manner changed.

"So, you fooled me, eh! Well, the next stop is Valdosta, Ga. You'll have to get off there," was the sharp retort.

A half hour later I was walking the streets of Valdosta, a much wiser man.

How true is the old saying: "A wise man keeps his tongue in his heart, but a fool keeps it in his mouth."

It was near daylight and bitter cold. A night cop directed me to a lodging house. After I had rung the bell several times the landlady appeared. She had hastily dressed and, with a frown on her face, stood shivering in the cold.

"Madam, have you any vacant rooms?"

"You might share a room with my son," she replied hurriedly.

"Thank you ever so much. What will it cost?" I asked.

"Twenty-five cents," was the pistol-like retort. "Do you want the room?"

"I now got to the point.

"Madam, the night is most over, and my money is low; would you accept 15 cents for the rest of the night?"

"I suppose I shall have to let you in," she said.

Five minutes later I had waked up her son, who began saying uncomfortable things about some people coming in at all times of the night; but the remainder of his remarks fell on deaf ears, for I was fast asleep.

It was the first bed I had been in since leaving home.

About 10 a. m. I awoke much refreshed.

The depot was close by, and the ticket agent informed me that the train bound for Madison, Fla., would pull out in a few minutes.

The fare from Valdosta to Madison is eighty-five cents, and I only had sixty cents.

Acting upon the impulse I boarded the train without purchasing a ticket.

Madison is on the main line between Jacksonville and Pensacola, and would, therefore, afford a better opportunity to catch a west-bound train than if I went to Montgomery.

In due time I was confronted by the conductor.

"How much to Madison?" I asked, feeling in my pockets.

"Eighty-five cents," said the conductor.

"I haven't but 60 cents, conductor; carry me as far as you can for that, and I'll walk the rest of the distance."

A well-dressed young man looked up.

"If you'll pardon me, I'll loan you 50 cents," said he.

"If you'll provide me with an address to which I can return the amount, I'll accept with thanks," I replied.

Taking my book, he wrote down, J. M. Turner, Jr., Gainesville, Fla. "I'm cigar salesman for a Gainesville house," he said.

About this time another passenger spoke out.

"I'll loan you twenty-five cents myself," said he, "if you need it."

Without loss of time, I handed over my book, and he wrote down K. T. Davis, Hopewell, Fla., and handed me twenty-five cents. (As yet I have been unable to locate one of these gentlemen since returning home.)

Madison is the Southern terminal of the road, and at this point I left the train in company with the conductor, who invited me to lunch.

The freight bound for Tallahassee pulled into Madison at 4 p. m.

I had no trouble in enlisting the sympathy of the conductor, a very genial sort of fellow, who told me to go back to the caboose and keep out of sight until we reached Tallahassee.

We reached the capital city sometime after dark.

Here are a few points about Tallahassee which are in great contrast to Jacksonville.

There are no paved streets in Tallahassee; if so, I didn't see them. They are all ill-lighted—one greasy street lamp post about every six blocks.

Little business. In fact, one store out of every three was vacant—those that were open were not selling anything. All the stores are on one big main street.

A street car line was started, but the town couldn't support it, and it went to smash.

The leaves and other rubbish had collected upon the sidewalks in great drifts.

The fine dust floating in the air came near giving me the asthma, and with a feeling of relief I wended my way back to the railroad yards.

To keep warm that night I helped the Negro fire the engine at the ice factory, which is located near the depot, until 10 p. m., when I boarded a freight train bound for Grand River Junction, ninety-nine miles away, at which place I landed about 3 a. m.

The next division was a stretch of a hundred miles or more from the Junction to Pensacola. This was the L. & N. road.

I have since learned that it is about the hardest road in the United States to beat. No long freights pass over the road—most of the trains are "mixed," that is to say, a few box-cars and a few passenger cars.

On this night the train for Pensacola had already made up. It consisted of two or three boxcars and the same number of passenger coaches.

The conductor was in the depot working on some freight bills, when I approached him, requesting permission to ride on the "blind baggage" to Pensacola.

"The same old story," said he, looking up. "Sorry, young man, but we can't carry you on this road."

I next went to the engineer, and there met with the same refusal.

Then to the express car I hurried, for the train would soon start; but again, I was met with a rebuff.

There were no stores in sight, and few houses. Surely Grand River Junction would be a most dismal place to get left in, especially in my condition—only fifty cents, and that borrowed money.

In desperation I ran to the front part of the engine.

In the intense darkness, both fireman and engineer failed to observe a silent form spring upon the cow-catcher.

The wheels began to revolve, and barring all accidents, I was due to reach Pensacola in time for dinner.

Being thinly dressed and facing the damp night winds at a fifty-mile an hour rate is certainly not an enviable position.

In a short time, my body was so benumbed with cold I could scarcely move. Another thing, it would soon break day, and unless I could hide myself better, a discovery would follow and I would be put off.

There's an old saying, which I afterwards learned:

"To hobo the roads successfully, one has to give up all thought of life or death."

That continued hardship lessens a man's fears of death, I have certainly learned by personal experience.

With slow deliberation, I worked my way under the boiler of the engine, and among the machinery. At last, I was stretched out full length under the boiler, with only one foot sticking out, which I must risk being seen. The boiler was rather warm, of course, and every moment I stayed under it, it was becoming warmer. Perspiration started out in huge drops. In running from the extreme of cold I had met the extreme of heat. Only a few moments sufficed to thaw me out and then a warm, hot time began in earnest. My clothes, pressed almost against the boiler, would become so hot every few minutes I was forced to turn over upon my side and ride for a while; only to revert to the original position and torture again.

Things were getting unbearable.

I had heard of hobos riding under the cowcatcher.

Yes, I would risk it! The train came to a standstill. The delay would hardly be a long one, for it was only a cross-roads station. I would have to work with lightning-like rapidity. About midway the boiler was an opening in the machinery, barely large enough to admit the passage of a man. Squeezing through this opening, I dropped upon the cross-ties under the engine. On all-fours I made my way along the track to the front axle of the engine, which I passed under. I had now reached the cow-catcher, but my trouble had been for naught. For some unexplainable reason the space under the cow-catcher had been nailed full of cross-beams, thus effectually barring further progress.

Now, fully realising the danger of my position, a sudden fear assailed me, and I began trembling from head to foot.

It had required scarcely thirty seconds to make the discovery, and within the same minute I had turned and was again squeezing under the terrible looking axle.

*Clang! clang!* sounded the engine bell.

Considerably bruised about the hands and knees, I reached the opening just as the engine pushed off.

Securing a firm grip upon a piece of machinery above the opening, and taking a step forward with the slowly moving engine, I drew myself up to safety.

About 8 a. m. we reached Chipley, Fla.

Here the station agent saw me, and I was pulled down. I was greasy and black, and my clothes were torn, but no limbs were missing.

The conductor, agent and others came hurrying to the engine to see the man who had dared hobo under the boiler.

Chipley is a fine little town of about 1,200 inhabitants, and a more sociable lot of people I've never met.

It was soon mouthed about the streets how I reached the town, and for a time I was the cynosure of all eyes, though no one offered to arrest me.

There are some five or six saw-mills around Chipley. About two miles from the town is a large saw-mill and brick kiln owned by J. D. Hall.

A young merchant of the town informed me that Mr. Hall was badly in need of labour and was paying good prices.

Even to hobo the roads, a man needs money, and I decided to stake up a bit before continuing my way.

Sometime before noon I arrived at the mill.

Mr. Hall looked me over quite critically.

"Did you ever do any hard labour?" he asked.

"Yes, sir," I untruthfully replied, for, to be candid, I had never done a day's hard work in my life.

"Well, you don't look it," was the compliment. "However, I'll give you a trial at $1.50 per day. You can board with Mr —— for thirty cents a day."

"That's unusually cheap for board," I said. "A man doing hard labour needs plenty to eat and I'm perfectly willing to pay at least $3.50 per week."

Evidently, he misconstrued my meaning.

"My men furnish plenty to eat for any man," said he, but you won't get any pie or cake," he retorted, eyeing me with undisguised disapproval.

"O, that's all right! I can eat anything," I hastened to say.

"Very well, Mr. Peele, you may come to work this afternoon. It's not far to your boarding place. Just keep the straight path through the woods there, and it's the first house you get to."

I'll not expose my landlord's name, but for the sake of convenience we'll call him Mr. Black.

In due time I reached the Black household. The scene which met my gaze was altogether uninviting and unappetizing. I can't describe the house. There was one living room, a kitchen, and a shed room.

The day was warm and several Black children were in the yard playing as I reached the gate.

Upon seeing a stranger approach there was a general stampede for the back yard, some of the smaller children taking refuge behind Mrs. Black, who at that moment appeared in the open doorway.

If appearances count for anything, Mrs. Black had certainly not combed her hair within several weeks, and the grime on her face and clothes was a sickening sight to contemplate.

"Good morning, madam; my name is Peele; I'm to work at the saw-mill, and Mr. Hall says you'll furnish me board."

"All right, just make yourself at home," she invited bashfully, and the next moment she disappeared into the dark recess of the only living room.

Strictly on time, Mr. Black arrived for the noonday meal, and forthwith we proceeded to the dining-room.

Both Mr. and Mrs. Black began making apologies, but, with a few jokes, I set them at ease, assuring them that I wouldn't be hard to please.

To see the hard side of life would make a better man of me anyway, I reflected.

There was no attempt to have clean dishes, for two sets or more of children had already eaten, and others were yet coming in.

The meal consisted of rice, honey and bread. So far as I could see there was nothing else. I now saw how a man could be boarded for thirty cents a day.

They'll have something more substantial for supper, I thought, beginning to crust the top of a black-looking, half-done biscuit. The biscuits were unusually large ones, weighing nearly two pounds each.

A little rice and honey and the huge top of the biscuit formed my meal.

There was no denying the fact, I was hungry and was enjoying my portion quite well, when Mr. Black took a sudden notion to either become funny, or spoil my appetite, I don't know which. He had been kicking up a great fuss drinking his coffee, when all at once the noise ceased. He had caught a fly in his cup. Holding up the fly by the hind leg high into the air, he smilingly announced:

"I've caught a sucker!"

To my astonishment Mrs. Black took it as a great joke, and began laughing heartily.

Thoroughly disgusted I kept silent.

It was not long before Mr. Black caught another fly.

Holding up the unfortunate fly between his thumb and forefinger, and with true Florida slowness, he drawled:

"Well, darlin', I've caught another sucker."

I'll not dwell upon all the funny things that happened during my short stay with the Blacks.

I slept in the little shed room, and every night went to bed at dark, for there was no way of obtaining anything to read.

Rice and honey continued in evidence on the table throughout.

Only twice was the menu changed. On these two occasions Mrs. Black's ten-year-old son varied the diet by visiting the lakes, which were near the house, and fairly teeming with fish.

Wild honey and fresh fish are both good, but at the end of a hard week's work at the saw-mill, I was ready for other fields of adventure, and settling my board bill, bade Mr. and Mrs. Black goodbye.

As a result of my week's labour, I now had the sum of seven dollars.

Mr. Hall seemed sorry at my leaving.

"You'd better be careful if you intend to beat to Pensacola," said he, "for I hear there are twenty-two white men working the county roads there for hoboing."

"Well, I can only wish for better luck, sir, and I must now bid you goodbye."

It was late Saturday afternoon when I reached Chipley.

Straightway I proceeded to the only restaurant in the little town, and my next half hour was indeed a busy one.

The bill was sixty cents, but I had no regrets.

The passenger train bound for Pensacola was due in Chipley just before dark.

Someone told me that I could catch the train at a long trestle about four miles from the town. I set out on foot at a rapid gait for the trestle and reached it slightly in advance of the train.

Having but three or four coaches and running at full speed, the engineer was unable to check the train's flight before running almost midway of the bridge.

Just in the nick of time I reached the brass handles, and swung upon the lower steps of the rear car, as the train once more resumed its journey.

The top part of the rear door had been let down—I suppose for ventilation.

Every moment, fearing discovery, my eyes were fastened in a steady stare upon the door.

I had been crouching upon the steps scarcely five minutes ere a lady passenger peered out into the fast gathering darkness.

For the space of a second the head was framed in the open doorway, when, with a quick jerk, it disappeared into the brilliantly lighted car.

There was no doubt she had seen me and was very much frightened.

"Hey! what the —— are you doing there?" shouted the conductor a moment later.

"Going to Pensacola, if you'll allow me, sir. I'll always appreciate it, Captain, if—"

"I'll wire to Caryville and allow you to be arrested if you don't either get down off this train or pay your fare," shouted the conductor.

As will be remembered, I was still on the L. & N. Road, and remembering Mr. Hall's caution, decided to pay my fare.

Ten minutes later I was riding on a first-class ticket to Pensacola. Out of the $5.00 bill I handed the conductor I received only twenty cents. He had taken out the full fare from Chipley, charging me for the four miles I had walked.

At 10 p. m. the train pulled into the station at Pensacola.

"Is there a night freight from here to Mobile?"

The question was directed to a young man about my own age, who had just come out of a barber shop.

"No, but there's a midnight freight to Flomaton, Ala., which is about half way, I believe. Going to hobo it?"

"Yes, I may do so."

"Then I'd advise you to be careful in this town, my friend. You're likely to get a job making "little rocks out of big ones." There are twenty-two of 'em at it now, and a night cop at the depot waiting to catch others. Now, the best thing you can do," he continued, "would be to walk from this town to Flomaton, and if you're going on to New Orleans, you'd better walk through all of Southern Mississippi to the State line of Louisiana, for if you're caught 'hoboing' in Mississippi, you'll get eleven months and twenty-nine days in prison. Upon being released you're allowed one day to get out of the town, and upon failing to do so, you're again arrested and thrown into jail for a like term for vagrancy.

Upon hearing this I admit that I was considerably frightened; but it would never do to give up in this manner, for the trip was hardly begun yet, and if I had heeded all the advice of this nature I had received since leaving Wilmington, the probabilities are I would not yet have reached Jacksonville.

"Nothing ventured, nothing gained," and I decided to either leave Pensacola on the next train or get thrown into jail for the attempt.

Accordingly, I started for the depot at which I had recently been landed as a first-class passenger, and reached it just as the Flomaton freight was pulling out.

There was no cop in sight, for which I was deeply thankful.

The train was an extremely short one and was rapidly getting under headway when I arrived.

A quick glance up and down the train sufficed to show that there were no empty or flat cars along. My ride must be either in the cold winds on top or between the cars. I chose the latter place.

In this position a man has to stick close to the end of only one of the two cars he is riding between, for there is always danger of the cars breaking loose and dashing him to instant death upon the tracks beneath. He can hold on to the break rod with his hands and the car bumper affords him a narrow standing room.

It was six long, weary hours later—just sunrise—when, more dead than alive, I stepped from the train in Flomaton, or rather I fell off the train in Flomaton.

My limbs had become cramped and stiff from standing in one position during the night's long ride, and in trying to jump off the train in the suburbs of the town, I was thrown violently to the ground, sustaining a badly bruised hand and several smaller hurts.

A Negro who lived nearby furnished me with soap and water, though I was minus a handkerchief and was compelled to dry my face with old newspapers.

Flomaton is a small town, not more than a mile from the Florida State line, and derives most of its importance from being a railroad centre.

I started down town in search of a restaurant, but had not proceeded far when I was overtaken by a man who inquired:

"Have you heard the news?"

"What news?" I asked.

"Why, a railroad man was shot and instantly killed near the depot this morning, just before light."

"Who shot him?" I asked.

"As yet they have no clew," replied the man, looking at me keenly, but it is thought he was shot by a stranger."

We were now near the depot. A passenger train was steamed up.

"Where does that train go," I asked.

"It leaves in a few minutes for Mobile," he replied, parting with me at a nearby street corner.

No sooner was he out of sight than I started on a 2:40 pace for the engine.

All thoughts of breakfast fled. A man had been shot dead in the town, and yet there was no clue as to the identity of the murderer. The citizens of the place would soon be up and astir on the streets, and I stood a fine chance of being arrested on suspicion.

With a single bound I was in the engine cab, and the next moment

186

I was pleading with the engineer to take me to Mobile.

That my pleading was earnest need not be said, for I won the case.

"Wait until we get a good start and then swing the 'blind baggage.' I won't see you," he grinned, "but its rather risky going into Mobile on a passenger train in broad open day, for there's generally two or three cops hanging 'round the depot, and the yard is full of detectives."

The word "detective" as used here is what is termed in North Carolina a town constable.

In making arrests of this kind the constable is not required by the State to show a warrant.

Southern Alabama and Mississippi are full of these detectives; and seldom it is that a man gets through without a scratch.

Sometime between 11 and 12 o'clock that day we ran into the suburbs of Mobile.

Darting from the closed doorway, in which I had been standing, to the car platform, I cautiously peeped out.

Several men standing on the sidewalk near a large factory saw me, and motioned violently with their hands for me to jump off, but the train was running too fast for that, and with a feeling of indescribable fear, I quickly sprang back and jammed myself tightly against the closed door—careful even to turn my feet sideways, with my face pressed flat against the door. All hopes of safely alighting in the suburbs was given out. The houses were fast getting thicker and stores began to flash by.

Presently, to my surprise, the train turned into one of the principal business streets of Mobile. Large mercantile houses towered above me on every side.

The train ran several blocks down this street before stopping at the depot.

A man stepped in front of me to uncouple the engine.

Not daring to move, I whispered:

"Which side is the depot on?"

"Get off on your right, quick!" he whispered, without glancing up.

In an instant I was upon the ground and walking towards the boat wharves, but a few blocks distant.

Only by prompt action in getting off the train, and knowing which side to alight on, had I been able to escape the wide-awake officials at Mobile.

I felt like laughing as I reached the wharves and noted that no one had pursued me.

Evidently, I was getting to be an expert "hobo"—but my joy was of short duration, for now I was as anxious to reach New Orleans as I had been to reach Mobile—and what if I was thrown in jail for a long term in Southern Mississippi? Well, my people should never hear of it, I resolved.

Going on a small vessel I asked for soap and water.

I was given a big cake of dirty looking soap, half as large as my head, and told to draw my own water. Seizing a water bucket to which a long rope was attached, I cast overboard and soon drew into view a big bucketful of slimy looking water, that at home my own dog would have sniffed at contemptuously. But a chap buffeting against the world, as I was now doing, soon learns not to be too choice. After a while he forgets the luxuries that were once his, and in most respects, life assumes a different aspect.

Having washed up, I thanked the boatman and left the wharves.

A good dinner made me feel better, and I decided to stay in town overnight and rest up.

After dinner I found a nice room and paid for a night's lodging in advance.

About one o'clock in the afternoon I retired to sleep, determined to get as much rest as possible for my money before next morning.

I slept probably two hours, and then awoke with an uncomfortable feeling. I had been dreaming of beating trains and of several narrow escapes from death.

A cop chasing me dangerously close had awakened me.

The bed seemed moving and the whole room whirling around. As soon as my eyes became accustomed to objects in the room and I saw that I was really safe from harm, I again tried to go to sleep, but it was no use, for the bed now seemed literally flying through space, and though lying in the middle, it seemed all I could do to maintain my position.

In disgust I arose and dressed.

The train for New Orleans would leave at 4:30, and I yet had over an hour to reach the depot.

The man who uncoupled the engine of the Flomaton passenger that morning showed up just before train time.

I told him I intended trying to beat the train to New Orleans.

He promised he would fix it up with the engineer for me, but that I must look out myself for the conductor, as he didn't know him.

"You'd better look out going through Mississippi, though," he said.

"The train makes but three regular stops—Scranton, Biloxi and Gulf Port. If you are not sharp, you'll get run in at one of those places."

"Don't turn your head! he suddenly whispered, "there's a detective under the depot looking at you now. We'd better not be seen talking together."

"Goodbye, young fellow, and I hope you may get through safe."

The 4:30 passenger arrived in Mobile on time, and a few moments later pulled out bound on its long journey to New Orleans.

Hidden between two box-cars farther up the road, I waited for the engine to pass.

The train was going at a rapid clip when I sprang out and made a headlong dash for the "blind baggage," which I caught safely.

Either the conductor had not seen me or was waiting for me to get picked up down the road.

The train's speed was increasing every moment, and Mobile was soon left miles behind.

Sunday evening just before dark we pulled into Scranton, Miss.

A great throng of people, including a good many beautiful young girls, had turned out to see the train. Their voices told me which side the depot was on.

No sooner had the train stopped than I was upon the ground on the opposite side.

I heard someone running towards the engine on the other side of the track.

Trembling with fear for a moment I stood still.

Another train filled to overflowing with passengers and headed towards Mobile had side-tracked for the New Orleans train. Jumping aboard the Mobile train, I mingled with the passengers.

In a few moments, by looking through the car window, I noted with satisfaction that the New Orleans train was again on the move.

One, two, three car lengths passed.

With a single bound I sprang from the Mobile train, and a never-to-be-forgotten race for the "blind baggage" ensued.

I soon passed from between the two trains, and now it was an open track race.

As I passed the last coach of the Mobile train two forms loomed up on the side-track.

"There he is! He is the fellow!" cried one of the men.

"Yes, I'm the fellow," and stiffening my forearm, I delivered the sheriff, who stepped out to intercept me, a right swing under the chin—*crack!*

The man received the full benefit of the motion of my body and went to the ground like a ten pin.

It was a blow I had been taught at the Ardell Club while taking boxing lessons under Cy Flinn, a pugilist of considerable local fame in Buffalo.

The engineer, sitting backwards in his cab, had witnessed the trouble, and as I vanished between two mail cars, the whole train jumped with a sudden burst of speed.

Evidently the kind-hearted engineer was keeping up his part of the contract to take me through.

It was dark when we reached Biloxi and Gulf Port, and by careful dodging I escaped the men who had searched the train at these points.

The biggest part of the journey was now over the Gulf waters, and at an extremely slow rate of speed.

At nine o'clock that night we crossed the Mississippi, and the train came to a standstill at the depot on Canal Street, New Orleans.

I stayed in New Orleans one week.

I arrived in the Crescent City with less than a dollar, and on the second night my money was gone and I was forced to sleep upon one of the wharves near the foot of Canal Street.

The next day I got a job unloading bananas off the boats at the I. C. wharves at two bits an hour.

I found a room now at No. 1006 Iberville Street, in a lodging house run by a Mrs. M. P. Westmoreland. Mrs. Westmoreland is a well-to-do widow, and also a very kind-hearted lady. She refused to accept anything for my lodging, saying she would be amply repaid if I would write her a letter when I got to Tucson.

"I shall always think you were accidentally killed if I never hear from you," she said.

I was always a poor writer, and have never sent her the letter, but if this little pamphlet is ever published, I shall take pleasure in sending her a copy, together with my best greetings.

Only three banana steamers arrived while I was in the city. The fruit is loaded in the West Indies. I made $4.50 at this job.

New Orleans is a fascinating town and the easiest place in the world to spend your money.

A few days later, when I made preparations to leave for Texas, my $4.50 had dwindled to $0.

There are more beautiful yellow girls to be seen on the streets of

New Orleans in one day than one would see in most cities in a lifetime. They are called Creoles, or something of the kind, and can be seen walking around, all over the town, in every direction. Even down at the wharves every afternoon about boat time you'll see them lined up in great numbers.

There was a lot of talk about the "Hoodlums" while I was in New Orleans. All the city newspapers, as well as some of the State papers, had long articles concerning the doings of this remarkable organisation. Nearly every section of the city had been visited at one time or another and terrorised by them.

I recalled the words of the engine coupler at Mobile. When I parted with him, his last remark was, "Look out for the Hoodlums."

They are a set of young city bloods and toughs of the worst stripe, banded together to rob, murder and steal.

I met a well-dressed young man in a large park there one night, who told me confidentially that he was a "Hoodlum"; said he thought he and I would make good friends, and that he might be able to get me in as a member, but I declined the invitation with thanks.

Yes, New Orleans is a great place in many ways. On the day I left, while standing on the street corner taking a last view of the place, a man bearing a large basket, carefully covered over, approached me and said:

"Crawfish? Crawfish?"

"What about crawfish?" I asked.

He looked at me in surprise.

"Good to eat," he said; "only five cents a pint."

I told him they were used down home for fish bait, whereupon he got mad and went strutting up the street.

I had caught a glimpse of the crawfish, though. There was no mistaking it; they were real crawfish all right, and were what we term "little teenie" ones. The man said they had been cooked very carefully and were well done. Of course, the head is thrown away, and it is only the tail part that is eaten.

## CHAPTER 5

# Nabbed by a Cop

Late one afternoon I crossed the river on a freight ferry to the Texas Pacific railroad yards.

That night I beat a freight train 208 miles to Boyce, La., reaching Boyce about 11 o'clock next morning. Another freight on the same day bore me to Marshall, Tex., 100 miles from Boyce.

All day long I had had nothing to eat and it was 9 o'clock at night when we reached the city of Marshall.

I had just one hour to get something to eat and get back to the depot, for the Dallas freight would pull out at 10 p. m.

I went four or five blocks up a side street and knocked on a cottage door. The occupants had retired, but a second knock brought the madam to the door.

I told the lady a sad story of how hungry I was, and ended up by asking for a pan of water to wash my face and hands, if it would not cause her too much trouble.

She called to her husband, who came hurrying into the hall in his stocking feet.

After I had told my story again a pan of water was brought into the hall and I was invited in.

They told me, while I was washing, they had nothing in the house to eat.

I took out my note book.

"If you will loan me five cents," I said, "I'll take your address and return it. I'm very hungry, sir, and will appreciate it more than I can tell you."

The man loaned me a dime, but would furnish no address; and hastily thanking them, I hurried out the gate and started on a run for the railroad restaurant.

A big, fat fellow runs the railroad restaurant at Marshall—a Dutchman or Irishman, I couldn't decide which, but he is as good natured as he is large.

There was nobody in but the proprietor when I entered.

"My friend, I am very hungry, and am broke—I have just ten cents, and am thousands of miles from home. Give me ten cents worth of supper, and please understand I want quantity and not quality."

The meal that good-hearted fellow spread out on the table caused me to blush with shame, but I was hungry, and shame was set in the background.

It was chicken *fricassee*, sausage, beef, etc., and more of each than I could eat, hungry as I was.

In a short time, I left the restaurant.

It was already time for the Dallas freight to leave, and I went hurrying down the track through the darkness to where the train was making up.

I came upon two brakemen struggling in a vain endeavour to close a tight car door. (From this point throughout the West the brakemen are white men.) The men were cursing and swearing at a great rate at their failure to close the door, but with the united effort of all three of us, it was finally pushed to and sealed.

"I want to go to Dallas. You fellows care if I get on?"

"We'll take you for $1.00," said the brakemen.

I told them I didn't have the money. (In this part of the country a brakeman makes almost as much carrying hobos as his wages amount to. A dollar is the usual charge for a division, which is anywhere from one hundred to two hundred miles, but when a hobo attempts to go without paying, he is generally treated pretty rough, if not thrown from the train and killed.)

"Four bits, and we'll carry you," said one of the brakemen.

"I give you my honest word, I haven't got a cent, fellows."

"Then don't get on this train. Do, you'll get kicked off," said the men.

I left them and went hurrying through the darkness down the long line of cars.

I found a car half full of cross-ties.

The door had not been sealed, and crawling into the back end of the car I pulled off my coat—for the night was very hot—and folding it up into a nice pillow, I lay down to sleep.

I never knew when the train started, but about forty miles down the road the brakemen found me, and shining their lanterns within a foot of my face, woke me up.

Instead of "kicking" me off, as threatened, they talked fairly sociable.

"We'll not put you down in this storm, here on the prairie, for there's nothing here but a side-track, but the next stop is Longview, and you'll have to get off," they said.

I went to the door and looked out. The rain was coming down in great sheets, and the heavens were lit up by an almost constant glare of lightning. It was the worst storm I had ever seen.

As far as I could see in every direction was a vast expanse of rolling prairie. It was the first time I had ever seen the prairies, and I felt deeply impressed. I noted that the air seemed purer and fresher too than any I had ever breathed before.

At Longview the men came to the car to put me down, but I had already gotten down, and not finding me, they left.

The train started, and rising up from the ground, where I had been hiding, I crawled into the car of ties again.

I was run out of the same car three times that night. The last time I was put off; the brakemen told me if I got back on the train again, they would shoot me.

I had reached the town of Big Sandy, Tex., and decided I had better wait for another train.

It lacked but a few minutes of 12 o'clock as I made my way over to a small drug store, not far from the depot.

A sharp featured man was talking to the druggist as I entered.

He slightly bowed at me, and presently said:

"You're a stranger here, are you not?"

Something told me he was a detective.

I told him yes, I was a stranger and trying to reach Dallas, and a good many other things I told him I don't remember.

He finally admitted he had just searched the train I had left, but as he hadn't caught me in the act, he would let me go, comforting me with the assurance that I would get caught anyway at Mineola.

"Why, they are so bad after hobos in Mineola they break open the car door seals, searching for them," he said.

Two hours later I was standing on the "blind baggage" platform, behind the coal tender of a passenger train bound for Dallas.

It was raining pretty hard when we got to Mineola, and no one came to bother me.

Shortly after daylight we steamed into Dallas.

I jumped from the train as it began to slow up at the State Fair Grounds in the edge of the city.

I had at last gotten to Dallas, but I was certainly in a bad fix—penniless, wet to the skin, cold, sick, and deathly sleepy.

I went over to a small grocery store, near the fairgrounds, run by a Mrs. Sprague.

A beautiful young girl about fifteen years old, who was clerking in the store, brought me a pan of water to wash.

"Didn't you beat that passenger train in town?" asked the elderly lady, as I began washing.

"I did, madam, and I am sorry that circumstances necessitated my doing so," I replied.

"I thought I saw you jump off," she said, whispering something to the young girl, who vanished into the back part of the store.

It took nearly twenty minutes of hard scrubbing for me to get the cinders and grease out of my hair and eyes. As I finished, the young lady re-entered the store and approached me.

"Come and have some breakfast," she said in a low voice, "it's all ready and the coffee's hot."

For a moment I felt worse than at any time since leaving home. I tried to refuse, but they allowed me no chance.

"I've got a dear son myself wandering somewhere over this big world," said the good woman, putting a handkerchief to her eyes.

There was no help for it, and I humbly assented to take a cup of coffee. The hot, steaming coffee was of the best quality, and four times did my beautiful young waitress see that my cup was filled.

Sometimes I think that coffee saved my life.

Upon leaving Mrs. Sprague's I walked down town from the fairgrounds, a distance of about three miles.

The first man I asked for a job was F. P. Holland, the rich editor of the *Texas Farm and Ranch*.

He said he had no work at present.

Before leaving, I told him I was sick, cold and hungry, and had nowhere to sleep that night.

I asked him to loan me $1.00 until I could get on my feet and pay him back. He loaned me 25 cents, which I was glad to be able to pay back in a few days.

Leaving the rich man and his luxury, I took a long tramp back to the fairgrounds, where someone said I could get a job.

Secretary Sidney Smith was in charge of the work, and after hear-

"Come and have some breakfast," she said in a low voice, "it's all ready and the coffee's hot."

ing my story, kindly furnished me a place to sleep and eat, and gave me a job helping to repair the fair grounds.

"I don't really need any more labour," he said, "but I believe in helping a man when he's down."

He secured me a place to board at No. 270 South Carroll Ave., with one of the foremen, Mr. R. A. Downey.

That night I was surprised to learn that the young lady, who had waited on me so nicely at the store, was Mr. Downey's daughter.

While at Mrs. Downey's I was taken down with a high fever, and for the first time since leaving home I had a hard spell of asthma. This only increased my desire to get to Arizona or New Mexico.

Good cotton choppers around Dallas are paid $1.75 per day and board.

About two weeks later I left the city.

After paying for my board and buying a few articles of clothing, I had but $3.00.

I left Dallas one Sunday evening on a street car for Fort Worth. The distance is about 22 miles.

That same afternoon an employment bureau run by Glenn & Co. shipped me for $1.00 from Fort Worth over the Fort Worth and Denver Road to Iowa Park, Tex., to do railroad construction work.

I was trying to reach El Paso, which is only 600 miles over the Texas Pacific Road from Fort Worth, but while in Fort Worth I was told it was almost as much as a man's life was worth to try to beat the T. P. Road between these points, on account of the extreme cruelty of the brakemen, so I decided to go around the longest way, which would take me through New Mexico.

On the way to Iowa Park, I fell in with a young man from Chicago, who had also shipped out.

That night we deserted the train at a small station just before reaching Iowa Park.

We were now nearly two hundred miles from Fort Worth and had ridden the entire distance for $1.00.

I have forgotten the young man's name, but will call him White. He said he had left his home in Chicago to settle somewhere in the West and make his fortune.

We decided to travel along together awhile.

About daylight we caught a freight train.

A long smokestack of some kind was loaded on a flat-car.

Into the smutty stack we crawled, he entering one end and I the

197

other, and crawled until our heads met in the middle.

When we came together White was trembling all over.

"I've done everything since leaving home but hobo," said he.

He reminded me of my own experience through South Carolina and Georgia.

We made a lot of noise getting into the stack, and had not more than become comfortable when a brakeman's lantern was thrust into one end.

"Hello! Hello! in the pipe there," he shouted.

We crawled out and asked him to let us go, but it was "no go."

"Give me a dollar apiece, or off you go at the next stop," said the brakeman, and he kept his word. We were put down at a little town sixteen miles from Vernon, Texas.

We immediately set out to walk to Vernon, and had proceeded along the track about ten miles when a large farm wagon containing seven or eight farmers overtook us.

They were going to Vernon and offered us a ride.

At this time of the year the farmers are walking up and down the streets of Vernon offering as high as $2.00 per day and board for men to work in the harvest fields. In fact, at no time of the year a farm labourer in this part of Texas is not paid less than $30.00 per month and board.

I had never heard of farm hands getting such high wages, and suggested to White that we work in Vernon long enough to pay our way to Arizona or New Mexico, but like all young fellows who stay in the West awhile, he had caught the fever of roving and rambling from one green pasture to another—content nowhere—and put up a strong kick.

He wanted to work in Vernon but a few days only.

"You're from the East, and you know nothing about good wages," he said. "Why this is nothing to what we can make in Roswell, New Mexico, gathering apples."

I had heard of the wonderful apple orchards around Roswell, and then, too, the climate would be better for me. I decided White was right, and that we would not stay long in Vernon.

Late that afternoon a ranchman took us out in his buggy to a ranch about five miles from town.

He had offered us $2.00 per day and board to shock wheat.

Neither of us had ever shocked any wheat, but he said we could soon learn.

Judging from my companion's conversation since I had met him, I had a suspicion he was a better pool player than he was wheat shocker, but the wealthy ranch owners of Texas at this season of the year, when their thousands of acres of land are lying in unshocked wheat, are glad enough to get a man, even if he is a slow worker and from the city.

Sometime after dark we came upon a small, one-room hut. Near the hut was a large, covered wagon.

"Here's where you sleep," said the ranchman. Just go right in and make your bed out of wheat."

Everything was very still in the hut, considering the fact that the one room contained some ten or a dozen men; but the men who had laboured long and hard under the hot Texas sun that day were now scattered here and there about the hut floor, wrapped in a deep, sweet sleep. (Each of these men was from a different city or State, as I afterwards learned.)

There was plenty of wheat strewn about the floor for us to lie upon, and soon two other weary, footsore travellers, lulled by the soft breeze blowing in the window, had fallen easy victims to the soothing caresses of Morpheus.

It was about 4 a. m. that we were roused out of bed by a man announcing that breakfast was ready.

"Come and get it, or I'll throw it out—Come and get it or I'll throw it out," yelled a loud voice from the vicinity of the wagon.

"What's he going to throw out?" I asked the fellow who had disturbed my sleep.

"It's the cook calling the men to breakfast," said he, "and you'd better hurry if you want any."

"Where is a place to wash?" I asked.

"Over there at the end of the wagon," said the man.

I reached the spot and found some seven or eight men washing from one small tin vessel about half full of soapy water.

Water is a scarce article on the prairies and but little of the precious fluid is used for washing purposes.

I washed the corners of my eyes, but there was no towel, comb nor brush to be had, and I made my way to the breakfast table.

The table was one long plank, supported at either end by a barrel.

The plates, saucers and knives were all made of tin.

The grub was well cooked and of good variety. The table was soon cleared and it was now to the wheat fields.

On the third day at noon both White and myself had gotten

enough of the harvest fields and, receiving our pay, set out on foot for Vernon.

That night we caught a passenger train and beat it one hundred miles to Childress, Tex., where we were put off.

But not to stay long. An emigrant, who was moving his household effects to the Indian Territory, allowed us to get in the car where his furniture was and carried us over two hundred miles to Dalhart, Tex., landing there late the next day.

I parted with White at Dalhart. He had changed his mind about going to Roswell, and now wanted to go to Denver, Colo.

Two hours after he had caught the Denver train, I was safely hid in a coke car on an El Paso freight train.

I had no trouble in catching the train at Dalhart, for just as it pulled out a rough fight took place on the depot platform, both parties using firearms, which served momentarily to take attention from me. It's doubtful though whether I'd have been bothered in Dalhart anyway, for it is one of those rough little Western towns 'way up in the Texas Panhandle, in which "everything goes."

And, say, that was a funny fight, too. A big, rough-looking fellow, presumably a miner, had been cutting up too much fuss on the depot platform. The agent came out and asked him to be quiet, but instead of quieting him, he made matters worse. The big fellow began cursing everybody on the platform. A cop was called and in a moment, there was a mix up. The cop pecked the fellow all over the head with his pistol, but the miner gamely came back at him with his own pistol, neither of them uttering a word. In a few minutes blood was streaming from both. The big fellow finally gave in and put up his gun.

"Come on now," said the cop, grabbing the man by the arm, and starting up the street.

I was wondering where the jail was, when to my surprise the cop released the man before they had gone a block.

The cop now came back to the depot, smiling.

"I got rid o' him," he said, but he was mistaken, for the other fellow, by this time, had also reached the depot.

Walking up close to the cop, he leered:

"Do you think I'm afraid of you?" and then another fight, even rougher than the other, began.

It was at this juncture, unobserved, I slipped into the coke car.

Within a short time after leaving Dalhart, we crossed the State line into New Mexico.

## CHAPTER 6

# Across the Line into New Mexico

The train had now entered a country that is simply indescribable for its bleak barrenness.

On every hand, as far as I could see, was nothing but barren sand hills, broken here and there by high mountain ridges.

In some places we would go forty or fifty miles without seeing a sign of human habitation, then suddenly we would come upon a small collection of *adobe* huts, that is, huts built of sun-dried, mud bricks.

These little houses have a flat roof, and some of them are no taller than a man's head. They are occupied by Mexicans and Indians.

A big rain would destroy all these dwellings; but rain is almost as scarce in this desolate, sun-baked region as snow is in the Torrid Zone.

When it does rain there and a man's clothes are wet, it takes but ten minutes for the air to dry him off again.

From where I was sitting in the door of the coke car thousands upon thousands of jack rabbits, cotton tails and prairie dogs could be seen dodging in and out among the rocks and cactus trees.

Once, just before dark came on, a solitary cowboy, wearing high boots and a big *sombrero*, mounted on a spirited young pony, dashed across the tracks ahead of the train and disappeared behind the low mountain ridges toward the sunset—and such a grand, beautiful sunset that was!—the sun slowly sinking behind the distant mountain peaks, and the whole heavens lit up with a perfect flood of golden beauty, was a scene, though I live to be a hundred years old, I shall never forget.

Nowhere else in all the world, I believe, are the sunsets so gloriously beautiful as in Arizona or New Mexico.

Lost in spell-bound admiration and silent reflection, I sat in the car door until long after dark.

The night air at home had always given me the asthma, but there was no asthma feeling about me now; instead, I felt that it would be an impossibility to wheeze.

I inhaled great draughts of the dry, pure air, which seemed to penetrate to my very toes, and open every air cell in my body.

Surely for those whose lungs are affected this is God's country, I thought.

Then and there I registered a solemn vow that when my parents were no more, I should return to this country and pass the remainder of my days.

All of this part of New Mexico is devoted to sheep raising. White men are in demand as sheep herders, and are usually paid $30.00 per month and board.

That night I slept in the coke car, and at sunup next morning we reached the first large town in all the 200-mile stretch from Dalhart—Santa Rosa—a town of 700 population.

No one discovered the poor, thirsty hobo in the coke car. (In this country three hours is a long time for a man to do without water.) Inside of an hour the train had changed crews, another engine had been coupled on, and the long 175-mile ride across the dreary waste to Alamogordo (the next division point) was begun.

During this long ride there was no change of scenery. I never went to the door without seeing thousands of jack rabbits and an occasional coyote. Once in a while a large tarantula (spider) as large as a man's hand could be seen scampering among the rocks for shelter.

Extreme thirst is caused by the alkali dust which floats in the air. Before the day was over my lips had become a fiery red and cracked open, and my tongue had swollen nearly twice its normal size.

Many a poor hobo has been put down in this country by a heartless brakeman, and left to die on the desert, of thirst, but, as yet no one on the train had seen me.

Once, as darkness was closing down, I heard a brakeman coming, and quickly crawled into the back end of the car, where it was very dark.

Slabs had been nailed across the open door within two feet of the top to prevent the coke from rolling out.

The brakeman climbed upon these slabs, and taking up a piece of coke, threw it into the dark end of the car, where I was hiding, with considerable force.

Though he could not see me, his aim was true, and the coke struck me a glancing blow upon the cheek, cutting a long gash, and starting the blood.

The pain was intense, and it was all I could do to keep from crying out, but the brakeman, unconscious of my hurt, hurled a piece of coke into the other end of the car, and upon hearing no one, sprang from the car door, and soon his footsteps could be heard going to some other part of the train.

Late that night we reached Alamogordo.

While here I wrote home to my folks.

Alamogordo is 4,000 feet above the sea level, and has one of the finest natural parks in the United States.

The town is also noted for the luscious fruit raised by the Mexican ranchers nearby.

My night's lodging was on a large pile of telegraph poles piled near the railroad.

No dew falls in that country and a good many of the people who live there would rather sleep on the ground during the summer months than on a good feather bed. A man can sleep on the ground there nine months in the year without taking a cold.

I left Alamogordo the next day on a passenger train as a "coal passenger," that is, I had to help the fireman shovel coal for my fare to El Paso.

About half of this trip lay in the foothills of the mountains, and then we reached the mountains proper.

Gradually the train rose foot by foot (the train was going very slowly now) until we had attained a height of over 5,000 feet above the level of the track.

The journey was now through the clouds, and in some places the fog was so thick I could not see the cars that were following behind us, but in a few moments the spiral winding tracks would carry us on the other side of the mountains, where the sun was shining brightly, and I could see far down the beautiful valleys to some distant mountain peak over seventy-five miles away.

It was the first time I had ever seen the mountains, and enraptured with their beauty, I forgot to throw coal down for the fireman.

The engineer, noticing my abstraction, called:

"Hey, come down here a minute."

I crawled into the cab.

"Where are you from?" he asked, good naturedly.

"I'm from North Carolina working my way to Tucson."

"I thought you were from the East," he said. "How far do you think it is to that mountain peak over there?"

"It looks to be about five miles," I answered.

"That's where this clear air fools you. Why that peak is over forty miles away," he laughed.

The rest of this trip I was treated exceptionally good. Both the fireman and engineer seemed to take a delight in pointing out to me things of interest.

Presently a very high mountain caught my eye.

"That's Mt. Shasta," said the fireman. It's over two miles high, and snow lies up there about nine months in the year. There's a railroad built up there now," he continued, "and it's an ideal summer resort."

About 8 or 9 p. m. we reached El Paso, Tex.

At one time, years ago. El Paso was one of the roughest border towns in the West, but the modern El Paso is altogether a different town.

The population now numbers over 50,000, of which 15 or 20 *per cent* are Mexicans.

Just across the Rio Grande River is the Mexican city, Ciudad Juarez. I spent nearly a day in this quaint looking city. In the centre of the town is a large park. Seated on one of the beautiful rustic benches, placed close together along the shaded avenues of the park, you are quite free from the hot, scorching sun beating down overhead. Just above your head a large frame work, extending over the entire park, has been constructed, and upon it a thick growth of vines and beautiful flowers are entwined in endless profusion.

Wherever I spent a small American coin, I was sure to receive nearly a handful of Mexican coins in change.

A toll bridge spans the river and connects the two cities.

An American collects the toll on the El Paso side and a Mexican on the Juarez side. It cost me two cents to cross each way.

While in El Paso I heard a great deal of talk about the high wages paid laborers in Bisbee, Ariz., and as it was only a few miles out of my way going to Tucson, I decided to stop over there a few days.

I shovelled coal on an El Paso and Southwestern freight train from El Paso to Douglas, a distance of 200 miles.

Douglas, Ariz., is a small place of about two thousand population, and is twenty-seven miles from Bisbee.

When we reached Douglas the engineer and the fireman invited me to take dinner with them.

The engineer offered to get me a place in the large railroad shops located there as apprentice boy at $2.50 per day, but I told him I would go on to Bisbee and try that town for a job first.

In this country a man willing to work can always find dozens of jobs waiting for him. Nearly everything is white labour, and its very seldom you are offered less than $3.50 to $4.50 per day for eight hours work.

The largest smelter plant in the world is located at Douglas. (It's the old plant removed from Bisbee.)

The ore train (heaviest tonnage train in the world) hauls the crude ore from the mines in Bisbee to the Douglas smelters.

I stayed over one night in Douglas, and the next morning at daylight caught the ore train with its long line of empty, iron-bound cars, bound for Bisbee.

At Osborne Junction a miner got into the car I was in. He was also going to Bisbee.

We left the cars on a side-track at Don Luis and started out to walk the remaining two miles to Bisbee, "The Greatest Mining Camp on Earth."

My first impression of Bisbee was certainly not a very favourable one.

The town is surrounded by high mountain ranges, making a sewerage system next to impossible. The waste matter of Bisbee is hauled away in wooden boxes with teams.

On account of this poor sewerage Bisbee suffers every summer with an epidemic of typhoid fever and smallpox. There is always the presence of a fearful stench upon the streets. All of the streets are very narrow, winding and short.

Most of the dwelling houses are built one above the other up the mountain sides, and are reached by narrow, winding paths.

Main street and Brewery Gulch are the two principal business streets.

On either of these streets, day or night, one always finds a large crowd of miners and gamblers—speaking of gambling, Bisbee is a typical Western town in this respect. There are over twenty public gambling halls there. Every saloon has its gambling hall, and in the rear a band of musicians. The doors are thrown wide open and the window shades are never drawn.

Strolling into one of these brilliantly lighted dens of iniquity, you'll find every known gambling device under the sun. "Dice throwing," "21," *"Faro,"* "Roulette," "Poker"— they are all there, and many others.

The Indian, Chinaman, Mexican and American all play at the same table, and unless you are a good poker player you had better stay out of the game.

In these games the ante is seldom less than $1.00.

The people in the Far West talk but little while the game is going on. There is no wrangling or misunderstanding. The cards are dealt quickly and deftly, and without a word the betting begins. Sometimes the pot swells to a thousand dollars or more, but even then, the same quiet among the players prevails.

The winner hardly smiles as he pockets his money, and the loser, if he goes broke, quietly gives up his seat and some other gentleman takes a hand.

On the 10th and 12th of every month the mines around Bisbee pay out to the employees the sum of $70,000, so it is no wonder the gambling halls do a good business.

There are no one cent pieces used in Bisbee, (not even in the post-office); nothing less than five cents.

Bartenders in Bisbee receive $6.00 for an eight-hour shift serving drinks.

There are no Negro people in Bisbee.

Board and room can be obtained for $30.00 per month and up. Clothing cost but little more than in the East.

## CHAPTER 7

# Smallpox Starts Me Off Again

It was an afternoon in July that I strolled into Bennett & Williams' law office on Brewery Gulch and asked for a job.

A sign in the window read:

"Stenographer Wanted."

It was in response to this ad I had entered.

Right here a description of me might not be out of place.

My spring suit had been ruined, and long since discarded for a suit of overalls that I had purchased in Dallas. Hard knocks had rent them in several places, and they were full of train grease. My shoes were worn completely out. For a hat I was wearing a wide-brimmed *sombrero*, purchased from a Mexican merchant at Alamogordo. I was strapped again, but that was a thing I was getting used to.

Taken all in all, I'm sure I looked anything but a stenographer.

Williams was typewriting when I entered and asked for the job.

He refused to look at the various references I produced, saying they would have no weight with him, but glancing up at me, broke out into a broad smile.

"So, you are a shorthand writer, eh! Well, come back tomorrow morning and I'll give you a trial," was the promise, but it was quite easy to see he thought I was more of a tramp than a shorthand writer.

Needless to say, though, I went back at the appointed time, and though I failed miserably in getting down the first letters he dictated, I was given the job.

"You'll soon get back in practice," he said, "and when you do, your salary will be $125.00 per month."

Three days later, as I began to improve, Williams bought me $17.00 worth of clothes and a nice dress suitcase. I was also given a $5.00 meal ticket on the English Kitchen, and room rent was paid for me one month in advance at the Le Grand Hotel. Both my employers provided me with spending money from time to time, but the most of this money I saved.

I had been in Bisbee nearly three weeks when several cases of smallpox and typhoid fever broke out.

Two cases of smallpox broke out in the Le Grand Hotel.

Several people deserted the town post-haste, and among the number was myself.

I resigned my position as stenographer, and bidding my kind-hearted employers and other friends goodbye, I purchased a ticket to Tucson. It took nearly all my money to buy this ticket, but I didn't like the idea of hoboing to the town I was to make my future home in.

I would, at least, have plenty of nice clothes when I got there, and if it came to a pinch about getting something to eat, I could sell some of my clothing.

The first thing that met me when I stepped from the train in Tucson was a sandstorm, filling my eyes, ears and nose full of fine dust and covering my clothes. (Sandstorms are of common occurrence in this section.)

It is a good deal warmer in Tucson at all times than at Bisbee, for Tucson is 2,000 feet lower. Tucson is on the Southern Pacific Railroad, and is but a few miles from the line of Old Mexico.

Climatic conditions render it a most desirable place to live, but owing to Mexican labour competition wages are not as good as at Bisbee. In Tucson the labouring man receives but $2.50 per day for eight hours. (This is just twice what is paid a labourer in North Carolina, South Carolina, or Virginia, however.)

Board is cheap in Tucson, $5.00 per week and up.

In the West Tucson is called the "lunger" town. The name comes from the large number of people who visit Tucson, every winter from all parts of the United States for lung troubles.

It is never cold enough in Tucson to wear an overcoat.

There are more hotels and boarding-houses there than in any other city of its size on the globe.

One hotel has a large sign up which reads:

"Any Day that the Sun Fails to Shine Upon this Hotel, we will Give Our Guests Free Board."

It's very seldom they have to give away any of their free board.

## CHAPTER 8

# "'For God's Sake, Give Me a Drop of Water"

I stayed in Tucson one night, and while knocking about the streets the next day I met a young man down at the depot who introduced himself as J. C. Allen, from some town in the East, which I have forgotten.

Allen had landed in Tucson but a few days before with about the same intentions I had, but for some reason had taken a violent dislike to the town, and now wanted to go to Los Angeles.

I had caught the fever of traveling pretty hard myself now, and as Allen was a sociable sort of chap as well as a good talker, it didn't take him long to convince me that Tucson was a poor town for us to remain in. Then, as two young fellows will, we soon came to an understanding that we would stick by each other through thick and thin and work our way to Los Angeles, Cal.

Like most fellows who stay in the West long, Allen was a great bull-conman (hot air man).

He told me they were already picking oranges around Los Angeles, and paying pickers the highest kind of prices.

My own common sense ought to have told me that this wasn't true, and that Allen merely wanted me to go with him for company, but I hadn't been in the West long, and the poorest kind of bull-con dealer found in me an easy mark.

I readily became as anxious to reach Los Angeles as Allen himself.

"How do you propose going?" I asked.

"A Mexican railroad foreman is going to ship me to Gila City, Ariz., tonight to do construction work, and I'll try to get him to ship you too," he promised.

Late in the afternoon the Mexican in question showed up at the depot.

Allen took him aside and had a long talk with him, during which time the Mexican glanced at me several times. Finally, he got up and went into the depot.

Allen now hurried over to me.

"——the luck," he exclaimed, "what are you wearing that white collar for? The Mexican has gone after me a pass, but he says you look too sporty. Hurry to your stopping place, quick! and get off them togs and I'll try him again."

I had put up within a block of the depot, and in a short time I had made the change and returned, bringing my dress suitcase.

Allen had already received his pass and was anxiously waiting for me.

"Hide your dress suitcase!" he whispered.

I had barely done so when the Mexican came out of the depot.

It was nearly dark now and there was a surging crowd of ladies and men on the depot yards waiting to meet the incoming train.

Allen pushed his way through the crowd and once more directed the Mexican's attention towards me.

The Mexican had no sooner glanced at me than he took out a pencil and wrote something on Allen's pass. A few moments later he left the depot and went hurrying up the street; and Allen approached me with a smile.

Upon his pass had been scrawled the two words, "And friend."

Shortly after, we were comfortably seated in a Southern Pacific passenger coach and bound far out upon the desert to Gila City, 180 miles away.

Allen had but thirty-five cents, while I was again stranded without a penny.

Just as day was breaking, we were roused by the conductor and put down at Gila City.

It's an unusual thing for a passenger to get on or off at Gila City.

Some of the passengers straightened up in their seats and watched us with interest, as we slowly got our things together and left the car at this desolate spot, located almost in the very middle of the desert.

We were yet 300 miles from Los Angeles, though Yuma, the next town, was but twenty miles away.

Gila City contains one small store, about the size of a man's hand; two small dwellings, and a miniature depot. The population numbers but four or five people.

One thing is plentiful there, though—long-eared jack rabbits and cotton tails by the thousand. This section abounds with thousands of quail, too, and on warm days not a few rattlesnakes can be seen sunning in the desert.

The shanty cars of the construction company stood on the sidetrack, and as there was nothing else to do, we went over to them.

The men were already up and the section foreman's wife was preparing breakfast.

We told the foreman that the Mexican had sent us down from Tucson, and were engaged by him at $1.50 per day and board.

Presently we were invited into one of the cars for breakfast.

The men seated around that table presented a picture seldom seen. Besides Allen and myself, there were three dark-skinned Mexicans, a half-breed Indian, the foreman, who was a Texan, and two ex-cowpunchers, besides an Irishman and a Chinaman.

As for the breakfast itself, I have never eaten better grub anywhere, and the cooking was splendid. Notwithstanding the motley crew around us, both Allen and myself made a hearty meal.

The teams were soon hitched, and after proceeding down the track about a mile the day's work commenced.

I was given a scraper team to drive, and Allen was put at pick and shovel work.

As soon as the sun rose it quickly got hot, and by 8 o'clock it began to sting through our clothes. At 10 o'clock the heat was so intense that all hands quit work and went back to the shade of the shanty cars.

Neither Allen nor myself had ever worked under such a hot sun before. Both of us came near fainting, and even when we reached the shanties, perspiration was still running from every pore.

All work was suspended until 4 p. m. (In this part of the world, owing to the intense heat, a day's work commences at 5 a. m. and lasts until 10 a. m. In the middle of the day, you take a six hours' rest. Commencing work again at 4 o'clock in the afternoon you work until 7 p. m., making an eight-hour day.)

On the morning of the second day, Allen got pretty badly hurt. A big bowlder, becoming dislodged from above his head, rolled down the cliff where he was at work, and struck him a painful blow upon the back of his hand. Already overheated from exertion in the hot sun, his injured hand threw him into a hard chill, and he was forced to quit work.

Some of the Mexicans and others standing around began laughing as if they thought it a great joke.

The foreman, instead of sympathizing with him, joined in the laugh. (The entire gang had put us down as tenderfeet.)

There was no use getting mad, for these tough-looking chaps were too many for us, and we did the next best thing.

We gave up our job and walked back to the shanties.

At 10 o'clock the men came in for dinner, when we informed the foreman that we had thrown up our job and that he could settle with us.

"Settle nothing," said the big fellow, laughing. "You've not worked enough to pay your fare from Tucson yet. You can get your dinner here, and after that, meals are fifty cents apiece, if you dine in these cars."

We walked over to the little store with the intention of investing Allen's thirty-five cents in groceries for our dinner, but there was nothing doing.

The man's stock consisted mostly of pop and cigars, which articles he probably got from Los Angeles.

"How much for pop?" I asked.

"Fifteen cents a bottle," was the reply.

A barrel of ginger snaps stood in one corner of the store.

"How much a pound?" I asked, giving the cakes a wistful look.

"Twenty-five cents a pound," said the grocer.

We left the store without purchasing anything and made our way back to the cars, forced to accept the ill-given hospitality of the section foreman.

That afternoon a lucky thought came to me. We yet had plenty of clothing, and why not auction it off?

In my grip was a mouth harp that I had bought in Bisbee.

Allen, who was a good harmonica player, struck up several lively airs, and in a few minutes every man in the camp had gathered around us, including the foreman.

Some were popping and slapping their hands in applause, and others were dancing jigs in time to the music.

I gave Allen the signal to stop and, opening up both our grips, began auctioneering off small pieces of goods.

Everything put up was sold to advantage, though the smaller articles brought the best prices.

The harmonica, which had cost me twenty-five cents, caused the liveliest bidding, and was finally knocked down to a cowboy for eighty

I gave Allen the signal to stop, and opening up both our grips, began auctioneering off small articles of clothing.

cents.

The foreman secured a nice comb and brush at a bargain, and was so well pleased with the music he invited us to take supper with him, and to play the harmonica again for him and his wife.

About nine o'clock that night a freight train stopped in Gila City, which we boarded with our grips and easily beat to Yuma.

Yuma has a population of 7,000 Indians, Mexicans and Americans, and like Bisbee, gambling forms a part of the revenue of the saloons.

Most of the houses in Yuma are built of wood or brick, though there are a good many adobe houses occupied by the poorer classes.

Some claim Yuma is fifty feet above the sea level; others say it is one hundred and fifty below the sea level. I don't know which of these statements is correct, but I do know that Yuma is by far the hottest town I was ever in. As early as half-past seven o'clock next morning the sun began to get uncomfortably hot, and by nine o'clock both Allen and myself were suffering from the heat.

We spent the biggest part of the day in the shade of the large Reservoir building opposite the depot, and but a few feet from the Colorado River.

That night a Mexican living in one of the *adobe* houses near the railroad yards supplied each of us with a large bottle of water for the long two hundred and eighty mile journey across the desert, but in dodging the brakemen while attempting to board a Los Angeles freight train, we became separated and it was the last I ever saw of my friend Allen.

I managed to hide in a car loaded with scrap iron.

Only once did I leave this car. We reached the first division point, Indio, Cal., about 3 o'clock in the morning.

My bottle of water had long since run dry, and I was once more beginning to suffer the acute pangs of desert thirst. With as little noise as possible, I slipped from the car and into the pump house (which is about the only building of any kind that Indio contains). In fact, between Yuma and Indio, for a distance of one hundred and fifty miles, there isn't a single town—nothing but desert and cactus trees.

The man in the pump house filled my bottle from a hydrant, and taking a big drink from a large tin cup, which I also filled from the hydrant, I hurried through the darkness to the scrap iron car nearly a half mile down the track.

I was about crawling in, when a low groan from under the car attracted my attention.

Peering under the car, I was amazed to see a man on the rods.

"For God's sake give me a drop of water," he begged piteously.

I passed him the bottle of water, and invited

The poor fellow eagerly took a long pull at it, him to drink half of it, passing it back scarcely half full, with a grateful "Thank you."

"I could drink five bottles like that," he said, smacking his lips.

The train now started, preventing further conversation, and I quickly crawled back into the scrap iron car.

The next day about 11 a. m. we pulled into the yards at Los Angeles.

As soon as the train stopped in the yards I jumped out of the car and looked for the man on the rods, but he was gone.

## CHAPTER 9

# Thrown Into Jail at Los Angeles

Upon seeing no one near, I lifted my grip from the car door and started down town in search of a lodging place. I found a nice place at No. 128 E. First street, and the following day I got a job with the S. P. Railroad Company, trucking freight at 20 cents per hour.

Los Angeles is probably the greatest fruit market in the world. Oranges, grapes, peaches and apricots are among the principal fruits raised.

During the orange season you can buy oranges for ten cents per dozen. A careful estimate places the number of oranges grown in California every year at 900,000,000. All fruit is cheap. The finest kind of Malaga grapes can be purchased on the streets of Los Angeles for 2½ cents per pound. You can live on fruit there over six months in the year.

The winters there are no ways as cold as in North Carolina.

The rainfall is scarcely ten inches a year, making it possible for the labouring man to work out doors every working day in the year.

Laborers get $1.75 to $2.50 per day, and are always in demand.

There are numerous restaurants in Los Angeles that set out a good, substantial meal for ten cents.

San Pedro is the port of entry for Los Angeles.

With the exception of Chicago, Los Angeles contains more employment bureaus than any other city in the United States.

While standing in one of these labour bureaus a few days later, I learned that a certain hotel in San Pedro wanted a hotel clerk. I gave up my job trucking freight and took the street car for San Pedro.

After having a short talk and showing my references to Jennings and White, proprietors of the Angelus Hotel, I was offered the place as clerk at $15.00 per month, board and room.

I accepted the position.

The little town of San Pedro bears the distinction of being one of the nine corners of the world.

The Pacific Ocean is in full view from the front entrance of the Angelus Hotel.

From this point it is only a two-hours run on the steamboat Cabrillo to the famous fishing grounds of Santa Catalina Island.

If you are a good fisherman with hook and line, two hours in these waters will supply you with from seventy-five to one hundred and fifty pounds of fish.

I had been clerking for Jennings & White about six weeks, when one day a man registered in the hotel from Searchlight, Nevada.

The man praised up Searchlight in glowing terms.

"Everything in Searchlight is on a boom," said he. "Wages are good, and it's the very place for a young man to make money."

I was not making anything and had already grown tired of the little, sleepy town of San Pedro.

The fever of travel was once more infused within me.

I would go to Searchlight, and if I found it like the man had said, I promised myself I would settle down there and stop traveling about.

To hold my position as clerk in the hotel I had been compelled to invest all of my small salary in clothing.

When I resigned the job, I had saved just $2.00.

Mr. Jennings said I was doing a bad thing starting to Searchlight broke, and that he would give me a letter of reference to a Los Angeles street car Superintendent. I reproduce his letter in this book, though I never used it, for I was bent now upon going to Searchlight, and that afternoon took the car for Los Angeles.

I knocked about the streets of Los Angeles three or four days trying to get up courage to begin beating trains again.

During my six weeks of ease and contentment at the hotel I had grown almost as timid as when I first left home.

Hardly before I knew it, I was stranded in Los Angeles without a penny.

My grip had been left in charge of Jennings & White, to be forwarded to me in case I reached Searchlight safely.

I told some kind-hearted gentleman on the street of my trouble, and he kindly advised me to apply to the Los Angeles Chief of Police.

"He'll get you a place to sleep tonight," said the man, giving me the street and number of the chief's office.

I lost sight of the fact that I was again dressed for hoboing the railroad, and that the chief might be unfavourably impressed with my appearance.

I reached his office, which was located in a large stone building, just after nightfall.

He listened to my story a moment or so, but instead of furnishing me with an address and the wherewithal to obtain a night's sleep at some lodging house, he tapped a bell on the desk.

The next moment a blue coat entered the office.

I now began to grow suspicious, but it was too late.

"Take that man around for a night's lodging," said the chief, and before I could gather my wits I was whisked from the chief's presence into another department.

"Search the prisoner," commanded the pompous looking individual presiding in this office.

The cop searched my pockets and all my things were put in a large envelope, sealed and locked in a large iron safe.

I now found my tongue and began using it pretty loud. The disgrace of spending a night in jail seemed more than I could bear.

"Turn me loose, I don't want lodging. Please let me go," I cried.

But it was no go.

"Dry up there!" came the command. "If the chief hears you, you may get thrown in a year for vagrancy."

I could have 'phoned to Jennings & White, and no doubt they could have gotten me out of the scrape, but I was ashamed for them to know of my predicament, and kept quiet.

A large book was thrust at me.

"Sign your name!" came the command.

Anyone looking over the Los Angeles records for 1906 will find the name "Robert Smith," signed for a night's lodging.

The city prison was in the back of the building, and a short time later I was locked behind the bars in an iron-bound cell containing twenty or more prisoners.

Within ten minutes every man of them had asked me what I had been "run in" for.

"You're liable to be kept in here several months for vagrancy," said the prisoners.

I'll not dwell upon the horrors of that night. I didn't sleep a wink throughout the long night, and was wideawake next morning at six o'clock when the prison warden approached the cage door and shouted:

"Robert Smith—is Robert Smith in there?" shouted the prison warden.

"Robert Smith"—

"Robert Smith in there?" he called to some of the prisoners a moment later.

I sprang up. I had forgotten that I had signed Robert Smith on the books.

"I'm the man!" I cried, and five minutes later I was a free man, again breathing the pure, fresh air of the outside world.

With rapid footsteps I hurried from this unpleasant locality and made my way down town.

At the time I write the railroad hadn't yet reached Searchlight.

The nearest point of construction was Manvel, Cal., twenty-three miles away.

By mere good fortune I learned that morning that the railroad company was shipping men through the Red Cross Employment Bureau to Manvel for construction work.

I lost no time in visiting the Red Cross Agency, and was given a pass over the Sante Fe Railroad to Manvel.

There were thirty-odd men in the crew I shipped with, mostly foreigners.

We rode all night, and about 12 o'clock next day we reached Manvel.

By keeping my eyes and ears open along the trip I easily spotted the men who had shipped out of Los Angeles as a means of reaching Searchlight.

At midnight when the rest of the camp was wrapped in deep slumber six men silently stole from the tents and struck out across the desert for Searchlight.

The lights of the town could be plainly seen from the railroad camps, and it hardly seemed possible that those bright looking lights were twenty-three miles across the desert.

Footsore, thirsty and tired we reached Searchlight next morning.

Searchlight contains fifteen business houses, and eleven of them are saloons, though it's a very quiet and well-governed little town, and about the only excitement is when some lucky prospector arrives with rich specimens of gold ore, discovered somewhere nearby in the surrounding desert—and this happens quite often. While I was there, Mike Walsh, a very poor man, discovered a rich gold claim three miles north of Searchlight and sold it for $10,000.

Anyone can prospect if he's able to buy a grub stake. Eighty dollars will buy two *burros* and a three-months' grub stake for two men, and

220

but little trouble is experienced in finding some veteran prospector who'll accompany you in search for gold on halves.

There are several good paying gold mines within a half mile of the town.

One gold mine there is in full operation within thirty feet of Main Street. It is worked by only three young men, who are the owners, and it is supposed they are making a small fortune.

I got a job with Cook & Co. assisting to survey town lots, for which I was paid $3.50 per day.

Later on, I got a job with Mr. Fred. Ullman, proprietor of the Searchlight Hotel. I was taken on as porter in the bar-room and hotel, but upon learning to mix drinks, I was engaged as bartender, which job I held until Mr. Ullman sold out a few weeks later to a firm in Los Angeles.

This threw me out of a job, but out of my salary I had placed $50.00 in the Searchlight Bank.

I now took a job at Doc's Kitchen washing dishes at two dollars and seventy-five cents per day.

While engaged in this work my brother wrote me a long letter from home, saying they were all very anxious to see me and that mother had been taken seriously ill, worrying about me.

For the first time since leaving home I began to feel homesick, so much so I had to give up my job.

I decided to make a short visit to San Francisco and then start home.

I bought a stage ticket to Nipton, Cal., and from that point purchased a ticket to Los Angeles. Next day I shipped from Los Angeles to Weed, Cal. Weed is in the Siskiyou Mountains, six hundred miles from Los Angeles. I deserted the train at Stockton, Cal., with another young fellow, and we took the boat from this point to 'Frisco.

By this manoeuvring I saved nearly half the fare from Searchlight to San Francisco.

I had a hard time finding a lodging house in 'Frisco, for over four-fifths of the hotels had gone up in the big fire. After several hours of weary tramping about the streets, I found the St. George Hotel, a large frame building, erected temporarily on Mission Street.

Lodging in 'Frisco was high and board brought fabulous prices.

Two weeks later I awoke to the realisation that my $50.00 had dwindled to $5.00.

Part of this money had gone for a new suit of clothes, but the other had been spent for living expenses.

I couldn't start for home with but $5.00, and only one other course was left—I must go to work. I didn't care to work in 'Frisco, though, for it was only skilled labour that was commanding high prices.

I met a young man in the hotel, P. A. Franck, from No. 3851 Juniata Street, St. Louis, Mo., who had left his St. Louis home to make a fortune in San Francisco, but disappointed with the poor wages paid for labour in 'Frisco compared with the high cost of living expenses, he readily agreed to leave with me.

Murray & Keady's Employment Bureau, on Tenth and Market streets, shipped us three hundred miles to the Sugar Pine Mountains, in central California to work at a saw-mill.

We left the train at Madera, Cal., at which town was located the Sugar Pine Company's office.

From Madera we took a sixty-mile stage ride through the Sugar Pine Mountains to the sawmill, arriving there late one afternoon.

That night we learned that the mill owners had decided to close down the mill until the following spring, and that, if we went to work, in all probability the job would give out by the time we had worked out our fare from San Francisco.

That night we slept on the bare floor of a little log hut up the mountain side, the man in the company store saying all his bed covering had been sold out.

The next morning, we were both frozen nearly stiff; we awoke before light and struck the trail back to Madera.

I had a thirty-pound grip of clothing and Franck was weighted down with a still heavier grip and an overcoat.

All day long we tramped over the mountains, and all the following night.

By morning of the second day, we were making scarcely a mile an hour, and were so near played out we were forced to rest every ten or fifteen minutes. Once Franck's shoe became untied, and in stooping to tie it he pitched heavily forward upon his hands and knees.

Only once did we get anything to eat, the half-way house sold us a scanty meal for 50 cents each.

At last, scarcely able to stand up, we reached Madera.

Afraid that the Sugar Pine Company would indict us for deserting, we spent our last penny for a ticket to Fresno, Cal.

We got a job at Madera's planing mill in Fresno and found a lodging house at No. 846 I street, run by a Mrs. Dora Harrell, a widow.

THE HOMEWARD JOURNEY.

Gooy-by, dear old Arizona.
Good-by, sunny California.
    (Pro tem) to you both.

Two days later we were discharged, Mr. Madera saying that we were the slowest two young men that had ever worked for him.

The fact is, the two days he paid us for was like finding money, for after that long tramp in the Sugar Pine Mountains we were too weak to work. It was about all we could do to stand around the mill and watch the others work.

Franck now placed his grip in the express office and bade me goodbye, saying he was going to hobo it to Los Angeles.

I refused to accompany him, relating my "Robert Smith" experience, but he was bent upon going, and with tears in our eyes we parted.

Not long after I was taken ill, and for two weeks I was unable to leave my room.

My money was all gone and I was in debt to my landlady for board.

About this time, I received another long letter from my brother, offering me a half interest in his grocery store, and advising me to come at once if I expected to find mother alive.

I lost no time in telegraphing the following reply:

Will come immediately if you send ticket; otherwise I can't.

Late the next day I received a telegraph order for ninety dollars.

The telegraph company wrote out a check, which I got the Principal of the Fresno Business College to endorse.

I purchased a ticket *via* Denver and Chicago, and after a long and tedious journey, I arrived in Tarboro.

My mother was sleeping and dreaming of her boy in far off sun-bathed California, when, with a light kiss, I awoke her. I will never forget the glad cry that escaped her lips when she saw me home once again, safe and sound.

It was Horace Greeley, the great American author, who said: "Young men go West."

From what little I saw of this great, grand country beyond the Mississippi, I think it is good advice. There are more opportunities to make money and more money to be made, and the climate is better; but unless father and mother are dead, take the well-meant advice of a young man who has recently been West; only to learn that there was but one place on. earth—"HOME."

San Pedro, Cal., Aug. 8th, 1906.

M. F. Vanranker, Esq., Supt.

Dear Sir:—This will introduce Mr. John Peele, who would like to make application with you for work. I know him personally, and can recommend him to be an honest, sober, and energetic young man, and will make you an A.1. conductor, for he is very bright and quick. If you can use him you will make no mistake.

Very respectfully yours,

J. W. Jennings.

St. Louis, Mo., Jan. 29, 1907.

My Dear Friend Jack:

I received your letter of the 11th inst. I have also been very busy—have been working steady since I got back home. I am very glad to hear that you appreciate my poor efforts at letter-writing.

Too bad about your girl getting married. You are right about the girls all wanting to marry a man with money. I guess that's the reason I'm not married. Never mind, old chap, you will find another girl—there are others, don't you know?

You state in your letter that since returning home you have been troubled with the asthma, and on account of the moist air and the land being so low and full of malaria you feared an attack of pneumonia. I hope you are well again and are rid of the cold.

I see you are in the grocery business. That proposition is all right, if you stay at home for a few years. Stick to it, old chap, for a while, anyway.

I intend to stay at home for a while, and any time I do go away I will let you know about it. Perhaps we may meet again out in the tall and uncut wild and woolly.

Say, Jack, do you remember in San Francisco "Murry & Ready," the "St. George" where we stopped, "Madera," the "Sugar Pine Co.," the sixty-mile "stage ride," the run-away, the comfortable little cabin on the side of the hill where we slept that night, the long tramp next day out of the Sugar Pine Mountains, and the boss we had in Fresno at the Madera Planing Mill? Them were some great old times.

My folks are all well, thank you. Trusting the same of yours, I will close, with kindest regards and best wishes. Your old side partner in California,

Phil.

P. A. Franck, 3851 Juniata St., St. Louis, Mo.
I was never in Paris or London, and have never crossed the
pond anywhere. My only experience on the deep blue was a
trip from Los Angeles to San Francisco.

I agree with you we did a foolish stunt when we parted at
Fresno, Cal.

I am getting along real nice, working hard, staying at home, and
saving my money.

Am still an advocate of Physical Culture, and take my daily
exercises, and perhaps this week will join the Central Y. M. C.
A. here.

I have not been able to find anything that weighs 35 lbs., so do
not know if I can muscle it out, but will let you know as soon
as I do. Pretty good work, old man, muscling out 35 lbs. Keep
up the good work.

www.ingramcontent.com/pod-product-compliance
Lightning Source LLC
Chambersburg PA
CBHW032051080426
42733CB00006B/237